D1335348

+. 10
n n

519.5

3453

CASS, Tom

Statistical Methods in Management 1

STATISTICAL METHODS IN MANAGEMENT 1

TOM CASS

CASSELL · LONDON

CASSELL LTD.
35 Red Lion Square, London WC1R 4SG
and at Sydney, Auckland
Toronto, Johannesburg
an affiliate of Macmillan Publishing Co. Inc., New York

First published November 1969
Second impression June 1970
Third impression June 1971
Second (enlarged) edition June 1973
Second impression September 1974
Third impression September 1977
Fourth impression December 1978

I.S.B.N. 0 304 29247 8

*Printed and bound in Great Britain at
The Camelot Press Ltd, Southampton*

PREFACE

During the last few years, particularly in larger companies, there has been a move towards combining the hitherto separate departments of Work Study, O & M, O.R. and Computer Services into one Management Services or Productivity Services department. This is a logical development, since as each of these areas has expanded and developed its activities, a great deal of overlap between them has inevitably occurred.

One of the implications of this amalgamation is the necessity for people in these departments to develop into Management Services staff, rather than remain comparatively narrow specialists in one area of the field. One of the essential requirements of such a broadening process is the acquisition of a knowledge of basic statistical methods, on which so many of the newer techniques are based.

As better information systems are developed (often computer-based), more and more quantitative data are becoming available to assist managers in their decision-making. A knowledge of statistical methods is necessary to interpret the meaning of such data and to use the information contained therein to the best advantage. Such knowledge also enables the manager to make the best use of the expertise available to him in the Management Services department.

The purpose of this book is to provide the introduction to statistical methods needed in both these areas. It has grown from a series of lecture notes written by the author for courses in Statistics at what was formerly the Cranfield Work Study School, and is now the Management Services Centre of the Cranfield School of Management.

The approach is essentially practical, each new idea being immediately illustrated by means of real-life examples. Further examples are given to be worked as exercises. Full solutions are given to all these exercises, thus making the book particularly useful to management students.

EDITOR'S FOREWORD

By the time the reader gets to page 25 of this book, he will have found himself considering staff turnover and training, the inspection of radio valves and transistors, a team of maintenance fitters, the problems of a computer punch room, a men's outfitter and an office with misplaced files, how many Kreemy-Krunch to expect in a box of sweets and how to assess the desirability of an extra minute in bed. If this is not enough to arouse his interest in applied statistics, he will, by persevering for another twenty-five pages, become involved in packing detergent and margarine, deciding what sizes of knitwear to manufacture and how opinion surveys are planned and conducted. It is this *universality* of statistical methods which makes them so valuable to the modern manager as well as imposing obligations upon him. The obligations are fourfold: he needs the ability to handle figures himself, to know when he requires professional help and, above all, to *communicate* with the statistician who supplies it; the nature of the managerial problem has to be explained and the methods of attacking it discussed; finally, the results of the investigation must be understood.

What gives this book its freshness of appeal is the author's speed in coming to grips with practical problems. No writer on statistics who seeks simplicity can afford to do without cards-in-a-pack, balls-in-a-bag and throws-of-a-die, but such devices are used no more than is necessary. Instead, we find ourselves 'piecening' during the doff cycle in a spinning mill and sharing a publisher's concern with his quire stock. The author is simple *and* lucid, but these virtues do not lead to any lack of rigour in his mathematics; indeed, his explanation of that tricky technicality, 'degrees of freedom', is a model of its kind, and its inclusion says much for the general thoroughness of his treatment.

Probability theory was born out of games of chance, and who will deny the gambling element in business? The great advances in statistical methods came in the nineteenth century, from the need to deal with the uncertainty and variability of living things—is not the skill of a manager centred upon the most complex living creature of them all, man himself? *Verbum sapienti.*

ALBERT BATTERSBY

CONTENTS

ACKNOWLEDGEMENTS

I would like to express my thanks to all the Cranfield staff, both academic and non-academic, who have helped in the preparation of this book, the former for their helpful comments and checking of the typescript, and the latter (particularly Brenda Clark) for more practical help in such matters as the preparation of the drawings.

I am indebted to the following people and organizations for allowing me to reproduce copyright material:

the McGraw-Hill Book Company, for permission to reprint Table I from *Handbook of Probability and Statistics with Tables*, by R. S. Burington and D. C. May, Jr;

Sir Isaac Pitman & Sons Ltd, for permission to reprint Tables II, III and V from *Modern Business Statistics*, by J. E. Freund and F. J. Williams;

Professor E. S. Pearson and the Biometrika Trustees, for permission to reprint Table IV from *Biometrika Tables for Statisticians*, Vol. I;

the Literary Executor of the late Sir Ronald A. Fisher, FRS, Dr Frank Yates, FRS, and Oliver & Boyd Ltd, Edinburgh, for permission to reprint Table VI from *Statistical Tables for Biological, Agricultural and Medical Research*;

Macmillan & Co. Ltd, for permission to reprint Table VII from *Logarithmic and Other Tables for Schools*, by F. Castle.

My gratitude (and admiration) go especially to my wife, who somehow managed to type the entire script while simultaneously coping with the demands of a young family.

Most of the examples used in the book are original, but some are not. They have accumulated over a period of time, and I have no record of their original sources. If anyone recognizes an example to which he can lay claim, I hope that he will accept this general acknowledgement.

T. C.

1 FREQUENCY AND PROBABILITY

Suppose you have just moved into a new house. You work in London and each morning you must drive to the local station to catch a train. How much time must you allow yourself for the journey? You know that the station is about 5 miles from home, so on the first morning, to be well on the safe side, you set off an hour before train time. You find that the trip, from house to platform, actually takes 20 minutes. Is it safe to conclude that the journey will always take 20 minutes?

Obviously not. All we can say with certainty is that it *took* 20 minutes on one occasion. When you repeat the journey the next day, it may take 18 minutes if road and traffic conditions are a little better, or perhaps 22 minutes if they are worse.

Suppose you were to make the trip 50 times. The times taken, rounded to the nearest minute, might be as follows:

17 minutes on		6	occasions	
18	,,	,,	8	,,
19	,,	,,	9	,,
20	,,	,,	12	,,
21	,,	,,	9	,,
22	,,	,,	4	,,
23	,,	,,	2	,,

We can represent this pictorially by means of a special kind of bar chart known as a **histogram**, shown in Figure 1.1 (page 2). The height of the bar representing each journey time is made proportional to the frequency with which that time was observed. The histogram thus shows the **frequency distribution** of journey time. For greater clarity, the frequencies have been written at the top of each bar.

Continuous Distributions

Notice that in order for the frequency distribution to arise at all, we had to round off the times to the nearest minute. If we had measured our 50 journey times very accurately, say to 3 decimal places of minutes, we would most likely have obtained 50 different times.

1

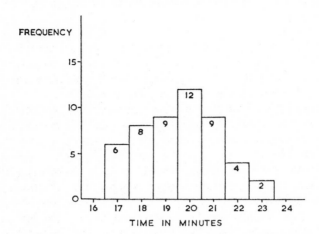

Figure 1.1. Distribution of journey times

Distributions of this nature, in which the measured variable can assume any value along a continuous scale, are known as **continuous** distributions. Height, weight, volume, time and temperature are all examples of continuous variables.

In such cases, we must always round off our measurements before they can be represented in histogram form. Any convenient grouping may be used which will give a reasonable number of bars (say about 6 to 12) in the histogram. Suppose, for example, that our journey times had varied from 10 minutes to 40 minutes. A more convenient grouping would then have been to take steps of 5 minutes to give 6 bars in the histogram. A more detailed discussion of grouping will be given later when we consider the calculation of various measures to represent our distributions.

Discrete Distributions

There is another type of distribution in which the variable can only be a whole number. Examples include the number of accidents per month in a factory, the number of goals scored per team in a set of football results, and the number of calls per day made on a breakdown repair gang. Distributions of this type are said to be **discrete** or **discontinuous**.

Populations and Samples

Figure 1.1. gives a far more comprehensive picture of the journey time situation than does any one particular time. To take another example, suppose we ask, 'How tall is a man?' Here again, there is no unique answer. We could take a group of, say, 100 men and draw a histogram of the distribution of their heights. This histogram would give a better answer than would any single height.

In neither of these cases, however, does the histogram give a *complete* answer. To be complete, the histogram of heights would have to contain the height of every man in the world. To contemplate obtaining all these measurements is, of course, ludicrous, but this is precisely the kind of problem which must be faced in practice. A balance has to be struck between the cost of obtaining the required information and the accuracy of answer required. More information will usually yield a more accurate answer, but the cost of obtaining more information may be prohibitive.

If we could produce a histogram which included the height of every man in the world, it would describe *exactly* the way in which height was distributed in the total **population** of men. A histogram giving the heights of, say, 100 or 1000 men would represent a **sample** of men from this population. The sample would describe *approximately* the way in which height was distributed in the population.

In most practical situations, the populations in which we are interested are very large. In a market research survey, for example, the population of interest would perhaps be all potential purchasers of our product. Inevitably, therefore, we must take samples and use them to make inferences about the populations from which they are drawn. A large proportion of this book is devoted to examining the way in which samples behave in order to discover what can (and often what cannot) be inferred about the populations from which the samples come.

Population in the statistical sense means the complete set of items which are of interest in any particular situation. This is a somewhat wider definition than the everyday one. Very often the population of interest is physically non-existent and is unlimited in size. In the journey time example, for instance, there is no limit to the number of journeys which can be made. However many times we made the trip, we should still only have a sample from the infinitely large population of journeys.

It is also necessary to define our population carefully. In the journey time example, the starting and finishing points of the journey would have to be specified. In the height example, what is meant by 'man' would have to be defined. Does it. for example, include women and children?

Using Histograms

Later on in this book, we shall develop much better ways of handling distributions than just drawing them as histograms, but even such a simple representation as this can be very useful. To illustrate how histograms can be used, let us look at two examples.

Example 1.1

One of the parts being manufactured in an engineering workshop is a shaft of 3 in nominal diameter. The specification allows tolerance limits of ± 0.006 in; that is, all shafts outside the range 2.994 to 3.006 in must be rejected.

A sample of 25 shafts is taken at random and the diameter of each is carefully measured. The 25 measurements are:

3·001	3·000	3·003	3·003	3·004
2·999	3·003	3·000	3·004	3·003
3·004	3·003	3·005	3·001	3·004
3·003	3·005	3·002	3·002	3·003
3·002	3·001	3·002	3·003	3·002

None of these is outside the tolerance range, so it would appear that things are working satisfactorily. However, a much more detailed analysis of the situation may be made if we construct a histogram. Grouping the measurements gives the frequencies shown at the top of page 5.

Constructing a histogram from these gives the results shown in Figure 1.2. The two vertical dotted lines in this diagram indicate the upper and lower tolerance limits.

Measurements	Frequency
2·999	1
3·000	2
3·001	3
3·002	5
3·003	8
3·004	4
3·005	2

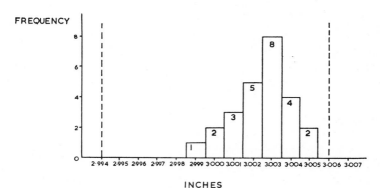

Figure 1.2. Distribution of shaft measurements

We can now see at a glance that although the process is not at the moment producing reject material, it is in imminent danger of doing so. The process could with profit be adjusted so that the distribution is centred at or near the middle of the tolerance range.

The width of the distribution is much narrower than the width of the tolerance range, indicating that the process is capable of producing parts to a greater accuracy than is required by the specification. It may be possible to use a cheaper, less accurate, machine for this work, provided that it is controlled properly. We shall see later how a quality control procedure could be devised to provide this control.

Example 1.2

Martin Wiberg* put forward the idea that the frequency distribution of the time taken by an operative to carry out a repetitive job

* M. Wiberg, *The Work Time Distribution*. McLure, Hadden, 1951.

provides useful information on the characteristics of that operative.

Look at the two distributions in Figure 1.3. They represent data obtained from time studies on two operatives. Neither of these distributions is symmetrical in shape. A distribution which is not symmetrical is said to be **skew**. Wiberg says that the direction of the skewness indicates how well the operative is motivated. Positive skewness (the long tail pointing to the right as in Figure 1.3 (*a*)) indicates positive motivation. There is a real incentive to work well. The negative skewness of Figure 1.3 (*b*) indicates an operative with a negative approach to his job.

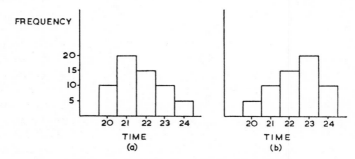

Figure 1.3. Distributions of time study data

In addition, claims Wiberg, the width of the distribution is an indication of skill; a narrow distribution indicates a skilled operative and a wide distribution an unskilled operative.

The times recorded in these distributions must, of course, be observed times unadjusted by any rating factor.

Probability

We have not yet answered the question with which this chapter started. Before we can do so, we must discuss one of the most important of all statistical ideas, namely **probability**. The concept of probability is an everyday one and is used frequently by everyone. We speak of rain being probable on a particular day, or of it being improbable that we shall win a fortune on the football pools. We even use a rough scale of measurement with expressions such as 'unlikely', 'likely' or 'very likely' as points on the scale.

In statistics, this scale of measurement is refined and a numerical scale added. The greatest degree of probability which any event can have is 'certainty'. Nothing can be more likely to happen than an event which is certain. It is, for example, certain that everyone will one day die. The probability scale assigns a probability of 1·00 to an event which is certain to occur.

At the other end of the scale, the lowest degree of probability which an event can have is 'impossibility'. Nothing can be less likely to happen than an event which is impossible. A probability of zero is assigned to such an event.

If we try to think of examples illustrative of certainty or impossibility, we soon realize that very few things are either certain or impossible. Most have some degree of likelihood in between. All events will therefore have a probability between 0 and 1, although we may not know precisely what it is. This is the reason for the great importance of probability calculations when considering real life problems. We can hardly ever be certain about the outcome of any particular course of action which we may choose. Very often, however, it is possible by means of statistical analysis to make an assessment of the probability of any outcome occurring. This enables decisions to be placed on a 'calculated risk' basis rather than on pure guesswork.

Exact Probability

With some events we can calculate the exact probability of occurrence. If, for example, we toss a coin, it can fall either 'head' or 'tail'. If the coin is unbiased and is tossed fairly, both are equally likely. We can therefore say that the probability of it falling 'head' is $\frac{1}{2}$.

Similarly, with a six-sided die it is easily seen that the probability of, say, a 5 being thrown is $\frac{1}{6}$. This again assumes that there is no bias present. Each of the six faces is equally likely to be uppermost. If we have a bag containing 80 white balls and 20 black, the probability of picking a black ball at random out of the bag is $\frac{20}{100}$ or $\frac{1}{5}$.

We can see that to calculate a probability in this way, two things must be known:

1. the total number of outcomes which can occur, all of which must be equally likely;

2. the number of these outcomes which will give rise to the particular event in which we are interested.

The probability that the event will occur is then simply the ratio of these two.

We can represent this concisely by using the letter n to represent the total number of possible outcomes, and the letter m to represent the number of outcomes which will give the required result. If we denote 'the probability that event A will happen' by P(A), we then have:

$$P(A) = \frac{m}{n} \qquad \qquad \ldots (1.1)$$

In the above examples:

When tossing a coin, $n = 2$ and $m = 1$ P(head) $= \frac{1}{2}$
When throwing a die, $n = 6$ and $m = 1$ P(5) $= \frac{1}{6}$
When drawing a ball, $n = 100$ and $m = 20$ P(black) $= \frac{1}{5}$

Approximate Probability

Very often it is not possible to calculate the n and m required in the above formula. In the journey time example with which this chapter started, what is the probability that the journey will take 20 minutes?

Without the information provided by the sample, we are unable even to guess at this probability. Having obtained our sample, however, we can use the proportion of occasions on which a time of 20 minutes was observed as an estimate of the probability. Out of our sample of 50, the journey took 20 minutes on 12 occasions. We can therefore estimate the probability at $\frac{12}{50} = 0.24$. This is known as the **relative frequency** approach to estimating probabilities. As one would expect, increasing accuracy of estimation is obtained as the sample size increases.

It is important to realize that the relative frequency approach requires the sample to be truly representative of the population. Just what is meant by representative is discussed more fully in Chapter 3. For the time being, the word may be considered to have its everyday meaning.

The Addition Rule

So far we have only considered the calculation of the probability of a single event, such as throwing a 5 with a six-sided die, but we are often interested in calculating the probability that any one of a number of events will occur.

Consider the probability of throwing an odd number with a die. Using formula (1.1),

$$P(\text{odd number}) = \tfrac{3}{6} = \tfrac{1}{2}$$

because of the 6 possible ways in which the die can fall ($n = 6$) there are 3 which are odd numbers ($m = 3$).

We can, however, look at this in another way. A throw of 1, 3 or 5 will do for our purpose.

$$P(1) = \tfrac{1}{6} \quad P(3) = \tfrac{1}{6} \quad P(5) = \tfrac{1}{6}$$

We can see that the sum of these 3 probabilities is also $\tfrac{3}{6}$ or $\tfrac{1}{2}$.

This is an illustration of the simplest form of the **addition rule** of probability, which states:

> The probability that any one of several possible, mutually exclusive, events will occur is the sum of the probabilities of the separate events.

Notationally,

$$P(A \text{ } or \text{ } B \text{ } or \ldots) = P(A) + P(B) + \ldots \qquad \ldots (1.2)$$

The words 'mutually exclusive' are important. They mean that the events under consideration cannot occur simultaneously.

The following example illustrates a situation in which the events being considered are not mutually exclusive. The example is phrased in terms of percentages. It is often useful to regard a probability as a long-run percentage. An event with a probability of occurrence of 0·5, for example, will occur in the long run 50% of the time.

A men's outfitter estimates from his invoices that 50% of his customers buy a shirt and 60% buy a tie. What percentage of them buy *either* a shirt *or* a tie? If we add the two percentages, we get

110%. This is incorrect because we have included some customers twice, namely those who buy both a shirt *and* a tie.

The reason why this happens becomes clear if we examine Figure 1.4. The rectangle represents the population of customers. The circle on the left encloses the proportion of those who buy a shirt. Similarly, the one on the right encloses the proportion who buy a tie. The area of overlap represents those who buy both, and is included twice in a straight addition of the two circles.

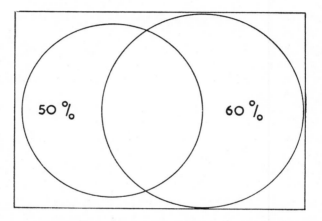

Figure 1.4. Illustration of the addition rule of probability

When the events which are being considered are *not* mutually exclusive, therefore, formula (1.2) must be modified. When only two events are being considered, it becomes:

$$P(A \ or \ B) = P(A) + P(B) - P(AB) \qquad \ldots (1.3)$$

where P(AB) is the probability of the joint occurrence of the two events.

This formula gives the probability that either A or B (or both) will occur. To calculate this in the case of our outfitter, we would also need to know P(AB), that is, the percentage of customers who bought both a shirt and a tie. If this is 30%, we then have 50% + 60% − 30% = 80% of customers who buy either a shirt or a tie (or both).

Conditional Probability

Suppose we have a bag containing 3 white and 7 black balls. What is the probability of picking out 2 white balls, if we make our selection without looking?

The probability of drawing 1 white ball is $\frac{3}{10}$. However, the probability of drawing a second white, *having already drawn 1 white*, is not $\frac{3}{10}$. There are now only 9 balls left in the bag of which 2 are white, therefore the probability of drawing a second white is clearly $\frac{2}{9}$. If we draw a black ball first, the probability that the second is white becomes $\frac{3}{9}$.

From this we can see that the probability of picking a white at the second drawing is dependent on what happens at the first drawing. The probability of the second event is said to be **conditional** upon the first event.

The conditional probability of drawing a black ball after a white has already been drawn is $\frac{7}{9}$.

The conditional probability of drawing a second black after a black has already been drawn is $\frac{6}{9}$.

Whenever we are interested in the probability that *both* of two events will occur, we must take these conditional probabilities into account. We do this in accordance with the **multiplication rule**.

The Multiplication Rule

This states:

> To calculate the probability of the joint occurrence of events A and B, multiply the probability of A by the conditional probability of B, given that A has occurred.

In the notation which we have developed,

$$P(A \textit{ and } B) = P(A) \times P(B \mid A) \qquad \ldots (1.4)$$

where $P(B \mid A)$ stands for the conditional probability of B, given that A has occurred.

To calculate the probability of drawing 2 white balls from the bag then, we have:

Probability that the first is white, $P(A) = \frac{3}{10}$
Conditional probability that the second
is white, given that the first is white, $P(B \mid A) = \frac{2}{9}$
The probability that both are white, $P(A \; and \; B) = \frac{3}{10} \times \frac{2}{9} = \frac{1}{15}$

Frequently, of course, the probability of event B will be independent of event A. Suppose we throw two dice. What is the probability of getting a total score of 2?

To obtain a score of 2, we must have a 1 on the first die (event A) and a 1 on the second (event B). Quite clearly the probability of event B is independent of event A. Whatever number comes up on the first die, the probability of throwing a 1 with the second is always $\frac{1}{6}$. The probability of a total score of 2 is therefore $\frac{1}{6} \times \frac{1}{6} = \frac{1}{36}$.

Applications

The concept of probability and the rules for calculating probabilities have been developed above by using simple examples such as throwing dice. To consolidate these ideas, a number of exercises are given at the end of the chapter. Let us now consider some practical examples of the use of probability theory.

Example 1.3

A complex piece of machinery contains 1000 components, all of which must function perfectly if the machine is to work. The probability that each individual component will not fail is 0·99. What is the probability that the machine will work?

Here we require the joint occurrence of 1000 events, each of which has a probability of 0·99. By the multiplication rule, the probability of their joint occurrence is $(0·99)^{1000}$ which works out to approximately 0·000 04. Thus, even though each individual component has a high probability of not failing, it is virtually certain that the machine will not work!

This illustrates a problem which is becoming increasingly important as technology advances. A relatively new branch of statistics, known as **reliability theory*** has been developed to help improve the

---

* D. K. Lloyd and M. Lipow, *Reliability: Management, Method and Mathematics*. Prentice-Hall, 1962.

reliability of complex equipment. The effect of possible groupings and duplication of components is examined, and also the way in which the probability of failure varies with the age of the component.

Example 1.4

A food manufacturer is considering the introduction of a new brand of instant coffee. What proportion of the instant coffee market would the new brand succeed in capturing?

This type of question is one of the most important in the field of marketing. One approach to its solution is through the use of **probability theory**. To illustrate this approach, let us consider a very over-simplified situation in which there is at present only one brand on the market. The same line of reasoning could be applied if there were a number of existing brands, but the arithmetic would be a good deal more complicated.

We put our new brand (Brand 2) on sale in a small test market area, and observe through market research the way in which consumers switch from one brand to another. This brand-switching pattern may be described by the set of probabilities in Table 1.1. If, for example, a consumer buys Brand 1 on one occasion, the probability that she will buy Brand 1 again on the next occasion is 0·2 (*from* Brand 1 *to* Brand 1). The probability that she will switch to Brand 2 after buying Brand 1 is 0·8 (*from* Brand 1 *to* Brand 2).

These probabilities would be estimated from our market research data by taking the relative frequencies with which these switches occurred in the test market.

TABLE 1.1

	Switch to *Brand*	
Switch	1	2
from 1	0·2	0·8
Brand 2	0·4	0·6

If these probabilities remain constant, it can be shown that the market will eventually settle down into a state of equilibrium, with a constant market share for each of the brands. We can estimate these equilibrium shares as follows.

Initially, Brand 1 has 100% of the market and Brand 2 has 0%. After the first round of purchases has been made following Brand 2's introduction, we can see from the table that 20% of the consumers will have bought Brand 1 again, while 80% will have switched to Brand 2. At this stage, then, Brand 2's market share is 80%.

At the next round of purchases, 60% of Brand 2's customers will buy Brand 2 again, and 80% of Brand 1's customers will switch to Brand 2. The market share of Brand 2 will therefore now be:

$$(0 \cdot 6 \times 0 \cdot 8) + (0 \cdot 8 \times 0 \cdot 2) = 0 \cdot 64, \text{ or } 64\%$$

Brand 1's share will therefore be 36%.

At the next round, 60% of Brand 2's customers will again buy Brand 2, while 80% of Brand 1's customers will switch to Brand 2. The new market share of Brand 2 will be:

$$(0 \cdot 6 \times 0 \cdot 64) + (0 \cdot 8 \times 0 \cdot 36) = 0 \cdot 672, \text{ or } 67 \cdot 2\%$$

At the next round, this will become:

$$(0 \cdot 6 \times 0 \cdot 672) + (0 \cdot 8 \times 0 \cdot 328) = 0 \cdot 665, \text{ or } 66 \cdot 5\%$$

At the next round it becomes:

$$(0 \cdot 6 \times 0 \cdot 665) + (0 \cdot 8 \times 0 \cdot 335) = 0 \cdot 667, \text{ or } 66 \cdot 7\%$$

We can see that the equilibrium position has now virtually been reached. An exact calculation (using the theory of Markov processes, of which this is an example) in fact shows it to be $66\frac{2}{3}\%$. Brand 2, therefore, will ultimately capture two-thirds of the market.

It should be emphasized that this example has been over-simplified. A number of the assumptions which have been made are, to say the least, a little questionable. It is very doubtful, for example, that the transition probabilities would remain constant, even for a relatively short period of time. Indeed, much of the marketing activity of a company is directed towards changing these probabilities in its favour. However, this kind of analysis provides a valuable indication of the way in which market trends are moving. It would be a useful exercise for the manufacturer of Brand 1 to undertake, since it tells him that if he does not mount a counter-attack against the new brand, it is likely to capture a large portion of his market. More complex models than this simple Markov one have been developed in which the basic assumptions are a little more realistic. Some of these are discussed in the book by Montgomery and Urban.*

Exercises

1.1. Two dice are thrown simultaneously. What is the probability that the total score will be:
    (*a*) 3;
    (*b*) 7;
    (*c*) 11?

1.2. A batch of 30 radio valves contains 3 which are defective. 2 valves are selected at random from the batch and put into a radio set. What is the probability that:
    (*a*) both the valves selected are defective;
    (*b*) only one is defective;
    (*c*) neither is defective?

1.3. 4 playing cards are drawn from a standard pack of 52. What is the probability that:
    (*a*) the 4 cards are all aces;
    (*b*) the aces are drawn in the order spade, heart, diamond, club?

1.4. The clerk in charge of a filing section claims that no more than 1% of records are misfiled. You look up two records at random and find that both are misfiled. Do you believe the clerk's claim?

1.5. Staff turnover in a Management Services Department is 40% per annum. 3 members of the department are given a joint assignment which will take a year to complete. What is the probability that all 3 will still be with the company at the end of the year? Assume that if they decide to leave, their decisions will be made independently of each other.

1.6. In a large consignment of bolts, 10% have faulty threads. If a sample of 5 is taken at random from the consignment, what is the probability that the sample contains:
    (*a*) no faulty bolts;
    (*b*) one faulty bolt?

1.7. There are 25 men on the field during a game of football (22 players and 3 officials). What is the probability that at least 2 of these 25 have the same birthday?

* D. B. Montgomery and G. L. Urban, *Management Science in Marketing*. Prentice-Hall, 1969.

2 PROBABILITY DISTRIBUTIONS

When we combine the two ideas (frequency distributions and probability), developed in Chapter 1, we obtain the most important concept in statistics, the **probability distribution**. Most of this book is concerned with various probability distributions and how they can be used.

We can easily convert a frequency distribution into a probability distribution by changing the frequencies into **relative** frequencies. In Figure 2.1 we have the probability distribution corresponding to the frequency distribution of journey times given in Figure 1.1.

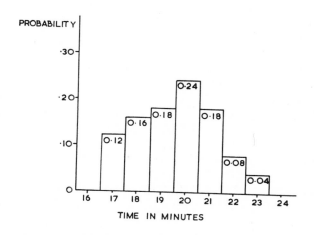

Figure 2.1. Probability distribution of journey times

In effect, all we have done is to change the scale on the vertical axis of the histogram by dividing it by 50, that is, the total number of journeys represented in the frequency distribution. It is in this probability form that the distribution is of most use to us. We can now use it to help us to decide how much time to allow each morning for the journey to the station.

Suppose we allow 23·5 minutes. None of the 50 journeys on which our distribution is based took longer than this. We can be fairly certain, therefore, that a time in excess of 23·5 minutes will occur very infrequently. It cannot, of course, be completely ruled out, because our distribution is only approximate.

However, we do not mind missing the train and being late occasionally. What will be the effect of having an extra minute in bed and reducing our allowed time to 22·5 minutes? The distribution tells us that the probability of exceeding 22·5 minutes for the journey is 0·04. In the long run, this means that we will miss the train about 4% of the time, or roughly 1 day in every 25.

This averages out at only once every 5 weeks. We do not need to achieve such a high standard of punctuality, so how about cutting a further minute off the allowed time? The probability of exceeding 21·5 minutes is $0·08 + 0·04 = 0·12$ or, as a percentage, 12%. This is an average of rather more than once a fortnight. This we feel is just about acceptable. We certainly could not get away with being late more often than this. Accordingly, therefore, we decide to allow 21·5 minutes every morning for the trip.

This example is somewhat frivolous, but it illustrates quite well how a probability distribution can help us to find a reasonable compromise between conflicting requirements. In this case we want to reduce the allowed time for the journey as much as possible without increasing the probability of missing the train to an unacceptable level.

Theoretical Distributions

The calculations we have done are necessarily approximate, because the probability distribution has been estimated from a sample of only 50 journey times. If we were to take a sample of 500, the resulting distribution would be that much more accurate. Fortunately it is not usually necessary to take a large sample and estimate the probabilities in this way. A number of standard theoretical probability distributions have been derived by statisticians which can often be taken 'ready-made' to fit particular situations. We shall be discussing a few of these and their applications in some detail later in this chapter.

To see how a simple theoretical distribution may be calculated, consider the number of heads which occur when 3 coins are tossed simultaneously. There are 8 possible ways in which the 3 coins can fall. Putting 'H' for head and 'T' for tail, these are:

	1	2	3	4	5	6	7	8
First coin	H	T	H	H	T	T	H	T
Second coin	H	H	T	H	T	H	T	T
Third coin	H	H	H	T	H	T	T	T

Of these eight possible arrangements of the coins, one shows 0 heads, three show 1 head, three show 2 heads and one shows 3 heads. The probabilities of getting the various numbers of heads per throw are therefore:

Number of heads	Probability
0	$\frac{1}{8}$
1	$\frac{3}{8}$
2	$\frac{3}{8}$
3	$\frac{1}{8}$

This probability distribution is shown in histogram form in Figure 2.2.

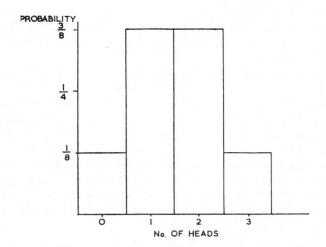

Figure 2.2. Probability distribution of number of heads obtained when tossing three coins

Exercises

2.1. Toss three coins 48 times and record the number of heads obtained on each throw. Construct the frequency distribution. Using the probability distribution of Figure 2.2, calculate the theoretical frequencies which are expected and compare them with the experimental results.

2.2. Construct the theoretical probability distribution of the score obtained when two dice are thrown simultaneously. Carry out an experiment by throwing two dice 72 times and comparing actual frequencies with theoretical frequencies as in Exercise 2.1.

The Binomial Distribution

One of the most important of the standard probability distributions is known as the **binomial distribution**. To see how it arises, let us consider a practical situation. There is nothing essentially new here; it is just an extension of the calculations already done in Exercise 1.6.

Of a large batch of transistors, 10% are defective. What are the probabilities of getting 0, 1, 2, 3 and 4 defectives in a sample of 4 taken at random from the batch? It will simplify the explanation if we imagine that each of the 4 items in the sample is selected in turn; not all 4 picked up at once.

From the fact that 10% of the batch are defective, it follows that if we pick a transistor at random, the probability that it is defective is 0·10. The probability that it is good is 0·90. Putting 'D' for defective and 'G' for good, we can write all the different ways in which a sample can be made up as follows:

First item	G	DGGG	DDDGGG	DDDG	D
Second item	G	GDGG	DGGDDG	DDGD	D
Third item	G	GGDG	GDGDGD	DGDD	D
Fourth item	G	GGGD	GGDGDD	GDDD	D

We can see from this that there is only one way in which a sample containing no defectives can arise. The probability of obtaining such a sample is 0·9 × 0·9 × 0·9 × 0·9 or (0·9)⁴, by the multiplication rule.

When we consider how 1 defective transistor can arise, the situation is rather more complex. The probability of getting the specific sequence DGGG is $0.1 \times 0.9 \times 0.9 \times 0.9$, or $(0.1)(0.9)^3$. This is not the only way in which 1 defective can appear in the sample, however. From the above listing of all possible sample compositions, we can see that there are 4 distinct ways of getting 1 defective; it could be obtained as either the first, second, third or fourth item in the sample. The probability of getting each of these specific arrangements will be $(0.1)(0.9)^3$, so by the addition rule the probability that any one of them will occur is:

$$(0.1)(0.9)^3 + (0.1)(0.9)^3 + (0.1)(0.9)^3 + (0.1)(0.9)^3 = 4(0.1)(0.9)^3$$

Similarly, we can see that there are 6 ways in which a sample containing 2 defective transistors can arise. The probability of any one specific arrangement being obtained is $(0.1)^2(0.9)^2$, so the probability that any one of the 6 will occur is $6(0.1)^2(0.9)^2$.

By the same reasoning, the probability of getting 3 defectives will be $4(0.1)^3(0.9)$ and of getting 4 defectives, $(0.1)^4$.

Summarizing these results, we have:

$$P(0 \text{ defectives}) = (0.9)^4 \qquad\quad\, = 0.6561$$
$$P(1 \text{ defective}) \ = 4(0.1)(0.9)^3 = 0.2916$$
$$P(2 \text{ defectives}) = 6(0.1)^2(0.9)^2 = 0.0486$$
$$P(3 \text{ defectives}) = 4(0.1)^3(0.9) = 0.0036$$
$$P(4 \text{ defectives}) = (0.1)^4 \qquad\quad\, = 0.0001$$

These are the successive terms in the expansion of the binomial expression $(0.9 + 0.1)^4$, from which fact the distribution gets its name.

The computation of binomial distributions by the method just described would be, to put it mildly, somewhat tedious. Imagine, for example, trying to write out all the possible ways in which 20 defectives could arise in a sample of 50. Better still, don't imagine it, try it!

A much better way of finding the required number of possible arrangements is to borrow a formula from the theory of permutations and combinations. This tells us that the number of ways in which x defectives can arise in a sample of size n is $\dfrac{n!}{x!(n-x)!}$. The exclamation mark means that the **factorial** of the number which precedes it is to be taken. The factorial of a number is obtained by multiplying together all the integers from 1 up to that number. We have, for example,

$$5! = 1 \times 2 \times 3 \times 4 \times 5 = 120$$

To see how this formula works, let us re-calculate the number of ways in which 2 defectives can arrange themselves in our sample of 4. Here, we have $x = 2$ and $n = 4$. The formula therefore gives the required number as

$$\frac{4!}{2!\,2!} = \frac{24}{2 \times 2} = 6$$

Exercise

2.3.   Calculate the number of ways in which 0, 1, 2, 3, 4, 5 and 6 defectives can arrange themselves in a sample of 6.

General Formula

The method of calculating binomial probabilities can be expressed in a concise formula. Letting sample size $= n$ and the probability of getting a defective $= p$, we have:

$$P(x \text{ defectives in sample}) = \left(\frac{n!}{x!(n-x)!} \right) p^x (1-p)^{n-x} \dots (2.1)$$

When n is small, calculating these probabilities is a fairly simple matter. As the sample size gets larger, however, the calculation involves a great deal of work. Comprehensive tables* have therefore been compiled for different combinations of values of n and p. However, it is not often necessary to use these, as much simpler approximate methods can frequently be adopted when n is large. Two of them will be described later in this chapter.

Conditional Probability

It should be noted that for the binomial distribution to apply, the probability of picking a defective must remain constant. Strictly speaking, in the situation we have considered this is not true. If the

* *Tables of the Binomial Probability Distribution*. National Bureau of Standards, Applied Mathematics Series No. 6, 1950.

batch contains 1000 components of which 100 are defective, p is initially $\frac{100}{1000} = 0 \cdot 1$. When we have picked a defective out, however, the conditional probability of picking a second one is $\frac{99}{999}$, which is not quite $0 \cdot 1$. To take this into account would complicate the calculation enormously and in the case of large batches would make virtually no difference to the answer. Provided the batches are large, therefore, it is sufficiently accurate to assume that p remains constant. In this context, 'large' means that the sample must be not more than 10% of the batch.

Example 2.1

One of the major uses of the binomial distribution is in the area of acceptance sampling. Each incoming consignment of material is sampled and a decision is taken on whether to accept the consignment or to reject it.

Suppose one such scheme specifies that a sample of 10 items be taken and that the consignment is to be accepted only if the sample contains no defective items. What is the probability that a consignment which is 10% defective will be accepted?

Here we have $n = 10$ and $p = 0 \cdot 10$.

$$\text{P(0 defectives)} = (0 \cdot 9)^{10} = 0 \cdot 3487$$

This means that in the long run $34 \cdot 87 \%$ of such consignments will be accepted. This is a most unsatisfactory state of affairs. We would almost certainly want to reject material which was as bad as this. Even if the defective rate is as high as 20%, the probability of acceptance is still fairly large, being $(0 \cdot 8)^{10} = 0 \cdot 1074$. A satisfactory sampling scheme must obviously have a low probability of accepting bad consignments.

Another aspect to be considered is the probability of rejecting good consignments. How does the scheme we are examining score on that count? Before we can answer this question, we must define a good consignment. Let us assume that a defective content of not more than 2% is acceptable.

The probability that our scheme will accept a consignment which is 2% defective is $(0 \cdot 98)^{10} = 0 \cdot 8171$. The probability of rejection is therefore $1 - 0 \cdot 8171 = 0 \cdot 1829$. This again is unsatisfactory. It means that in the long run almost 1 batch in every 5 of acceptable material will be returned to the supplier.

A satisfactory scheme will have a low probability of rejecting good material and a low probability of accepting bad. If we specify these probabilities, together with a definition of good and bad material, it is possible to calculate the corresponding sampling scheme. These computations are rather complicated, but tables have been compiled which are readily available and easy to use. Information on these is contained in the very comprehensive *Quality Control Handbook* edited by Juran.*

Example 2.2

So far in our discussion of the binomial distribution we have referred almost exclusively to defective items in samples taken from batches of components. This is by no means the only type of situation in which this distribution occurs, as the following example shows.

Company XYZ operates a twelve-month training scheme for school-leavers. The probability that an individual selected for the scheme will leave before completing the training period is estimated from past records at 0·2. The company wants to be reasonably sure that at least 4 trainees will complete the course. How many should be selected for the scheme?

Suppose only 4 are selected. This is equivalent to taking a sample of 4 from the population of school-leavers. The probability that any individual will not complete the course is 0·2, so the probabilities that 0, 1, 2, 3 or 4 will leave will follow the binomial distribution with $n = 4$ and $p = 0·2$. We are only interested in the probability that all 4 complete the course.

$$P(0 \text{ leavers}) = (0·8)^4 = 0·4096$$

If 5 are selected, we have:

$$P(0 \text{ leavers}) = (0·8)^5 \qquad\qquad = 0·3277$$

$$P(1 \text{ leaver}) = \frac{5!}{1!\,4!}(0·2)(0·8)^4 = 0·4096$$

* J. M. Juran, ed., *Quality Control Handbook*. McGraw-Hill, 1962.

The probability that at least 4 will remain is the sum of these, which is 0·7373.

If 6 are selected, we have:

$$P(0 \text{ leavers}) = (0·8)^6 \qquad\qquad = 0·2622$$

$$P(1 \text{ leaver}) = \frac{6!}{1!\,5!}\,(0·2)(0·8)^5 = 0·3932$$

$$P(2 \text{ leavers}) = \frac{6!}{2!\,4!}\,(0·2)^2(0·8)^4 = 0·2458$$

The probability that at least 4 will remain is again the sum of these probabilities, which is 0·9012.

If 7 are selected, we have:

$$P(0 \text{ leavers}) = (0·8)^7 \qquad\qquad = 0·2098$$

$$P(1 \text{ leaver}) = \frac{7!}{1!\,6!}\,(0·2)(0·8)^6 = 0·3671$$

$$P(2 \text{ leavers}) = \frac{7!}{2!\,5!}\,(0·2)^2(0·8)^5 = 0·2753$$

$$P(3 \text{ leavers}) = \frac{7!}{3!\,4!}\,(0·2)^3(0·8)^4 = 0·1147$$

The probability that at least 4 will remain is now 0·9669.

These results may be summarized as follows:

Number selected	Probability that at least 4 will complete the course
4	0·4096
5	0·7373
6	0·9012
7	0·9669

These figures will help the company to decide on what it means by 'reasonably sure'. The additional cost of taking on more trainees must be balanced against the consequences of ending up with fewer than 4 at the end of the course. In some instances, the risk of approximately 10% which would be run by starting with 6 trainees may be acceptable. In others, the risk of rather less than 4% involved by starting with 7 may be considered too great. In that event, the calculation could be done for 8, 9, and so on until an acceptably small risk level had been reached.

It would probably also be necessary to investigate the probability that more than 4 would complete the course. The ease with which more than 4 could be absorbed by the company could then also be taken into account.

Exercises

2.4.   In a computer punch room 5% of the cards which are punched contain errors. A spot check is made on the work of a certain operator by taking 4 cards at random from her output. Two of these cards are found to contain errors. Would you consider that this is convincing evidence that the operator's work is sub-standard?

2.5.   The probability that a school-leaver taking up employment in an office will leave within twelve months is 0·4 in Company ABC. What is the probability that out of 5 school-leavers entering the company:

   (*a*) 0,
   (*b*) 1,
   (*c*) at least 1 will leave within twelve months?

2.6.   The game of Russian roulette is played by placing one bullet in a six-shooter and leaving the other five chambers empty. The cylinder is given a spin, the pistol pointed at the player's head and the trigger is pressed. If a group of 6 army officers each have one turn, what is the probability that:

   (*a*) 0,
   (*b*) 1,
   (*c*) more than 1 of them will be killed?

2.7.   A certain brand of wrapped sweets contains a number of different centres. The most popular centre in the assortment is known as 'Kreemy-Krunch'. The retailer receives this brand in large boxes in which all the centres are mixed together. When weighing them out for sale, he picks at random from the box. If the manufacturer puts 10% of Kreemy-Krunch centres into the boxes, what is the probability that a customer who buys $\frac{1}{4}$ lb of the sweets will get at least 1 ? $\frac{1}{4}$ lb contains 20 sweets.

    2.8.   Calculate the complete binomial distributions for:

      (a) $n = 5$, $p = 0.10$;

      (b) $n = 5$, $p = 0.50$.

    2.9.   Draw the histograms of the distributions calculated in Exercise 2.8.

The Poisson Distribution

When the probability of a certain event occurring is constant, we have seen that the probabilities of the event occurring 0, 1, 2 . . . n times in a series of n trials (that is, in a sample of size n) follow the binomial distribution. In order to determine these probabilities, we need to know the probability p that the event will occur in a single trial, and the total number n of trials made.

There are cases where the number of times an event occurs can be counted, but no real meaning can be attached to n and p. Consider, for instance, the number of goals scored in a football match. We can count the number of times the event 'scoring a goal' occurs, but we cannot say how many trials were made. In other words, no value can be assigned to n. Similarly, we can count how many knots there are in a ball of knitting wool, but again no meaning can be found for n and p.

We can, however, make n and p meaningful if we think of this type of situation in the following somewhat artificial way. Imagine the ball of wool as being made up of thousands of equal, very short, lengths of wool. Some of these will contain a knot and the remainder will not. We may have, for example, 10 000 short lengths, of which 5 contain a knot. Another ball of similar size may have 3 knots in 10 000 short lengths.

We can think of these balls as samples of 10 000 short lengths of wool from the population of short lengths which comprises our total production. A proportion of these contain a knot. The distribution of the number of knots per sample, that is, the number per ball, will therefore follow the binomial distribution, with $n = 10\,000$ and p being the proportion of short lengths in the population which contain a knot. The actual value of p will not be known, but it will certainly be very small: a ball containing 3 knots would estimate it at $\frac{3}{10\,000}$.

We can similarly regard a football match as being a sample of thousands of instants of time, some of which, perhaps 4 or 5, will contain a goal. Again n will be very large, and p (the probability that any particular instant contains a goal) will be very small.

It can be shown mathematically that as n gets larger and p gets smaller, the binomial distribution merges into another one called the **Poisson distribution**, named after the French statistician who was one of the first to derive it.

The Poisson distribution can thus be expected to apply to many practical situations similar to the ones just discussed. The essential requirement is that the probability of the event under consideration must be constant. If the number of goals scored per match is to follow the distribution, this implies that a goal must be equally likely to be scored at any time during the ninety minutes of playing time. If the distribution of knots is Poisson, this implies that a break is just as likely to occur at any time during the making up of the wool into balls.

All that is needed to calculate the Poisson distribution is the *average number* of occurrences of the event. The probabilities of getting 0, 1, 2, . . . occurrences on any particular occasion may then be found by putting x successively equal to 0, 1, 2, . . . in the following formula:

$$P(x) = \frac{e^{-m}m^x}{x!} \qquad \ldots (2.2)$$

In this formula, m is the average number of occurrences and e is the mathematical constant (equal to approx. 2·7183). It is not too difficult to calculate probabilities from this formula, especially when tables of e^{-m} are available. However, it is not necessary to do so because tables of the Poisson probabilities themselves have been compiled for a comprehensive range of values for m. These may be found in Table I at the end of the book.

Example 2.3

We examine 100 balls of knitting wool and find a total of 150 knots, giving an average per ball of 1·5. Consulting Table I for $m = 1·5$, we can read off the following probabilities:

Number of knots (x)	Probability
0	0·2231
1	0·3347
2	0·2510
3	0·1255
4	0·0471
5	0·0141
6	0·0035
7	0·0008
8	0·0001

From these probabilities we can calculate how many balls in our 100 we would theoretically expect to contain each number of knots. These are obtained simply by multiplying the probabilities by 100.

By comparing these theoretical frequencies with those actually observed in our 100 balls, we are able to check on how well the theoretical distribution fits the observed data. A close correspondence between the two sets of frequencies confirms that the event being investigated does occur in a random way. How close is 'close'? Chapter 4 describes a test which answers this question.

Table 2.1 shows that there is a close correspondence between observed and theoretical frequencies, indicating that knots do occur in a random way. When this investigation was carried out, it was hoped that the observed frequencies would not agree with the theoretical ones. This would have meant that there was some systematic cause of knots which could perhaps have been tracked down and eliminated.

TABLE 2.1

Number of knots	Observed frequencies	Theoretical frequencies
0	21	22·31
1	34	33·47
2	26	25·10
3	13	12·55
4	5	4·71
5	1	1·41
6	0	0·35

It will be noticed that the theoretical frequencies are not whole numbers. That is because they represent average values. In other words, if the distribution of knots is Poisson, we will get an average of 22·31 balls in every 100 containing no knots.

Example 2.4

A pool of fitters is to be established to deal with emergency plant breakdowns. How many fitters should be in the pool?

This type of problem can often be resolved by using the Poisson distribution. Breakdowns, by their very nature, tend to occur in a random way. The probabilities of getting 0, 1, 2, . . . breakdowns per day may be calculated and used to balance the cost of breakdowns having to wait for attention against the cost of additional fitters in the pool.

Let us suppose that an analysis of past records reveals that, on average, 3·2 breakdowns occur daily. For the sake of simplicity, we will assume that once a fitter has been called out, he is not available again on that day.

Referring to Table I, with $m = 3·2$, the probabilities of x breakdowns per day may be read off for $x = 0$, 1, 2, . . . These are given in the second column of Table 2.2 (page 30). Column 3 shows the *cumulative* probability of getting x *or more* breakdowns on any day. These are calculated from column 2 as follows.

Clearly the probability of 0 or more breakdowns occurring must be 1·0000, which is therefore the first entry in column 3.

The probability of 1 or more will be $\{1·0000 - P(0)\}$, which is $(1·0000 - 0·0408) = 0·9592$.

The probability of 2 or more will be $\{P(1 \text{ or more}) - P(1)\}$, which is $(0·9592 - 0·1304) = 0·8288$.

Each entry in column 3 is thus obtained by subtracting the entries in columns 2 and 3 on the line above.

The cost of a breakdown having tó wait until the following day for attention is estimated at £100, and the cost of providing an extra fitter (or presumably a fitter-mate pair) is £10 per day.

Suppose we have 5 fitters in the pool. What will be the cost of unattended breakdowns? These will occur whenever more than 5 fitters are needed on a particular day. When 6 breakdowns occur, 1 will have to wait at a cost of £100. When 7 occur, 2 will have to

TABLE 2.2

Number of breakdowns (x)	Probability	Cumulative probability of x or more
0	0·0408	1·0000
1	0·1304	0·9592
2	0·2087	0·8288
3	0·2226	0·6201
4	0·1781	0·3975
5	0·1140	0·2194
6	0·0608	0·1054
7	0·0278	0·0446
8	0·0111	0·0168
9	0·0040	0·0057
10	0·0013	0·0018
11	0·0004	0·0005
12	0·0001	0·0001

wait at a cost of £200 and so on. Now from Table 2.2 we can see that 6 breakdowns will occur with probability 0·0608, or on 6·08% of days. This means that the *average daily* cost arising from these will be £100 × 0·0608 = £6·08.

Similarly, the average daily cost arising from occasions when 7 breakdowns occur will be £200 × 0·0278 = £5·56, and so on.

The total cost of breakdowns if 5 fitters are in the pool will thus be:

$$
\begin{aligned}
& 0\cdot0608 \times £100 \\
+\, & 0\cdot0278 \times £200 \\
+\, & 0\cdot0111 \times £300 \\
+\, & 0\cdot0040 \times £400 \\
+\, & 0\cdot0013 \times £500 \\
+\, & 0\cdot0004 \times £600 \\
+\, & 0\cdot0001 \times £700
\end{aligned}
$$

which comes to £17·53.

If we increase the pool to 6 fitters, the cost of breakdowns will be reduced to:

$$0{\cdot}0278 \times £100$$
$$+ 0{\cdot}0111 \times £200$$
$$+ 0{\cdot}0040 \times £300$$
$$+ 0{\cdot}0013 \times £400$$
$$+ 0{\cdot}0004 \times £500$$
$$+ 0{\cdot}0001 \times £600$$

which adds up to £6·98.

The £10 per day which will be paid for the sixth fitter can thus be more than offset by the saving of £17·53 – £6·98 = £10·55 which will result.

We can now go on to assess what would happen if a further fitter were added. There is no need in this particular case to do the detailed calculations, because we could not possibly save more than £6·98. This would not justify an extra fitter, so the size of the pool is established at 6.

It should be emphasized that this simple approach provides only an approximate solution to the problem. In particular, we have always assumed that when more breakdowns occur than can be dealt with on one day, the surplus can always be handled on the following day, in addition to that day's breakdowns. This will not always be the case. A more sophisticated approach, using an advanced development of probability theory known as **queueing theory,** would enable this to be taken into account.

We have also ignored the small cost which will arise from breakdowns very occasionally having to wait for two days.

Example 2.5

Because of the awkwardness of the calculations involved when working with the binomial distribution, particularly when n is large, the Poisson is often used as an approximation. Earlier in this chapter we saw how, as n increases and p decreases, the binomial merges into the· Poisson. It can be shown that by the time p is as small as 0·1 and n is larger than about 30, the two distributions are almost identical.

Suppose that a screw manufacturing machine produces 1 % of its output without a slot cut in the top. These defective screws are randomly scattered throughout the production. The screws are packed into boxes of 250. The manufacturer offers to supply another box free to any customer who buys one and finds that it contains more than 5 slot-less screws. How much will this offer cost if the sales forecast of 100 000 boxes over the next year is achieved, and each box costs the manufacturer 25 new pence to produce?

Each box is in effect a sample of 250 from the total production. This total production contains 1 % of slot-less screws. The number of slot-less screws per box will therefore follow the binomial distribution with $n = 250$ and $p = 0.01$. Formula (2.1) could be used to calculate the proportion of boxes which will contain more than 5 slot-less screws by successively putting $x = 6, 7, \ldots$ with $n = 250$ and $p = 0.01$.

It is, however, much easier to use the Poisson approximation. To do this, we need to know the average number of slot-less screws per box. 1 % of the population has this defect, so on average, we would expect to get 1 % of the sample showing the defect. In other words, the average of a binomial distribution is np.

Putting $m = np$ will then enable us to calculate the required probabilities using formula (2.2), or to read them off from the appropriate section of Table I. We have $np = 250 \times 0.01 = 2.5$, so the probabilities of getting 6, 7, . . . defective screws in a box are:

x	Probability
6	0·0278
7	0·0099
8	0·0031
9	0·0009
10	0·0002

The probability of getting more than 5 per box will be the sum of these probabilities, which is 0·0419. Interpreting this as a percentage, 4·19 % of all the boxes will contain more than 5 slot-less screws.

Of the expected sales of 100 000 boxes, then, 4190 will qualify for a free replacement. Assuming that all customers ask for their free box, this will cost the manufacturer 4190×25 new pence, which is approximately £1050.

Exercises

2.10. The average demand on a factory store for a certain type of electric motor is 6 per week. When the storekeeper places an order for these motors, delivery takes one week. If the distribution of demand is Poisson, how low can the storekeeper allow his stock to fall before ordering a new supply? He wants to be at least 95% certain that he can meet requirements while waiting for the new supply to arrive.

2.11.   The number of telephone calls coming into a switchboard during each minute of the morning busy period follows the Poisson distribution with an average of 10. The switchboard can handle a maximum of 20 calls per minute. What is the probability that in one particular minute the switchboard will be overloaded?

2.12.   Customers enter a supermarket randomly at an average rate of 240 per hour.

(a) What is the probability that during a one-minute interval no one will come in?

(b) What is the maximum number likely to enter during any two-minute period?

Take 'likely' as meaning with 0·95 probability.

2.13.   Assume that 1 in every 10 000 cars travelling along a stretch of motorway requests assistance on the roadside telephones. During a peak holiday Saturday, it is estimated that 60 000 vehicles will use the motorway. What is the maximum number of calls which may be expected, with 99% certainty?

2.14.   The following data were compiled from an analysis of two weeks' football results. Calculate the theoretical frequencies, assuming a Poisson distribution.

Number of goals (x)	Number of teams scoring x goals
0	32
1	52
2	44
3	29
4	13
5	6
6	2

Draw the histogram of observed frequencies and superimpose the theoretical frequencies on to it.

The Normal Distribution

Both the distributions which we have so far considered have been concerned with **discrete** variables. In other words, the variable could only be a whole number. These distributions may be represented exactly by means of a step-wise histogram such as the one in Figure 2.2. (Incidentally, you should now be able to recognize this distribution as a binomial.)

In Figure 2.1, on the other hand, the steps in the histogram are purely arbitrary. This is because the variable concerned, time, is a **continuous** variable. If we had measured our journey times to the nearest half-minute, the bars would have been half as wide and there would have been twice as many of them. Measurement to the nearest quarter-minute would again double the number of bars and halve their width. Eventually, as the accuracy of measurement increased, the outline of the distribution would merge into a smooth curve. This is shown pictorially in Figure 2.3.

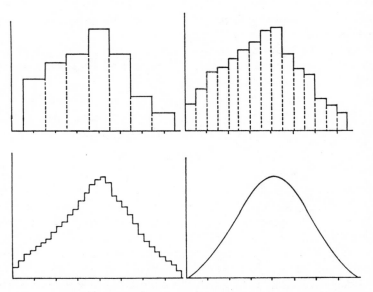

Figure 2.3. Successive approximations to a continuous distribution

The true probability distribution of a continuous variable will therefore always be some sort of smooth curve. The probability that a member of the population selected at random will fall within any specified range will be given by the corresponding proportion of the total area under the curve.

To clarify this point, look at Figure 2.4. This represents the probability distribution of the height in inches of adult males. The probability that the height of a man selected at random will be between 65 and 70 in is the shaded portion of the distribution. Another way of looking at this is to say that the percentage of the population who are between 65 and 70 in is found by expressing the shaded area as a percentage of the total area under the curve.

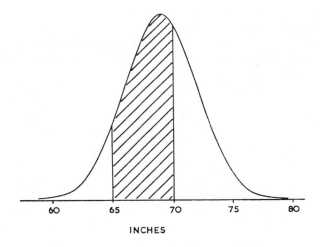

INCHES

Figure 2.4. Probability distribution of height

Before this area can be determined, it is necessary to know the mathematical equation of the curve. In any given practical situation, it is virtually impossible to find this equation. Its calculation would usually require an examination of the entire population. Fortunately there are once again a number of standard theoretical distributions to one or other of which many practical distributions conform very closely. By far the most important of these is known as the **normal distribution**.

This distribution was developed on the hypothesis that whenever a thing is measured, the measurement is subject to the influence of many sources of error. Each of these is in itself very tiny but they combine together purely at random to produce a noticeable total error.

In practice, these conditions are never fulfilled completely, so it is very doubtful if the normal distribution ever applies exactly. However, it is surprising how often it provides a satisfactorily close approximation.

Parameters of the Normal Distribution

The normal curve has a characteristic bell shape and is symmetrical. The ends of the curve are asymptotic to the x axis, that is, they get closer and closer to it but never quite touch it.

There are two fundamental measurements which specify any particular normal curve completely. One of these indicates the centre of the distribution and the other measures its width. These two measurements are known as the **parameters** of the distribution. The measurement of the centre is the arithmetic **mean** or average of the population. The measurement of width is a kind of average of the deviations from the mean. It is called the **standard deviation**. To calculate these parameters exactly would involve measuring every member of the population. This is hardly ever possible, and so we must estimate them from a sample. The necessary calculations are described in detail in Appendix A.

Each different pair of numbers for the mean and standard deviation defines a different normal curve. Unless some other way could be found, therefore, we should have to compile separate probability tables for all possible pairs of values of the mean and standard deviation. Fortunately this is not necessary, because the proportion of the population which falls between the mean and a specified number of standard deviations away from the mean is always constant, regardless of the actual numerical values of the mean and standard deviation.

Look at the distributions in Figure 2.5. The top one has a mean value of 12 and a standard deviation (S.D.) of 2. The bottom one has a mean of 16 and a standard deviation of 4. In each case, the shaded portion covers the area between the mean and one standard

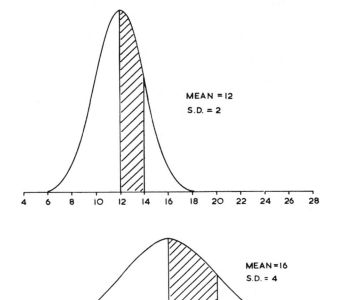

Figure 2.5. Normal distributions

deviation above the mean. This area covers the same proportion of both distributions. It is in fact 0·3413 or 34·13%.

One table of probabilities is therefore sufficient, provided that it is expressed in terms of distances in standard deviations from the mean. This table appears as Table II at the end of the book. An example will clarify this and illustrate how the table is used.

An automatic detergent packing machine produces packages whose weights are normally distributed with a mean of 8·000 oz and a standard deviation of 0·010 oz. What is the probability that a package selected at random will be between 8·000 oz and 8·015 oz?

It is conventional to denote the mean of a normal distribution by the Greek letter μ (mu) and the standard deviation by the Greek letter σ (sigma). We have in this example $\mu = 8·000$ and $\sigma = 0·010$, and we require to find the shaded portion of the distribution in Figure 2.6.

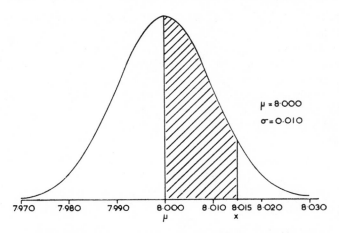

Figure 2.6. Distribution of weights of packages of detergent

To find this probability from the table, we must first calculate how many standard deviations away from the mean the point 8·015 lies. Calling this 'number of standard deviations' z we have:

$$z = \frac{8·015 - 8·000}{0·010} = 1·50$$

Consulting Table II with $z = 1·50$, we find that the required probability (area) is 0·4332.

We may generalize the way in which z was calculated to give us the formula:

$$z = \frac{x - \mu}{\sigma} \qquad \qquad \ldots (2.3)$$

where x stands for any specified value of the variable.

Various ways in which the table may be used to calculate the areas of other sections of the curve are:

(a) What proportion of packages are between 7·985 oz and 8·000 oz?

The required section of the distribution is shaded in Figure 2.7 (a). Using formula (2.3), we have:

$$z = \frac{7·985 - 8·000}{0·010} = -1·5$$

The negative sign of z indicates that the point we are considering is less than the mean. In Table II, only positive values of z are given. Since the distribution is symmetrical, however, areas under the left-hand half of the curve will be identical with the corresponding areas under the right-hand half.

The shaded area in Figure 2.7 (a), then, corresponds exactly to the shaded area in Figure 2.6, which has $z = +1 \cdot 5$, although the distributions are drawn to different scales. The required area is therefore $0 \cdot 4332$.

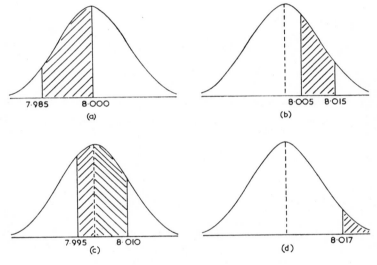

Figure 2.7. Areas of the normal curve

(b) What proportion are between $8 \cdot 005$ and $8 \cdot 015$?

Here the required area does not have the mean as one of its boundaries. We must first find the area from the mean up to $8 \cdot 015$ and then subtract from this the area from the mean up to $8 \cdot 005$. Figure 2·7 (b) illustrates this.

$$z_1 = \frac{8 \cdot 015 - 8 \cdot 000}{0 \cdot 010} = 1 \cdot 5$$

Area between $8 \cdot 000$ and $8 \cdot 015 = 0 \cdot 4332$

$$z_2 = \frac{8 \cdot 005 - 8 \cdot 000}{0 \cdot 010} = 0 \cdot 5$$

Area between $8 \cdot 000$ and $8 \cdot 005 = 0 \cdot 1915$

The area between $8 \cdot 005$ and $8 \cdot 015$ is the difference between these, which is $0 \cdot 4332 - 0 \cdot 1915 = 0 \cdot 2417$.

(c) What proportion are between $7 \cdot 995$ and $8 \cdot 010$?

In Figure 2.7 (c), we can see that the mean lies inside the required area. This time then, we must find the areas from the mean up to each of the boundaries and add them together.

$$z_1 = \frac{7 \cdot 995 - 8 \cdot 000}{0 \cdot 010} = -0 \cdot 5$$

Area between $7 \cdot 995$ and $8 \cdot 000 = 0 \cdot 1915$

$$z_2 = \frac{8 \cdot 010 - 8 \cdot 000}{0 \cdot 010} = 1 \cdot 0$$

Area between $8 \cdot 000$ and $8 \cdot 010 = 0 \cdot 3413$

The area between $7 \cdot 995$ and $8 \cdot 010$ is the sum of these, which is $0 \cdot 1915 + 0 \cdot 3413 = 0 \cdot 5328$.

(d) What proportion are above $8 \cdot 017$?

The area above $8 \cdot 000 = 0 \cdot 5000$. For the point $8 \cdot 017$,

$$z = \frac{8 \cdot 017 - 8 \cdot 000}{0 \cdot 010} = 1 \cdot 7$$

Area between $8 \cdot 000$ and $8 \cdot 017 = 0 \cdot 4554$

The area above $8 \cdot 017$ is the difference between these, which is $0 \cdot 5000 - 0 \cdot 4554 = 0 \cdot 0446$.

Example 2.6

One of the garments produced by a knitwear manufacturer is a men's sweater. It is made in a range of sizes based on chest measurement. The size ranges are 32–34 in, 34–36 in and so on. The average chest measurement of the male population is $37 \cdot 5$ in with a standard deviation of 2 in. What proportion of his total output should the manufacturer put into each size category? Before using the normal distribution to estimate these proportions, we must satisfy ourselves that the normal curve does provide a good approximation to the distribution of chest measurements. This remark applies to all the exercises and examples in this section. The appropriate test is described in Example 4.1 on page 107.

Assuming that this test has been successfully applied, our problem is to calculate the proportions of the distribution which fall into each of the sections marked in Figure 2.8.

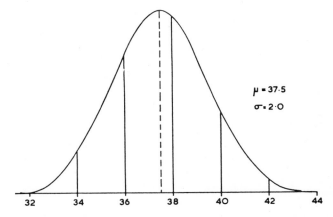

$\mu = 37.5$
$\sigma = 2.0$

Figure 2.8. Breakdown of chest measurements into size categories

The first step is to calculate the z values corresponding to each size-range boundary. These are obtained by successively putting $x = 32, 34, \ldots$ in formula (2.3).

$$\text{Putting } x = 32, \text{ we have } z = \frac{32 - 37.5}{2.0} = -2.75$$

$$\text{Putting } x = 34, \text{ ,, ,, } z = \frac{34 - 37.5}{2.0} = -1.75$$

$$\text{Putting } x = 36, \text{ ,, ,, } z = \frac{36 - 37.5}{2.0} = -0.75$$

$$\text{Putting } x = 38, \text{ ,, ,, } z = \frac{38 - 37.5}{2.0} = +0.25$$

$$\text{Putting } x = 40, \text{ ,, ,, } z = \frac{40 - 37.5}{2.0} = +1.25$$

$$\text{Putting } x = 42, \text{ ,, ,, } z = \frac{42 - 37.5}{2.0} = +2.25$$

Using Table II, we now find the areas between each of these points and the mean. They are:

z	Area
− 2·75	0·4970
− 1·75	0·4599
− 0·75	0·2734
+ 0·25	0·0987
+ 1·25	0·3944
+ 2·25	0·4878

The proportions of the distribution falling into each size category will therefore be:

Category		Proportion
32–34	0·4970 − 0·4599 =	0·0371 or 3·71%
34–36	0·4599 − 0·2734 =	0·1865 or 18·65%
36–38	0·2734 + 0·0987 =	0·3721 or 37·21%
38–40	0·3944 − 0·0987 =	0·2957 or 29·57%
40–42	0·4878 − 0·3944 =	0·0934 or 9·34%

Example 2.7

Margarine is automatically made up into 8 oz packages. If the machine doing this work is set to produce an 8 oz package, what it actually produces is a population of packages whose weights are distributed around an average value of 8 oz. This means that 50% of the packages will be under 8 oz. If these are offered for sale as 8 oz packages the manufacturer is liable for prosecution under the Weights and Measures regulations.

It is impossible for the manufacturer to be certain that no underweight packages at all are produced, but he can ensure that they are reduced to an acceptably small percentage. To do this, he must increase the average setting on the machine so that the 8 oz mark falls well down in the lower tail of the distribution. Figure 2.9 illustrates this.

The important question is, just how high must the average setting be? The higher it is, the smaller will be the percentage of underweight packages. On the other hand, the amount of margarine 'given away'

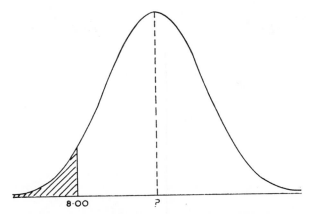

Figure 2.9. Distribution of package weights

with each pack will be larger. Some compromise must be found between these two conflicting objectives of small percentage of underweight packages and small amount of 'give-away'. To help find this compromise, the cost of the give-away for a range of percentages of underweights may be calculated.

Suppose we make the shaded area of Figure 2.9 5% of the distribution. We must then have 45% between 8 oz and the mean. Consulting Table II, we find that the z value associated with an area of 0·4500 is between 1·64 and 1·65. The mean of the distribution (that is the setting on the machine) must therefore be about 1·64 standard deviations above 8 oz.

Assuming that we have estimated the standard deviation at 0·10 oz (in practice it would be much smaller than this), the machine setting would be 8·164 oz. The amount given away per pack is thus 0·164 oz. This can easily be converted into a cash figure. If the company sells 500 tons a year at 5 new pence per pound, the calculation will be as follows:

Quantity given away per pound sold $= 0·164 \times 2$ $= 0·328$ oz

,, ,, ,, ,, ton ,, $= \dfrac{0·328 \times 2240}{16} = 45·92$ lb

,, ,, ,, ,, year $= 45·92 \times 500$ $= 22\,960$ lb

The cost of this at 5p per pound $= \dfrac{22\,960 \times 5}{100}$ $= £1148$

Similar calculations for smaller percentages of underweight packages produce the following results:

%	z value	Cost per year
5	1·64	£1148
4	1·75	£1225
3	1·88	£1316
2	2·05	£1435
1	2·33	£1631

It is interesting to see the way in which the cost increases more and more rapidly as the percentage of underweight packages gets smaller. A 1% reduction from 5% to 4% costs £77. A 1% reduction from 2% to 1% costs £196.

It is now necessary to try to assess the costs of the various percentages of underweight packages. This is essentially the same kind of calculation as was done in Example 2.4 on page 29, but here the costs are not so easy to assess. Presumably one of the major considerations would be the cost of the fine in the event of a prosecution!

Binomial Approximation

The normal curve provides an approximate method of calculating binomial probabilities if n and p fulfil certain conditions. The mean of a binomial distribution is np. As this becomes larger, the binomial approaches nearer and nearer to the normal. It has been calculated that by the time np becomes as large as 5, the two distributions are sufficiently alike for the normal to be used. A further condition is that p must not be smaller than about 0·1.

Before we can use a normal distribution, we need to know its mean and standard deviation. When using it as an approximation to the binomial, therefore, we need to know the mean and standard deviation of the binomial. We have already seen that the mean of a binomial distribution is np. Its standard deviation is also very easy to calculate; it is $\sqrt{np(1-p)}$.

Figure 2.10 shows the binomial distribution for $n=15$, $p=0\cdot4$. Superimposed on it is the normal distribution with $\mu=np=6\cdot0$ and $\sigma=\sqrt{np(1-p)}=1\cdot9$.

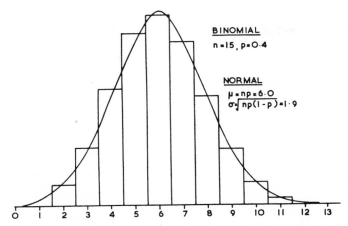

Figure 2.10. Corresponding binomial and normal distributions

In order to see how close the approximation is in this instance, let us calculate the probability of getting 4 defectives in our sample of 15 by both methods.

(a) *Binomial*
Substituting in formula (2.1), we have:

$$P(4) = \frac{15!}{4! \, 11!} (0.4)^4 (0.6)^{11} = 0.1268$$

(b) *Normal*
The normal distribution is continuous, whereas the binomial is discrete. To use the normal approximation, therefore, the discrete variable (number of defectives per sample) must be 'spread' over a continuous scale. This is easily done by regarding the discrete values as continuous ones which have been rounded to the nearest whole number. Thus 4 defectives on the discrete scale corresponds to the range 3·5 to 4·5 on the continuous scale.

We therefore require to find the z values corresponding to the points 3·5 and 4·5 when $\mu = 6·0$ and $\sigma = 1·9$. They are:

$$z = \frac{3·5 - 6·0}{1·9} = -1·32$$

$$z = \frac{4·5 - 6·0}{1·9} = -0·79$$

The areas between these points and the mean are respectively 0·4066 and 0·2852 (from Table II). The required probability is therefore:

$$0·4066 - 0·2852 = 0·1214$$

This differs from the true binomial probability only in the third decimal place.

Poisson Approximation

As the mean value m of a Poisson distribution becomes larger, it too approaches the normal. The normal may thus be used as an approximation to the Poisson when m has become sufficiently large. In this context, 'sufficiently large' means more than about 10.

The standard deviation of a Poisson distribution is $\sqrt{m}$, so the corresponding normal will have $\mu = m$ and $\sigma = \sqrt{m}$.

Combining Normal Distributions

It is frequently necessary to add together a number of normal distributions. In network analysis, for example, the critical path consists of a number of jobs which must be carried out sequentially. The mean and standard deviation of the duration of each job are known, but we wish to know the average or expected time for the whole project, together with its standard deviation.

Let us suppose there are just two jobs, the first of which has an average duration of 10 days with a standard deviation of 3 days while the second has an average of 15 days with a standard deviation of 4 days. What will be the overall average duration and its standard deviation?

The rule is that the average of the sum of a number of distributions is the sum of the individual averages. In our example this gives an overall average duration of $10 + 15 = 25$.

To get the overall standard deviation σ, the rule is:

$$\sigma^2 = \sigma_1^2 + \sigma_2^2 + \ldots$$

where σ_1, σ_2, ... are the individual standard deviations.

In our example we have:

$$\sigma^2 = 9 + 16 = 25$$
$$\therefore \sigma = 5$$

It is sometimes useful to be able to calculate the resulting distribution when two distributions are subtracted. One example of this is given in Exercise 2.17. In such cases the resulting mean is found by subtracting the two original means. Somewhat surprisingly, however, the standard deviation is still found by *adding* the original squared standard deviations and taking the square root.

Exercises

2.15. A normal distribution has a mean of 20 and a standard deviation of 4. Calculate the proportions of the distribution which are in the following intervals:

(*a*) 20 to 23;

(*b*) 17 to 19;

(*c*) 18 to 23;

(*d*) below 15;

(*e*) outside the range 20 ± 6.

2.16. One way to standardize examinations is to ensure that the same percentage of candidates is placed in each grade every year. In such an examination there are five grades, numbered 1 to 5. The first four are passing grades and the fifth is a fail. Each year, 10% of the candidates are placed in Grade 1, 20% in Grade 2, 40% in Grade 3, 20% in Grade 4 and 10% in Grade 5.

In one particular year, the average mark of all the candidates is 60 and the standard deviation is 15. Calculate the marks corresponding to the grade boundaries, assuming that the marks are normally distributed.

2.17. In the manufacture of parts for an engine, the pistons are made with an average diameter of 3·000 in and a standard deviation of 0·004 in. The cylinders into which they fit have an average diameter of 3·010 in with a standard deviation of 0·006 in. If pistons and cylinders are paired off in a random way:

(*a*) what proportion of pistons will be too large to fit into the cylinder?

(*b*) the amount of 'slack' in the fit must be between 0·003 and 0·020 in; what proportion will not meet this requirement?

2.18. In compiling synthetic data in Time Study, the time which a competent operator takes to perform short elements of work is established. These short elemental times are then used to synthesize the time required for complete jobs which are made up of a number of these basic elements.

Such a job consists of 10 elements, each of which takes an average time of 0·5 minutes with a standard deviation of 0·05 minutes. What is the overall average time for the job and its standard deviation?

2.19. The weekly demand for a certain stores item is normally distributed with an average of 100 and a standard deviation of 10. When an order is placed for a replenishment of stock, the time taken before the new supply is received is one week.

(a) How low can the stock level be allowed to fall before placing an order, to be 95% certain that the new supply will arrive before stocks are exhausted?

(b) Do the same calculations for a delivery period of four weeks.

The negative exponential distribution

When events are occurring at random in some continuum such as time, the number of events which occur in intervals of constant length will conform to the Poisson distribution. In example 2.4 on page 29 we considered the distribution of the number of machine breakdowns per day in a production department. Because breakdowns were occurring at random, the Poisson distribution enabled us to calculate the probability of a given number of breakdowns occurring on any given day.

A rather more detailed study of that situation would require us to look at the distribution of the time which elapses *between* breakdowns, and relate this to the time taken by a fitter to effect a repair. In fact the queueing theory approach referred to on page 31 does just that.

In many contexts, it is more useful to concentrate on the time between successive occurrences of the event, rather than on the number of occurrences in some fixed unit of time. Suppose, for example, that a component in an electronic device has an average life of 2000 hours. What is the probability that it will operate satisfactorily for at least 1000 hours? This kind of assessment plays an important part in reliability calculations and in determining replacement and planned maintenance policies.

The Poisson distribution, being essentially a count of the number of times the event of interest happens in a fixed interval, is a discrete distribution. The length of time between occurrences, however, is a continuous distribution, ranging in theory from zero to infinity. This distribution is known as the **negative exponential distribution.**

Suppose that events are occurring at an average rate m per unit time. The average number of occurrences in a time of length t will be mt. From the Poisson distribution, the probability of no occurrences in a random length of time t is e^{-mt}.

Whenever there are no occurrences of the event in an interval of length t, there must be an interval of at least t between two successive events. The cumulative form of the negative exponential distribution may thus be stated as:

$$P(\text{time between occurrences} > t) = e^{-mt}$$

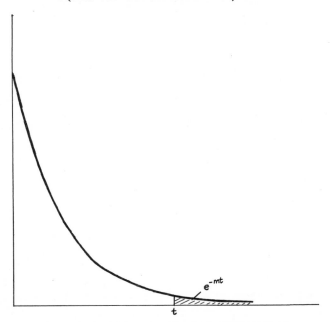

Figure 2.11. A Negative Exponential Distribution

Figure 2.11 shows this pictorially. Notice that the distribution is very heavily skewed. The parameter m is the average number of occurrences per unit time. The average time between occurrences will thus be $\frac{1}{m}$. In the reliability context of the example quoted earlier, this is often referred to as 'mean time between failures'.

To return to that example, we have $\frac{1}{m} = 2000$ hours.

Putting $t = 1000$, therefore, $mt = \frac{1000}{2000} = 0\cdot5$

and P(time to failure > 1000 hours) $= e^{-0\cdot5}$.

From Table IX, $e^{-0\cdot5}$ is found to be $0\cdot6065$.

Example 2.8

It is sometimes useful to calculate the complete distribution for comparison with observed data, as a test of randomness. Let us consider the following data, relating to the interval of time which elapsed between 100 successive arrivals of motor cars at a service station:

Time between arrivals (minutes)	Observed frequency
0–1	46
1–2	24
2–3	15
3–4	7
4–5	4
>5	4

If cars are arriving at random, this distribution should conform to the negative exponential.

We first calculate the approximate average inter-arrival time by using class mid-points. The final class is assumed to have an upper boundary of 6:

$$\frac{1}{m} = \frac{(0\cdot5 \times 46) + (1\cdot5 \times 24) + (2\cdot5 \times 15) + (3\cdot5 \times 7) + (4\cdot5 \times 4) + (5\cdot5 \times 4)}{100}$$

$$= 1\cdot61$$

This gives $m = \frac{1}{1\cdot61}$ minutes $= \left|0\cdot62\right.$

A more accurate average could be calculated if we had the 100 actual inter-arrival times available.

The remaining calculations are summarised below:

Class	t Class boundaries	$e^{-0.62t}$ $P(>t)$	Class probability	Theoretical frequency	Observed frequency
	0	1·0000			
0–1			0·4621	46·21	46
	1	0·5379			
1–2			0·2485	24·85	24
	2	0·2894			
2–3			0·1337	13·37	15
	3	0·1557			
3–4			0·0720	7·20	7
	4	0·0837			
4–5			0·0387	3·87	4
	5	0·0450			
>5			0·0450	4·50	4
	∞	0·0000			

The probability that the inter-arrival time exceeds t is $e^{-0.62t}$. By putting t successively equal to each class boundary and using Table IX, we find the probability of exceeding the time represented by each class boundary. Subtraction of successive items in this column gives the class probabilities. For example, the probability of exceeding 2 minutes is 0·2894 and of exceeding 3 minutes is 0·1557. The probability of a time between 2 and 3 minutes is therefore $0.2894 - 0.1557 = 0.1337$.

The theoretical frequencies for a sample of 100 inter-arrival times are compared with the observed frequencies in the final two columns. There is a close correspondence between these two sets of frequencies, indicating that cars do arrive in a random fashion.

Exercise 2.20

If the length of a local telephone call conforms to the negative exponential distribution with an average of 3 minutes:

(a) What is the probability that a call will exceed 10 minutes?

(b) How many calls in every 100 will last between 1 and 2 minutes?

Exercise 2.21

Calculate the complete probability distribution for the life of an electronic component which conforms to the negative exponential with an average of 2000 hours. Use class intervals of 1000 hours.

3 SAMPLING DISTRIBUTIONS

Very rarely is it possible to examine an entire population. Usually we must take a sample and base our conclusions about the population on the sample results. The study of the way in which samples behave is thus an extremely important branch of statistics.

It is immediately apparent that before any sound inferences can be made, the sample must be representative of the population. If we were to use a sample of tomatoes taken from the front of a market stall to estimate the general quality, we should be very likely to get a wrong impression. Our sample would be biased. It is essential that any samples we take are unbiased and truly representative of the population.

To ensure this, it is usually stipulated in sampling theory that a sample must be **random**. We have used this word a number of times already in rather a loose way. The precise definition of a random sample is that every member of the population must have an equal chance of being selected.

We have seen that a normal distribution is completely identified by two parameters, its mean and its standard deviation. If we take a sample from the population and calculate the mean and standard deviation of the sample, these will be estimates of the population parameters. A sample estimate of a population parameter is called a **statistic**.

In sampling theory, we are concerned with the problems of estimating population parameters from sample statistics. Questions such as 'How close to the required parameter can a statistic be expected to lie?' 'How sure can we be that our estimate is not more than a specified quantity out?' can be answered by studying the appropriate **sampling distribution**.

The concept of a sampling distribution is one of the most important ideas in statistics. Every sample statistic has a sampling distribution which must be investigated before any interpretation of the sample results is possible. We shall be looking at the most important ones in this chapter and the next.

The Sampling Distribution of a Percentage

To establish this concept of a sampling distribution let us consider a practical situation. Out of a random sample of 1000 electors, 500 say that they will vote Conservative at the next election. What conclusions can we draw from this about the percentage of the total electorate who hold this view?

Our sample has estimated this percentage at 50%. We cannot claim, however, that this is the exact population percentage. Another sample, taken at the same time, may well contain 45% or 55% of electors who hold this view. In other words, although the population percentage is constant (at least for a short period of time), sample estimates of it will vary.

The way in which sample estimates are likely to vary is of great importance. In particular, we must know how much difference there is likely to be between the population percentage and our estimate of it. Without this knowledge, we are not able to assess the possible error in our sample estimate.

The aggregate of all possible sample estimates which could occur for a sample of a given size comprises the sampling distribution. If the sample size is large, the sampling distribution may be closely approximated by a normal curve.

It will be convenient at this point to introduce some notation. We need to be able to distinguish between the true population percentage and a sample estimate of that percentage. Accordingly, we shall use different symbols to denote these. The true percentage we shall call π (the Greek letter pi) and the sample estimate will be P.

To be able to make use of the sampling distribution, we must know its mean and standard deviation. As might be expected intuitively, the mean is the true population percentage π. In other words, if we took a very large number of sample estimates and took their average, we should expect this to be the true percentage.

The standard deviation of a sampling distribution is usually known as the **standard error** of that particular statistic. This is rather a good name, since it emphasizes the fact that it enables us to assess the extent to which a sample estimate is likely to be in error. The standard error of the sampling distribution of a percentage is

$$\sqrt{\frac{\pi(100 - \pi)}{n}}$$

where n is the size of the sample.

Estimating an Unknown Percentage

Let us now return to the problem of interpreting the 50% estimate in our sample of 1000. The sampling distribution enables us to calculate limits between which the true percentage is almost certain to lie. These limits are known as **confidence limits.**

In any normal distribution, 95% of the population lies within ±1·96 standard deviations of the mean. Another way of saying this is that there is a probability of 0·95 that an item picked at random from the population will lie within this range.

Our sample estimate P is in effect a random selection from a normal distribution with mean $= \pi$ and standard error (standard deviation) $= \sqrt{\dfrac{\pi(100 - \pi)}{n}}$. There is thus a probability of 0·95 that P is within ±1·96 standard errors of π.

Now the actual value of π is not known, but because of the foregoing statement, we can be 95% certain that it is not more than 1·96 standard errors away from P. For ease of calculation, this is usually rounded off to 2. Accordingly, therefore, we can say with 95% confidence that:

$$\pi \text{ lies between } P \pm 2 \sqrt{\frac{\pi(100 - \pi)}{n}}$$

To evaluate this expression, we need to know π, which is the very thing we are trying to estimate! Fortunately, P may be substituted in the standard error formula without any serious loss of accuracy. We then have:

$$\pi \text{ lies between } P \pm 2 \sqrt{\frac{P(100 - P)}{n}} \qquad \ldots (3.1)$$

In our example, we have $P = 50\%$ and $n = 1000$. We can therefore say with 95% confidence that:

$$\pi \text{ lies between } 50\% \pm 2 \sqrt{\frac{50 \times 50}{1000}}$$

which is $50\% \pm 3\cdot1\%$, or within the range $46\cdot9\%$ to $53\cdot1\%$.

These are known as the **95% confidence limits** for π. In the long run, the true value of π will lie outside the calculated range 5% of the time. 95% limits are nearly always used in practice, but limits may be calculated for any chosen confidence level. 99% confidence limits, for example, would require us to take $\pm 2 \cdot 58$ standard errors.

Calculating the Sample Size

In the example just calculated, we have seen that our estimate of 50% is likely to be within $3 \cdot 1\%$ of the true percentage. Suppose that this is not accurate enough for our purpose. How can it be improved?

The answer clearly lies in the size of sample. In the standard error formula, n appears as the denominator. Increasing n will therefore reduce the standard error, which will in turn reduce the width of the confidence band.

If an answer which is not likely to be in error by more than 1% is required, we have:

$$2\sqrt{\frac{P(100-P)}{n}} = 1 \qquad \ldots (3.2)$$

Squaring this and transposing it gives:

$$n = 4P(100-P)$$
$$= 4 \times 50 \times 50 = 10\ 000$$

Notice that this calculation requires that a provisional estimate P be available. If an estimate is not available, a sample which is at least large enough may be ensured by putting $P = 50\%$, since the maximum value of $P(100-P)$ is 2500, which only occurs when $P = 50$. Where P subsequently turns out to be substantially different from 50%, however, it means that a sample much larger than necessary has been taken.

In the above example, if $P = 30\%$ then the required sample size for $\pm 1\%$ accuracy would be:

$$n = 4 \times 30 \times 70 = 8400$$

which is substantially less than the 10 000 required if $P = 50\%$.

A better way is to take a smallish sample first to get a preliminary estimate for P. This may then be used to calculate the full sample required. The original sample may, of course, be incorporated into the complete sample. If it turns out that the provisional estimate of P was very inaccurate, a revised calculation of n may be done to make sure that the sample size will be adequate. This will only be necessary if P is nearer to 50% than was the original estimate.

Equation (3.2) enables us to calculate the sample size required to give ± 1% accuracy. This may be generalized to give n for any specified percentage accuracy. Calling this specified percentage L, equation (3.2) becomes:

$$2\sqrt{\frac{P(100-P)}{n}} = L$$

Squaring and transposing gives:

$$n = \frac{4P(100-P)}{L^2} \qquad\qquad \dots (3.3)$$

Example 3.1

In order to evaluate the success of a television advertising campaign for a new product, a company interviewed 400 housewives in the television area. 120 of them knew about the product. How accurately does this estimate the percentage of housewives in the area who know of the product? How many more interviews must be made in order to establish this percentage, with ± 2% accuracy, at the 95% confidence level?

In the original sample, $n = 400$ and $P = 30$%. Substituting these values in formula (3.1) gives:

$$\pi \text{ lies between } 30\% \pm 2\sqrt{\frac{30 \times 70}{400}}$$

$$= 30\% \pm 4\cdot6\%$$

To find the sample size needed to reduce this to ± 2% accuracy, we must use equation (3.3) with $L = 2$ and $P = 30$. This gives:

$$n = \frac{4 \times 30 \times 70}{4} = 2100$$

Exercises

3.1. A cigarette company wishes to establish the percentage of smokers who prefer its brand to any other. The percentage is thought to be about 30%.

(a) Using this as an estimate for P, calculate the sample size which will be necessary to estimate the true percentage to within 2%.

(b) When the sample has been taken, P is found to be 25%. Will the sample need to be enlarged to ensure the required accuracy?

3.2. Activity sampling is a widely used Work Study technique which enables an estimate to be made of the percentage of the total time which a machine or operator spends on various activities. Observations are taken at random times and the activity on which the subject is engaged at each observation is noted. The percentage of occasions on which each activity was observed is then used as an estimate of the percentage of the total time which is spent on that activity.

A sample of 1000 observations was taken on a machine and the following numbers of observations were recorded for each of the specified classifications:

Activity	Number of observations
Working	700
Idle	200
Setting up	100
	——
	1000

(a) Calculate 95% confidence limits for the percentage of total time spent on each of these activities.

(b) An estimate of each of these percentages is required which is not more than 2% away from the true value. How many more observations ·must be taken to ensure this at the 95% confidence level?

Testing a Specified Population Percentage

It is often useful to be able to test whether some specified value for a population percentage is likely to be correct. A mail order firm stipulates that 80% of orders received must be dispatched within three days. It is suspected that this degree of efficiency is not being achieved, so a sample is taken to check the situation. It is discovered that, out of a random sample of 100 orders, only 70% were dispatched within three days. Does this indicate that the required standard of service is not being achieved?

The mere fact that our sample estimate is less than 80% tells us nothing. What we want to establish is whether the difference of 10% could reasonably be expected to arise, given that the 80% is correct. If it could, we would not be justified in claiming that the sample indicated a deterioration in service standards.

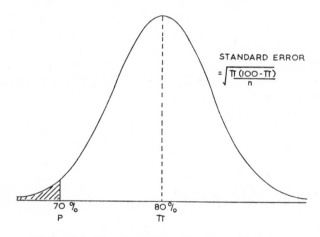

Figure 3.1. Sampling distribution of a percentage

To evaluate the significance of this observed difference, we can calculate the probability that our sample result would be 10% or more below the population figure of 80%. Figure 3.1 shows pictorially what this probability is. It is the area of the sampling distribution to the left of 70%. Before we can calculate this probability, we need to know the parameters of the sampling distribution when $n = 100$ and $\pi = 80\%$.

Remembering that the mean $= \pi$ and the standard error (S.E.)
$= \sqrt{\dfrac{\pi(100 - \pi)}{n}}$, we have:

$$\text{Mean} = 80$$
$$\text{S.E.} = \sqrt{\frac{80 \times 20}{100}} = 4$$

The z value for the point 70 is:

$$z = \frac{P - \pi}{\text{S.E.}} = \frac{70 - 80}{4} = -2 \cdot 5$$

From Table II, the probability associated with a z value of 2·5 is 0·4938, giving the shaded area as $0 \cdot 5000 - 0 \cdot 4938 = 0 \cdot 0062$. What this means is that if the true percentage really is 80%, only about 6 samples in every 1000 of a similar size ($n = 100$) would estimate it at 70% or less. We are therefore faced with two alternative decisions.

(a) *Either:* A very rare event has occurred, and by chance we have got a sample which will only occur about 6 times in every 1000 such samples.

(b) *Or:* This low sample percentage has arisen because the population percentage is less than the 80% which we assumed it to be.

Which of these alternatives we choose depends on how much of a risk we are prepared to take. The first of these alternatives has a probability of 0·0062 of being correct. In rejecting it and accepting the second alternative, therefore, we are running a 0·62% chance of being wrong. In the long run we could expect to be wrong about 6 times in every 1000 similar situations. It would be perfectly reasonable to discount such a small risk and accept the second alternative.

Suppose, however, that our chance of being wrong had worked out to 10% instead of 0·62%. Now acceptance of the second alternative means that in the long run we shall be wrong 10 times in every 100 similar situations. Is this a reasonable risk to run?

What is or is not a reasonable risk will depend on the consequences of being wrong. Through custom and practice, a number of standard risk levels, known as **significance levels**, have become established. By far the most commonly used of these are the 5% and 1%, or 0·05 and 0·01 significance levels. The process of calculating if the probability of making a wrong decision is greater or less than the required significance level is known as **significance testing**.

Significance Testing

The idea of significance testing has been introduced in connection with a specific problem regarding a percentage. It is, however, one of the cornerstones in the whole structure of statistical reasoning. Whenever an assumption about a population is tested, the reasoning processes always follow the same general lines. The procedure may be stated as a logical series of steps.

1. A statistical **hypothesis** is set up.

This is the initial assumption, which is almost invariably an assumption about the value of a population parameter. In the example just discussed, the hypothesis was '$\pi = 80\%$'.

These hypotheses are usually referred to as **null hypotheses,** since they almost always state that no change has occurred from known or specified conditions.

2. An alternative hypothesis is defined which is to be accepted if the test permits us to reject the null hypothesis.

In our example, the alternative hypothesis was 'π is less than 80%'. Steps 1 and 2 must be carried out *before* the sample is analysed.

3. An appropriate significance level is fixed.

In industrial situations, this is usually the 5% or 0·05 significance level. Occasionally, if the consequences of wrongly rejecting the null hypothesis are serious enough to warrant it, the 1% or 0·01 level is used.

In our example, the 0·05 level would probably be satisfactory. If, however, it had been decided that 'heads would roll' as a result of the test showing that service had deteriorated, it might be fairer on the staff to use the 0·01 level!

4. On the assumption that the null hypothesis is true, the appropriate sampling distribution is defined and the area which will lead to rejection of the null hypothesis is identified. The probability that the sample result will fall into the rejection area is made equal to the specified significance level.

In our example, the appropriate sampling distribution is shown in Figure 3.1 and in Figure 3.2 (page 62). The only difference between these figures is that in 3.2, the shaded tail corresponds to the rejection area of the test. As the 0·05 significance level is being used, this area

is the bottom 5% of the distribution. There is thus a probability of
0·05 that our sample percentage will fall in the rejection area when
the true percentage really is 80%.

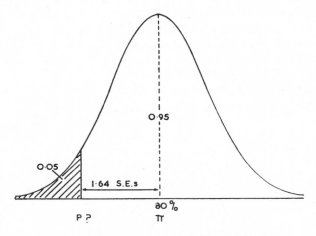

Figure 3.2. Illustration of a 0·05 significance level test

5.   The position of the sample result in the sampling distribution
is calculated. If it falls in the rejection area, the null hypothesis is
rejected and the alternative hypothesis is accepted. The result is
then said to be **statistically significant**.

The necessary calculation usually entails finding how many
standard errors away from the mean the sample result lies. If this
exceeds the number of standard errors corresponding to the boundary
of the rejection region, then the sample result lies in the rejection
area.

In our example, all we need do is determine whether the sample
estimate of 70% is more than 1·64 standard errors below 80%. We
have:

$$z = \frac{P - \pi}{\text{S.E.}} = \frac{-10}{4} = -2·5$$

which indicates that the sample result lies in the rejection area.

6.   If the sample result does not lie in the rejection area, then we
are not able to reject the null hypothesis without incurring a greater

risk than has been defined as acceptable by the chosen significance level.

It does not follow from this that the null hypothesis is therefore true. It merely means that there is insufficient evidence against it, and is equivalent to a verdict of 'not proven' rather than 'not guilty'.

Because of the great importance and wide application of significance testing, we have digressed somewhat in order to discuss the stages in the reasoning process in general terms. Let us now discuss two examples which relate specifically to the application of this reasoning to the sampling distribution of a percentage.

Example 3.2

A company manufacturing a certain brand of breakfast cereal claims that 60% of housewives prefer its brand to any other. A random sample of 300 housewives contains 165 who do prefer the brand. Is the true percentage lower than the company claims?

We have $n = 300$ and $P = 55\%$. Follow the steps in the previous section.

1. Null hypothesis: $\pi = 60\%$.
2. Alternative hypothesis: $\pi < 60\%$.
3. Significance level: 0·05.
4. If the null hypothesis is true, the sampling distribution will have a mean of 60 and a standard error of $\sqrt{\dfrac{60 \times 40}{300}} = 2\cdot83$. This distribution is shown in Figure 3.3 (page 64).

As in the previous example, the rejection area will be the lowest 5% of the distribution, which means that once again our sample result P must be more than 1·64 standard errors below 60%, before the null hypothesis can be rejected.

Because we are only interested in one tail of the distribution, this is usually referred to as a **one-tail test**.

5.
$$z = \frac{P - \pi}{\text{S.E.}} = \frac{55 - 60}{2\cdot83} = -1\cdot77$$

Our sample result is thus more than 1·64 standard errors below the mean. This enables us to reject the null hypothesis at the 0·05

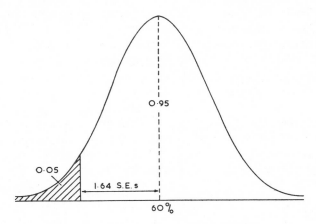

Figure 3.3. Illustration of a one-tail test

significance level. We therefore accept the alternative hypothesis: this sample establishes that the manufacturer's claim is exaggerated.

Example 3.3

A coin is suspected of bias. It is tossed 100 times and 57 heads occur. Does this establish that the coin is biased?

The sample has $n = 100$ and $P = 57\%$. Again follow the usual sequence.

1. Null hypothesis: the coin is not biased, therefore $\pi = 50\%$.
2. Alternative hypothesis: $\pi \neq 50\%$.

Notice that this is rather different from any previous alternative hypothesis which we have had. We are seeking to detect bias in the coin, and this can manifest itself either in unusually high or low percentages of heads in the sample. If we knew for certain that any bias present could only be such as to produce more heads than expected, the alternative hypothesis would be: $\pi > 50\%$.

This illustrates the importance of defining the alternative hypothesis before the sample is analysed (it should preferably be done before the sample is taken). If no clear formulation of the alternative is made beforehand, there is a danger of using the sample result itself to suggest the alternative hypothesis. Having, for instance, found more heads than expected in our sample, we would be tempted to formulate the alternative hypothesis as $\pi > 50\%$. This would ignore the very important fact that before we took the sample we had no idea what to expect as the percentage of heads.

3. Significance level: 0·05.

4. If the null hypothesis is true, the sampling distribution will have a mean of 50 and a standard error of $\sqrt{\dfrac{50 \times 50}{100}} = 5$. The distribution is shown in Figure 3.4.

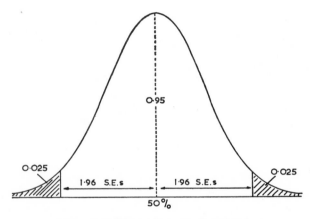

Figure 3.4. Illustration of a two-tail test

The effect on the rejection area of the different formulation of the alternative hypothesis can be seen in Figure 3.4. We are interested in both unusually high and unusually low percentages of heads. Our rejection area must therefore occupy both tails of the distribution. To keep the risk of wrongly rejecting the null hypothesis at 0·05, we must have 0·025 in each tail. Our z value must therefore be more than 1·96 to enable us to reject the null hypothesis.

This type of test is often referred to as a **two-tail test** to distinguish it from the **one-tail test** which is appropriate when only one tail of the distribution is of interest to us, as in the previous example.

5.
$$z = \frac{P - \pi}{\text{S.E.}} = \frac{57 - 50}{5} = 1·40$$

This is less than 1·96 and we cannot therefore reject the null hypothesis.

6. The result is inconclusive. Because we are unable to reject the null hypothesis, it does not follow that it is true. All we have established is that there is a greater than 5% chance that the result we have got could have come from an unbiased coin.

Exercises

3.3. A new method of operating a group of machines should enable them to operate 80% of the time, the remaining 20% being needed for maintenance and setting up. It is suspected that one machine is not achieving this standard. An activity sampling study of 400 observations estimates the utilization of this machine at 75%. Is this significantly less than standard?

3.4. On the basis of the results of a door-to-door canvass, support for one of the candidates in an election is estimated at 60% of the electorate. An independent random sample of 500 people is interviewed and 270 of them support the candidate. Is this evidence consistent with the 60% estimate?

Comparing Two Sample Percentages

Frequently we have two sample estimates of a percentage which we wish to compare. A significance test may be devised to enable this comparison to be made. In connection with its marketing policy, a company wishes to know if its product is used more in town areas than in the country. A sample of 500 people is interviewed in each of two areas, one town and one country. There are 125 and 95 users of the product respectively in each sample. Does this establish that the overall percentage of users is higher in the town than in the country?

Once again, we develop the test by following the sequence of steps described on page 61. To distinguish between our two samples, we will use the following notation:

	Town	Country
True percentage	π_1	π_2
Sample estimate	$P_1 = 25\%$	$P_2 = 19\%$
Sample size	$n_1 = 500$	$n_2 = 500$

1. Null hypothesis.

In situations of this type, the null hypothesis always states that there is no difference between the true percentages in the populations from which the samples come. This may be stated concisely as:

$$\pi_1 = \pi_2 = \pi$$

where π is the unknown percentage common to both.

2. Alternative hypothesis.

Here we are testing specifically to find out if usage is greater in the town than in the country. We know that it is certainly not less. Our alternative hypothesis is therefore: $\pi_1 > \pi_2$.

3. Significance level.

Let us assume that if we do decide that usage is heavier in town areas, an expensive advertising campaign is to be mounted in country areas. We need to be fairly certain of our ground before taking such a step. The significance level is the risk of deciding that there is a difference when there is not, so we would probably want to make it 0·01 in this case.

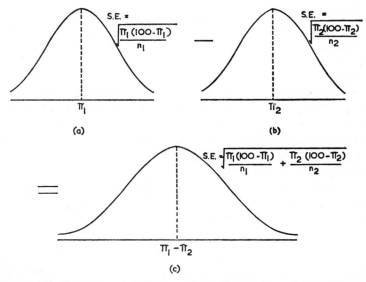

Figure 3.5. Derivation of the sampling distribution of the difference between two percentages

4.   Our first sample estimate P_1 is in effect a random selection from the sampling distribution in Figure 3.5 (*a*). The second estimate P_2 is a random selection from the distribution in Figure 3.5 (*b*).

We are interested in evaluating the *difference* between these two estimates $(P_1 - P_2)$. If we subtract these two distributions, therefore (using the rules given on page 46 to get the resulting mean and standard error), we will get the distribution in Figure 3.5 (*c*). Our difference $(P_1 - P_2)$ is in effect a random selection from this distribution.

Now under the null hypothesis, $\pi_1 = \pi_2 = \pi$, so the mean of this distribution will be zero, and its standard error will have both π_1 and π_2 equal to the assumed common value π. This is shown in Figure 3.6.

We must now consider the rejection area. We are interested only in large *positive* values of the difference $(P_1 - P_2)$, so we are only interested in the upper tail of the distribution in Figure 3.6. In other words, a one-tail test is appropriate. As we have decided on a significance level of 0·01, only 1 % of the distribution will be in the rejection area. The z value corresponding to the boundary of this area will therefore be 2·33.

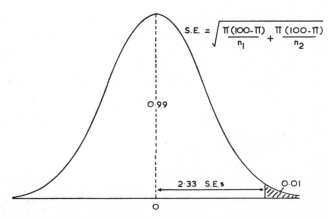

Figure 3.6. A one-tail test of the difference between two percentages

5. We must now see if our particular difference $(P_1 - P_2)$ is further away from the mean than this. If it is, the null hypothesis will be rejected.

$$z = \frac{(P_1 - P_2) - 0}{\text{S.E.}}$$

$$= \frac{P_1 - P_2}{\sqrt{\left(\dfrac{\pi(100 - \pi)}{n_1} + \dfrac{\pi(100 - \pi)}{n_2}\right)}} \qquad \ldots (3.4)$$

In this formula, the values of n_1, n_2, P_1 and P_2 are known, but π is unknown. We must get the best estimate of it we can from our sample data. Remember that we are working under the assumption that both our samples come from populations with a common value for π. To estimate this common percentage, we may pool our samples to give 220 users in a sample of 1000. This gives an estimate for π of 22%.

When sample sizes are equal, as in this case, the estimate of π is simply the average of P_1 and P_2. This will not be the case, however, when the two samples differ in size.

Using this estimate of π in formula (3.4),

$$z = \frac{25 - 19}{\sqrt{\left(\dfrac{22 \times 78}{500} + \dfrac{22 \times 78}{500}\right)}} = \frac{6}{2 \cdot 62} = 2 \cdot 29$$

This is smaller than 2·33, so our sample point $(P_1 - P_2)$ does not fall in the rejection area of the distribution in Figure 3.6. Accordingly, therefore, we are unable to reject the null hypothesis. These data do not establish that the percentage of users of our product is higher in the town than it is in the country.

Exercises

3.5. The results of two market surveys in consecutive years were as follows:

	Year 1	*Year 2*
Sample size	650	500
Number possessing Product XYZ	338	230

Does the second survey indicate that Product XYZ has lost ground?

3.6. Two factories of the same combine are located in different parts of the country. In making a decision on which factory to expand, one factor to be taken into account is labour turnover. The following figures relate to the previous year:

Factory	1	2
Number of leavers	180	250
Labour force	1000	1200

Do these figures indicate that there is any difference in labour turn-over between the two factories?

Summary of Formulae

The calculations involved in the various ways of using the sampling distribution of a percentage have been described above at some length in order to explain fully the reasoning processes behind them. Once these processes are understood, however, the tests may be applied very quickly and easily by substitution of the sample details in the appropriate formulae. These may be summarized as follows.

1. Calculation of confidence limits for an unknown percentage π.

$$\pi \text{ lies between } P \pm z \sqrt{\frac{P(100 - P)}{n}}$$

where n = sample size,
P = sample estimate of π,
$z = 1 \cdot 96$ for 95% confidence limits,
$z = 2 \cdot 58$ for 99% confidence limits.

These values of z are frequently rounded off to 2 and 3 for ease of calculation.

2. Estimation of sample size required for a specified degree of accuracy in the estimate of an unknown percentage π.

$$n = \frac{4P(100 - P)}{L^2}$$

where n = sample size required,
P = provisional estimate of π,
L = specified limit of accuracy.

3. Testing a specified population percentage.
   (a) Null hypothesis: the specified value of π is correct.
   (b) Alternative hypothesis: this could be any one of the following.
      (i) $\pi \neq$ the specified value.
      (ii) $\pi >$ the specified value.
      (iii) $\pi <$ the specified value.
   If it is (i), a two-tail test will be appropriate. If it is (ii) or (iii), a one-tail test will be appropriate.
   (c) Significance level: usually either 0·05 or 0·01, depending on the consequences of wrongly rejecting the null hypothesis.
   (d) Calculate z from the formula:

$$z = \frac{P - \pi}{\sqrt{\left(\dfrac{\pi(100 - \pi)}{n}\right)}}$$

   where P = sample percentage,
            π = specified population percentage,
            n = sample size.
   (e) Interpret z for significance.
   The null hypothesis may be rejected if z exceeds the appropriate value from the following table:

Significance level

		0·05	0·01	
	(i)	± 1·96	± 2·58	two-tail test
Alternative hypothesis	(ii)	+ 1·64	+ 2·33	one-tail tests
	(iii)	− 1·64	− 2·33	

4. Comparing two sample percentages P_1 and P_2.
   (a) Null hypothesis: $\pi_1 = \pi_2 = \pi$.
   (b) Alternative hypothesis: this could be any one of the following.
      (i) $\pi_1 \neq \pi_2$.
      (ii) $\pi_1 > \pi_2$.
      (iii) $\pi_1 < \pi_2$.

If it is (i), a two-tail test will be appropriate. If it is (ii) or (iii), a one-tail test will be appropriate.

(c) Significance level: usually either 0·05 or 0·01, depending on the consequences of wrongly rejecting the null hypothesis.

(d) Calculate z from the formula:

$$z = \frac{P_1 - P_2}{\sqrt{\left(\dfrac{\pi(100-\pi)}{n_1} + \dfrac{\pi(100-\pi)}{n_2}\right)}}$$

where P_1 and P_2 = sample percentages,
n_1 and n_2 = sample sizes.
π is obtained by pooling both samples.

(e) Interpret z for significance.
The null hypothesis may be rejected if z exceeds the appropriate value from the following table:

Significance level

		0·05	0·01	
	(i)	±1·96	±2·58	two-tail test
Alternative hypothesis	(ii)	+1·64	+2·33	one-tail tests
	(iii)	−1·64	−2·33	

The Sampling Distribution of the Mean

In example 2.6 on page 40, we needed to know the average chest measurement of the adult male population. Let us now consider the problem of getting that information. One way would be to measure the entire population and thus obtain an exact answer. This, of course, is out of the question. We must rely on a sample estimate. So we take a sample and calculate its average, $\bar{x}$. This is an estimate of the population average μ just as P was an estimate of π in the previous section. Although μ is constant, $\bar{x}$ will vary from sample to sample. We need to know how large this variation is likely to be.

All the possible values which $\bar{x}$ can assume for a given sample size comprise the **sampling distribution of the mean**. Any particular sample mean which we get is in effect a random selection from this distribution. We must therefore know the parameters of this distribution in order to evaluate our sample results properly.

There is a simple relationship between the parameters of the population and those of the sampling distribution of the mean. Figure 3.7 illustrates this relationship. The population distribution with mean $= \mu$ and standard deviation $= \sigma$ is at the top. The mean of the sampling distribution is also μ, as one would expect intuitively. In other words, the average of all possible sample averages which could arise will be the population average.

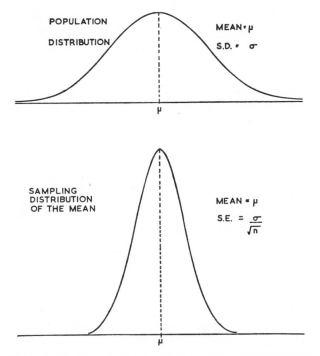

Figure 3.7. Relationship between population distribution and the sampling distribution of the mean

The standard deviation of the sampling distribution is again referred to as the standard error to avoid confusing it with the population standard deviation. It is related to the population standard deviation σ by the simple relationship:

$$\text{S.E.} = \frac{\sigma}{\sqrt{n}}$$

where n = sample size.

So far nothing has been said about the shape of the sampling distribution. If the population is normally distributed, then, as might be expected, the sampling distribution of the mean is also normal, as indicated in Figure 3.7.

However, even if the population is not normal it is a remarkable fact that the sampling distribution of the mean will be normal, or very nearly so, provided that the sample is fairly large. This explains why, even though we may not know the shape of the population distribution (and usually we do not) we can confidently apply normal curve theory to the sampling distribution of the mean, particularly when we are concerned with large samples.

'Large' in this connection means more than about 30. It is impossible to be precise, as a sample does not remain 'small' until it gets to 29 and then suddenly become 'large' at 30. The sampling distribution of the mean, based on samples from a non-normal population, gradually becomes more and more normal as the sample size increases. By the time the sample size reaches 30, the errors introduced by assuming the sampling distribution to be exactly normal are negligible.

For this reason, and another which will be mentioned shortly, two sets of formulae have been developed, one of which applies to large samples and the other to small.

Estimating an Unknown Mean (Large Sample Method)

We have seen that usually the population mean is not known and must be estimated from a sample. The sampling distribution of the mean can be used to calculate confidence limits for the population mean in precisely the same way as limits are calculated for π.

From the table of the normal curve, we know that 95 % of a normal distribution lies within 1·96 standard deviations (or standard errors) of its mean. It is therefore 95 % certain that any sample $\bar{x}$ which we get is within 1·96 standard errors of μ. This gives us a formula for 95 % confidence limits for μ which is similar to formula (3.1). The 1·96 has been rounded off to 2 as before:

$$\mu \text{ lies between } \bar{x} \pm \frac{2\sigma}{\sqrt{n}} \qquad \dots (3.5)$$

Unfortunately these limits can only be calculated if σ, the population standard deviation, is known. Much more often than not, σ will not be known. We are able, however, to estimate σ from our sample by calculating s, the sample standard deviation. So long as s is calculated from a large sample (more than about 30) we can use s in place of σ in the standard error formula. This is the second reason why different methods are required for small samples. The s of a small sample is not accurate enough to enable us to use it in place of σ. Small sample tests allow for this possible inaccuracy.

Example 3.4

A sample of 36 tyres from a certain manufacturer lasted an average of 18 000 miles, with a standard deviation of 1200. What are the 95% confidence limits for the average life of all tyres supplied by the manufacturer?

We have $\bar{x} = 18\ 000$, $s = 1200$ and $n = 36$. For 95% limits,

$$\mu \text{ lies between } \bar{x} \pm \frac{2\sigma}{\sqrt{n}}$$

We do not know σ, but as we have a large sample, s may be used instead.

$$\mu \text{ lies between } 18\ 000 \pm \frac{2 \times 1200}{\sqrt{36}}$$

$$= 18\ 000 \pm 400, \text{ or between } 17\ 600 \text{ and } 18\ 400$$

Calculating the Sample Size

It is possible to calculate the sample size which is necessary to achieve any specified degree of accuracy in the resulting estimate of the mean. With 95% certainty, the sample mean $\bar{x}$ will be within 2 standard errors of the population mean. As sample size increases, the standard error decreases. If, therefore, we equate 2 standard errors to the degree of accuracy we require, it will enable us to find the sample size which will give us that accuracy.

In the chest measurement problem, for example, suppose that we wish to estimate the average to within $\frac{1}{4}$ in. We must find n so that:

$$\frac{2\sigma}{\sqrt{n}} = \tfrac{1}{4}$$

Before we can proceed any further we must have an estimate for σ. A small pilot sample of about 30 is therefore taken to get this estimate, which turns out to be 2 in. We now have:

$$\frac{2 \times 2}{\sqrt{n}} = \tfrac{1}{4}$$

$$n = 256$$

This formula may be generalized by putting L for the limit of accuracy which is required. The formula then becomes:

$$\frac{2\sigma}{\sqrt{n}} = L$$

which when transposed is:

$$n = \frac{4\sigma^2}{L^2} \qquad\qquad \dots (3.6)$$

Exercises

3.7.   36 samples of a new yarn are tested to breaking point. The average breaking strength is 30 lb with a standard deviation of 4 lb. Calculate 95% and 99% confidence limits for the true average breaking strength of the yarn.

3.8.   In some ergonomics experiments, an estimate of average reaction time is required. If the standard deviation is first estimated at 0·05 seconds, how many measurements of reaction time must be made to ensure that the resulting estimate of the mean is not more than 0·01 seconds in error at the 95% confidence level?

3.9.   The average I.Q. of a sample of 30 students from a large college is 120 with a standard deviation of 10. How accurately does this estimate the average I.Q. of all the students?

How many more students must be tested in order to ensure that the estimate is not more than 2 points out with 99% confidence?

Testing a Specified Population Mean (Large Sample Method)

A test may be constructed to establish if a specified value for a population mean is likely to be correct. Once again, the standard procedure for significance testing described on page 61 is used. To illustrate how the test may be constructed, let us consider an example. An average life of 1000 hours is claimed for his product by a manufacturer of electric light bulbs. A sample of 36 bulbs is tested and it is found that they have an average life of 920 hours, with a standard deviation of 150 hours. Does this disprove the manufacturer's claim?

We have $n = 36$, $\bar{x} = 920$, $s = 150$.

1. Null hypothesis.

In situations of this kind, the null hypothesis always states that the specified value of the mean is correct, or: $\mu = 1000$.

2. Alternative hypothesis.

We are interested in seeing if the average is less than is claimed, so our alternative hypothesis will be: $\mu < 1000$.

3. Significance level.

We will use the 0·05 significance level.

4. Identify the rejection area in the appropriate sampling distribution, assuming the null hypothesis to be true.

The sampling distribution is shown in Figure 3.8 (page 78). It will have a mean of 1000 and a standard error of $\dfrac{\sigma}{\sqrt{36}}$. Because σ is unknown, we must use s as an estimate. Our sample is large, so this is permissible. Using s, we have:

$$\text{S.E.} = \frac{150}{6} = 25$$

Our alternative hypothesis indicates that we are only interested in unusually small values of $\bar{x}$, so the rejection area will all be in the lower tail of the distribution. In other words, this is a one-tail test. As we are using the 0·05 significance level, the rejection area will be 5% of the distribution. There is then a 5% chance that $\bar{x}$ will fall in the rejection area, even if μ does equal 1000.

The boundary of the rejection area is 1·64 standard errors below the mean of the distribution, so $\bar{x}$ must be at least this far away from 1000 to enable us to reject the null hypothesis.

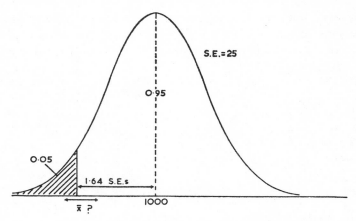

Figure 3.8. A one-tail test of a population mean

5. Find the position of the observed sample mean in the sampling distribution. If it falls in the rejection area, the null hypothesis may be rejected and the alternative accepted.

We can calculate how many standard errors $\bar{x}$ is from μ by using the formula:

$$z = \frac{\bar{x} - \mu}{\text{S.E.}} \qquad \ldots (3.7)$$

$$= \frac{920 - 1000}{25} = -3 \cdot 2$$

This is well inside the rejection area, so we may conclude that the manufacturer's claim is over-optimistic.

Example 3.5

In Example 1.1 of Chapter 1, we saw how the construction of a histogram could help to determine when a machine producing 3 in shafts needed to be adjusted. A much better method of controlling industrial processes has been developed, based on the significance test which we have just derived.

The machine in Example 1.1 was required to produce shafts with a diameter of $3 \cdot 000$ in $\pm 0 \cdot 006$ in. The most efficient way to operate the machine is to control it so that it produces a population of parts with an average diameter of 3 in. This would be even more important if the width of the tolerance range approximately equalled the width of the distribution. In that event, any movement of the mean away from 3 in would result in a sharp increase in the amount of reject material produced.

Figure 3.9 illustrates this. The dotted vertical lines indicate the tolerance limits, and the machine when it is correctly controlled will produce parts following the solid-line distribution. Virtually all of this distribution falls inside the tolerance range. However, if the machine 'drifts' slightly so that the dotted distribution is being produced, the shaded portion will have to be rejected.

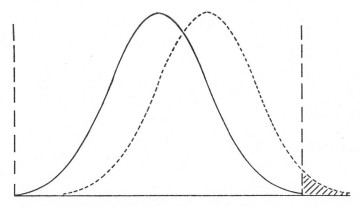

Figure 3.9. Defective material produced because of a shift in the mean

The problem, then, is to detect when the average has moved away from its specified value, which in this case is 3 in. Suppose we take a sample and find that $\bar{x} = 3{\cdot}001$ in. Does this indicate that the population average is not $3{\cdot}000$ in?

This is precisely the kind of question which the test we have just developed is designed to answer. The procedure has been reduced to a simple routine.

Samples are taken at regular intervals and the mean is plotted on a chart as in Figure 3.10 (page 80). The centre line on the chart indicates the required population mean. The pair of lines marked 'W.L.' automatically carry out a $0{\cdot}05$ significance level test on $\bar{x}$. There is only a 5% chance that $\bar{x}$ will fall outside the range enclosed by them, if the process mean is what it should be. This means that

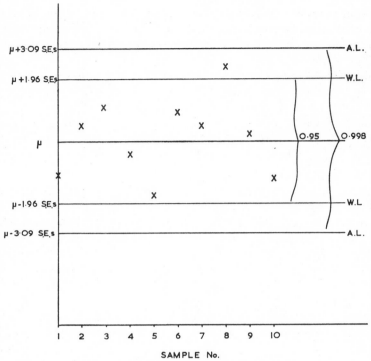

Figure 3.10. A quality control chart

on average we can expect to get 1 sample in every 20 falling outside this range, even if the process is under control. A point which does come outside, therefore, is not of itself sufficient justification for concluding that the process has gone out of control. It is interpreted as a warning. These limits are therefore called 'warning limits' (W.L.). If the next sample falls back in control, no action would be taken. If, however, the next sample also falls outside the warning limits, action would be taken.

Similarly, the pair of lines marked 'A.L.' effectively carry out a 0·002 significance level test on $\bar{x}$. There is only a 0·2% chance that $\bar{x}$ will fall outside this range. If a sample point does come outside, the probability that the process is still under control is so small that immediate action would be justified. These limits are therefore known as 'action limits' (A.L.).

Process and quality control is a subject in its own right, with its own extensive literature. The work by Juran* already mentioned provides one of the most comprehensive accounts available.

Exercises

3.10.   The average performance level of the operatives in a large factory is 90 (on the B.S.I. scale) with a standard deviation of 8. The performance of one department is suspected of being below this average. A sample of 36 operator performance records is taken from this department, and the sample average is 85. Does this prove that the department is below average?

3.11.   The average time taken for the reaction to take place in a chemical process is 35 minutes and the standard deviation is 4 minutes. The quality of the product may be improved by changing one of the raw materials, but it is not known if this would affect reaction time. 30 batches are made with the new ingredient, and the average reaction time is 38 minutes. Does this indicate, at the 0·01 significance level, that the new ingredient affects the reaction time?

Comparing Two Sample Means (*Large Sample Method*)

The construction of an appropriate significance test to evaluate the difference between two sample means may again best be described by means of an example. Two methods of operating a production process are under consideration. To see if they differ in average output per hour, a trial of both methods is arranged with the following results:

	Method 1	*Method 2*
Number of operators	$n_1 = 32$	$n_2 = 36$
Average output per hour	$\bar{x}_1 = 50$	$\bar{x}_2 = 54$
Standard deviation	$s_1 = 2$	$s_2 = 3$

Do these results establish a difference between the two methods?

1.   Null hypothesis.
There is no difference between the true average output per hour of the processes, or: $\mu_1 = \mu_2$.

* *Quality Control Handbook, op. cit.*

2. Alternative hypothesis.

We do not know which, if any, of the processes is the better one. Our alternative hypothesis will therefore be: $\mu_1 \neq \mu_2$.

3. Significance level: 0·01.

4. The appropriate sampling distribution is that of $(\bar{x}_1 - \bar{x}_2)$. Figure 3.11 (*a*) shows the sampling distribution of $\bar{x}_1$, and Figure 3.11 (*b*) that of $\bar{x}_2$. To obtain the distribution of $(\bar{x}_1 - \bar{x}_2)$, we must subtract these.

The resulting distribution is shown in Figure 3.11 (*c*). In accordance with the rules on page 46, its mean will be $\mu_1 - \mu_2$ and its standard error will be $\sqrt{(\text{S.E.}_1^2 + \text{S.E.}_2^2)}$.

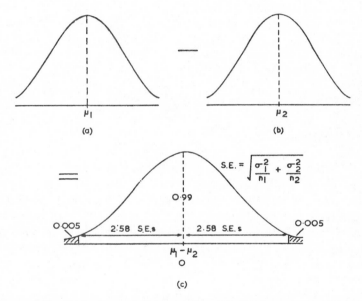

Figure 3.11. Derivation of the sampling distribution of the difference between two means

Under the null hypothesis, $\mu_1 = \mu_2$ so the average of the distribution is zero. The alternative hypothesis indicates that we are interested in both tails of the distribution. As we are using a significance level of 0·01, therefore, the rejection area will consist of the extreme $\frac{1}{2}\%$ of both tails, as indicated in Figure 3.11 (*c*). In order to fall in the rejection area, $(\bar{x}_1 - \bar{x}_2)$ must be at least 2·58 standard errors away from the mean.

5. We must now find the z value corresponding to our particular $(\bar{x}_1 - \bar{x}_2)$. The necessary calculation is:

$$z = \frac{(\bar{x}_1 - \bar{x}_2) - 0}{\text{S E.}} = \frac{\bar{x}_1 - \bar{x}_2}{\sqrt{\left(\dfrac{\sigma_1^2}{n_1} + \dfrac{\sigma_2^2}{n_2}\right)}} \qquad \ldots (3.8)$$

Again we do not know σ_1 and σ_2, but as we have large samples, s_1 and s_2 may be used instead. Substituting in formula (3.8) gives:

$$z = \frac{50 - 54}{\sqrt{\left(\dfrac{4}{32} + \dfrac{9}{36}\right)}} = -\frac{4}{\sqrt{0\cdot375}}$$

$$= -\frac{4}{0\cdot612} = -6\cdot5$$

The difference between our sample means is thus large enough to enable us to reject the null hypothesis and claim that there is a significant difference between the two methods, the second one obviously being superior.

Exercises

3.12. A new petrol additive is being tested, with the hope that it will increase m.p.g. A series of trials is carried out, both with and without the additive. 30 trials without the additive show an average petrol consumption of 35 m.p.g. with a standard deviation of 3. With the additive, the average of 30 trials is 38 m.p.g., also with a standard deviation of 3. Do these figures establish, at the 0·01 significance level, that the additive increases m.p.g.?

3.13. In the testing of cake recipes, a quality assessment is made based on awarding marks for taste and texture. Two recipes are tested to find out if they differ in quality. The first recipe is tested by 40 people whose average mark is 50 with a standard deviation of 10. The second recipe is tested by 30 people whose average mark is 45 with a standard deviation of 8. Does this establish, at the 0·05 significance level, that there is a difference in appeal between the two recipes?

Summary of Large Sample Formulae

1. Calculation of confidence limits for an unknown mean μ.

$$\mu \text{ lies between } \bar{x} \pm \frac{z\sigma}{\sqrt{n}}$$

where $\bar{x} =$ sample mean,

$\sigma =$ population standard deviation (usually this will not be known, and s the sample standard deviation will be used instead),

$n =$ sample size,

$z = 1.96$ for 95% confidence limits,

$z = 2.58$ for 99% confidence limits.

These z values are frequently rounded off to 2 and 3 for ease of calculation.

2. Estimation of sample size required for a specified degree of accuracy in the estimate of an unknown mean μ.

$$n = \frac{4\sigma^2}{L^2}$$

where $n =$ sample size required,

$\sigma =$ population standard deviation (here again the standard deviation s of the sample will usually have to be used as a substitute),

$L =$ specified limit of accuracy.

3. Testing a specified population mean μ.

(*a*) Null hypothesis: the specified value of μ is correct.

(*b*) Alternative hypothesis: this could be any one of the following.

(i) $\mu \neq$ the specified value.

(ii) $\mu >$ the specified value.

(iii) $\mu <$ the specified value.

If it is (i), a two-tail test will be appropriate. If it is (ii) or (iii), a one-tail test will be appropriate.

(*c*) Significance level: usually either 0.05 or 0.01, depending on the consequences of wrongly rejecting the null hypothesis.

(*d*) Calculate z from the formula:

$$z = \frac{\bar{x} - \mu}{\frac{\sigma}{\sqrt{n}}}$$

where $\bar{x}$ = sample mean,

μ = specified population mean,

σ = population standard deviation (use s when σ is not known),

n = sample size.

(e) Interpret z for significance.

The null hypothesis may be rejected if z exceeds the appropriate value from the following table:

Significance level

		0·05	0·01	
	(i)	±1·96	±2·58	two-tail test
Alternative hypothesis	(ii)	+1·64	+2·33	one-tail tests
	(iii)	−1·64	−2·33	

4.   Comparing two sample means $\bar{x}_1$ and $\bar{x}_2$.

(a) Null hypothesis: $\mu_1 = \mu_2$.

(b) Alternative hypothesis: this could be any one of the following.

(i) $\mu_1 \neq \mu_2$.

(ii) $\mu_1 > \mu_2$.

(iii) $\mu_1 < \mu_2$.

If it is (i), a two-tail test will be appropriate. If it is (ii) or (iii), a one-tail test will be appropriate.

(c) Significance level: usually 0·05 or 0·01, depending on the consequences of wrongly rejecting the null hypothesis.

(d) Calculate z from the formula:

$$z = \frac{\bar{x}_1 - \bar{x}_2}{\sqrt{\left(\frac{\sigma_1^2}{n_1} + \frac{\sigma_2^2}{n_2}\right)}}$$

where $\bar{x}_1$ and $\bar{x}_2$ = sample averages,

σ_1 and σ_2 = population standard deviations, for which s_1 and s_2 will usually have to be substituted,

n_1 and n_2 = sample sizes.

(*e*) Interpret z for significance.

The null hypothesis may be rejected if z exceeds the appropriate value from the following table:

Significance level

		0·05	0·01	
	(i)	±1·96	±2·58	two-tail test
Alternative hypothesis	(ii)	+1·64	+2·33	one-tail tests
	(iii)	−1·64	−2·33	

Practical Problems of Sampling

In developing all the formulae in this chapter, the assumption has been made that the samples concerned are selected at random. In practice, however, this apparently simple assumption poses a number of problems, particularly when human populations are concerned.

Suppose that we manufacture shirts and wish to obtain opinions concerning materials and styles. How do we define the population which we wish to sample? Is it the aggregate of people who wear shirts? More than 50% of men's shirts are bought by women, so the population of wearers might not be the best for our purpose. If it is not, how can the population of interest to us be defined? Frequently this is not an easy task, but it must be done before we can hope to select a representative sample.

Let us assume that we are seeking political opinions and have defined our population to be the electorate. Having decided on the sample size required, we may choose a random sample from the electoral register by using random numbers. In effect this means that we assign a number to every member of the electorate, put all these numbers into a hat and draw out as many as are needed for our sample. In practice, it would not be necessary to use a hat. Tables of random numbers are available which enable us to read off as many as are required.

This would be very satisfactory from a theoretical point of view, but has many snags when the interviewers subsequently try to contact the people listed in the sample. It will take several calls to find some of the people at home, thus inflating the cost of the exercise. Others may have moved, or be away on holiday or ill in hospital. Some will refuse to be interviewed, giving rise to the problem of non-response. Out of a sample of 1000, perhaps only 900 will respond. Can we regard this as a random sample of 900? It would be very dangerous to do so, since we would be making the implicit assumption that the non-responders would hold similar views to the responders. The very fact that they are non-responders makes them different to the others. This difference probably extends to their opinions on the subject of the questionnaire.

Various ways of reducing the labour and cost of random sampling are used. These include **systematic sampling**, where every tenth or twentieth name is selected from the list, and **cluster** or **area sampling**. Cluster sampling first requires that the population be broken down into convenient sub-groups (these are often geographical areas). A random selection of a number of these sub-groups is then made, and an appropriate portion of the sample is selected from within each sub-group. This would mean that in obtaining a sample from the electorate, we should only have to visit perhaps 40 or 50 constituencies instead of the 600 or so which would arise in a fully random sample.

Another alternative to random sampling which removes the problem of non-response is **quota sampling**. The interviewer is given a description of types of people to be interviewed and the number of each type required. The selection of the actual individuals is then left to the interviewer. Usually the proportion of each type of person in the sample is the same as the proportion in the population, but sometimes weighting factors are used, particularly when a certain type includes only a small proportion of the population.

4 MORE SAMPLING DISTRIBUTIONS

In most practical situations, the population standard deviation is unknown. This is of no great consequence when dealing with large samples because, as we have seen, the sample standard deviation can be used instead with no serious loss of accuracy.

This cannot be done with small samples, and so a corresponding theory has been developed, based on the sample estimate of the standard deviation and not on the population standard deviation itself. One of the pioneers in this work, most of which was done in the early part of this century, was W. S. Gosset. He published his work under the pen-name 'Student'. In particular he developed the formula for the sampling distribution of the mean when σ is unknown. He gave it the name 't-distribution' and it has been known as the **Student-t** distribution ever since.

The Student-t Distribution

The sampling distribution of the mean when σ is unknown is a t-distribution with mean $= \mu$ and standard error $= \dfrac{s}{\sqrt{n}}$. It is similar in general outline to the normal distribution, as may be seen from Figure 4.1. However, the shape of the curve varies with sample size, becoming increasingly wider and flatter than the normal as sample size is reduced. This is to be expected, because the distribution allows for variation in s from sample to sample. This variation increases as the samples get smaller.

In the normal curve, there is a constant relationship between the area under part of the curve and the distance away from the mean of the boundaries of that area, measured in standard deviations or standard errors. We saw, for example, that 95% of the sampling distribution is always contained within ± 1.96 standard errors of the mean.

In the t-distribution, however, this 'number of standard errors away from the mean' will vary with sample size, becoming larger as the sample size gets smaller. It is, for example, 2·131 for a sample of 16 items and 2·776 for a sample of 5 items.

We called the number of standard errors away from the mean z in the normal curve. In the t-distribution, it is denoted by the

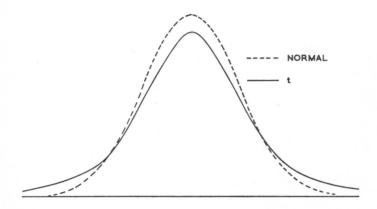

Figure 4.1. Comparison between normal and t-distributions

letter t. Because z is always constant for a given probability, one table of normal curve probabilities and their corresponding z values is sufficient. Because the t value varies with sample size for a given probability, however, a separate table would be necessary for each sample size if a complete tabulation were to be made.

Usually, all we are concerned with is discovering if a particular value of t is significant at a chosen significance level, or calculating confidence limits for a population mean. The only values of t which

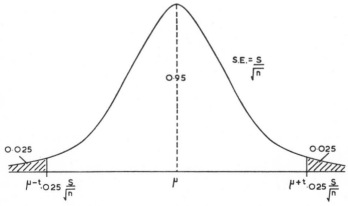

Figure 4.2. Illustrating the 2·5 percentage point of the t-distribution

are tabulated, therefore, are those which have 10%, 5%, 2½%, 1% and ½% of the distribution above them. The particular values of t relating to these percentage points are identified by using a suffix. We have, for example, $t_{.025}$ as the value of t which has 2½% of the distribution above it. In other words, 2½% of the distribution lies above the point $\mu + t_{.025} \dfrac{s}{\sqrt{n}}$. As the distribution is symmetrical, 2½% of it also lies below $\mu - t_{.025} \dfrac{s}{\sqrt{n}}$. This is illustrated in Figure 4.2.

There is one further complication in that the t values are not tabulated under sample sizes, but according to the number of 'degrees of freedom' on which s is based.

Degrees of Freedom

In order to obtain an estimate of σ, at least two members of the population are required. One member would give a very vague estimate of the mean, but would give no information about the standard deviation at all. Thus, if we have two items from the population, only the second one is useful in providing an estimate of σ; the first acts as a kind of 'marker'. In statistics, the number of items which contributes usefully towards an estimate of a parameter is referred to as the number of **degrees of freedom** on which that estimate is based. If we have a sample of size n, therefore, we can say that $\bar{x}$ is based on n degrees of freedom as an estimate of μ, but s is based on only $(n-1)$ degrees of freedom as an estimate of σ. This is why $(n-1)$ appears in the formula for the calculation of s.

Another way to look at this is to consider how the standard deviation is calculated. To start with, the deviation of each item from the mean is found. Before this can be done, obviously the mean must be fixed. Now if the mean of a set of, say, 8 numbers is fixed, then only 7 of the numbers have the freedom to assume any value. Once the first 7 numbers are decided upon, then the eighth number is automatically determined. It has no freedom at all.

Suppose, for instance, that the mean of the 8 numbers is 2. The total of the numbers must therefore be 16. The first 7 are free to be assigned any value we wish, but once their values are decided upon, the last one must be chosen so that the total of the 8 numbers is 16. The fixing of the mean 'uses up' one degree of freedom.

The general rule is that whenever the calculation of a statistic requires the prior calculation of other quantities from the sample data, the number of degrees of freedom on which that statistic is based is reduced by the number of quantities so calculated.

In the case of the standard deviation, only one quantity, namely the mean, must be calculated first. This uses up one degree of freedom, leaving $(n - 1)$. In other cases, several quantities must first be calculated, as we shall see later in this chapter.

Uses of the t-distribution

When we are dealing with small samples (n less than about 30) and the population standard deviation σ is unknown, the t-distribution may be used to calculate confidence limits for population means and to carry out significance tests in precisely the same way as the normal distribution was used for large samples.

Strictly speaking, the t-distribution should be used whenever σ is unknown, regardless of sample size. However, as sample size increases, the t-distribution approaches nearer and nearer to the normal. By the time $n = 30$, the two distributions are almost identical. Because the normal distribution is easier to work with, it is therefore used whenever n is large enough.

In the next few sections, formulae to estimate means and carry out significance tests with small samples are developed. These are an exact parallel of the large sample formulae developed in Chapter 3.

Estimating an Unknown Mean (Small Sample Method)

The average life of 9 car batteries is 30 months with a standard deviation of 4 months. How accurately does this estimate the true average life of this type of battery?

Here we have $\bar{x} = 30$, $s = 4$ and $n = 9$. In effect, this particular $\bar{x}$ is a random selection from a t-distribution with mean $= \mu$, the unknown population mean, and standard error $= \dfrac{s}{\sqrt{n}} = \dfrac{4}{\sqrt{9}} = 1\cdot33$. We are 95% certain that $\bar{x}$ is not more than $t_{\cdot025}$ standard errors away from μ (see Figure 4.2) so for 95% confidence limits we have:

$$\mu \text{ lies between } \bar{x} \pm t_{\cdot025}\frac{s}{\sqrt{n}} \qquad \dots (4.1)$$

In this formula, we know the values of $\bar{x}$, s and n. It only remains to find $t._{025}$. This may be found from Table III at the end of the book. To use this table, all we need to know is the number of degrees of freedom on which s is based. This is $(n-1)$, which in our sample is 8. Entering the $t._{025}$ column of Table III with 8 degrees of freedom (d.f.), we find that $t._{025} = 2\cdot306$.

Substituting in formula (4.1), the 95% confidence limits are:

$$\mu \text{ lies between } 30 \pm 2\cdot306 \times \frac{4}{\sqrt{9}}$$
$$= 30 \pm 3\cdot07, \text{ or between } 26\cdot93 \text{ and } 33\cdot07$$

The formula for 99% confidence limits will have $t._{005}$ in place of $t._{025}$ in formula (4.1). Consulting the $t._{005}$ column of Table III with 8 degrees of freedom, the appropriate value in this case is $3\cdot355$. The 99% confidence limits are therefore:

$$\mu \text{ lies between } 30 \pm 3\cdot355 \times \frac{4}{\sqrt{9}}$$
$$= 30 \pm 4\cdot47, \text{ or between } 25\cdot53 \text{ and } 34\cdot47$$

Calculating the Sample Size

To be 95% certain that $\bar{x}$ is not more than a specified amount L away from the true mean, we must have:

$$t._{025} \frac{s}{\sqrt{n}} = L$$

Transposing this gives:

$$n = \left(\frac{t._{025}\, s}{L}\right)^2 \qquad \qquad \ldots (4.2)$$

As before, we must have a provisional estimate s available in order to use this formula.

Suppose that in the car battery example above, an estimate of average battery life which is accurate to within 1 month is required. The necessary sample size may be obtained by substituting in formula (4.2) the appropriate values for $t._{025}$, s and L:

$$n = \left(\frac{2\cdot306 \times 4}{1}\right)^2 = 85$$

Testing a Specified Population Mean (Small Sample Method)

The appropriate test of a specified population mean may again be derived by using the standard procedure for significance testing described on page 61.

Suppose that, for expenses purposes, a representative receives 500 miles per week car allowance. Over an eight-week period, his actual weekly mileage averages 510 with a standard deviation of 20. Is it likely that the allowance is inadequate?

Follow the sequence of steps on page 61.

1. Null hypothesis.

This always states that the specified population value is correct, or: $\mu = 500$.

2. Alternative hypothesis.

We are only concerned with the possibility that the allowance is inadequate. Our alternative hypothesis will therefore be: $\mu > 500$.

3. Significance level.

The 0·05 level will be satisfactory.

4. Identify the rejection area in the appropriate sampling distribution, assuming that the null hypothesis is true. The appropriate sampling distribution will be a t-distribution with mean = 500 and

standard error $= \dfrac{s}{\sqrt{n}} = \dfrac{20}{\sqrt{8}} = 7\cdot07$.

The alternative hypothesis indicates that we are only interested in unusually large values of $\bar{x}$. The rejection area will thus consist of the upper tail of the distribution. Because our significance level is 0·05, the rejection area will contain 5% of the distribution. This means that even if the population mean really is 500, there is a 5% chance that our sample mean will fall in the rejection area. This is illustrated in Figure 4.3 (page 94).

The boundary of the rejection area will be $t_{.05}$ standard errors above the population mean. If our sample mean is further than this above 500, it will fall in the rejection area. From Table III, the value of $t_{.05}$ with 7 degrees of freedom is found to be 1·895.

5. Find the position of the observed sample mean in the sampling distribution. If it falls in the rejection area, the null hypothesis may be rejected and the alternative accepted.

To establish the position of $\bar{x}$, we need to find how many standard errors above 500 it lies. We may do this by using the formula:

$$t = \frac{\bar{x} - \mu}{\text{S.E.}} \qquad \qquad \dots (4.3)$$

$$= \frac{510 - 500}{7 \cdot 07} = 1 \cdot 41$$

This is less than the value of 1·895 necessary for $\bar{x}$ to be in the rejection area. Accordingly, the null hypothesis cannot be rejected.

6.   This is an inconclusive result. It does not necessarily mean that the null hypothesis is true. It merely means that there is a greater than 5% chance that the observed sample results could have come from a population with a mean value of 500.

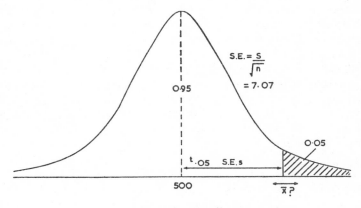

Figure 4.3. A one-tail t-test

Comparing Two Sample Means (Small Sample Method)

We will again develop a test for assessing the significance of the difference between two sample means by referring to a specific example. A sample of 6 operatives from Department A of a factory have an average performance (on the B.S.I. scale) of 96 with a standard deviation of 4·0. A sample of 5 from Department B have an average of 92 with a standard deviation of 3·5. Do these samples establish that the overall averages of the operatives in these two departments differ?

$$\bar{x}_1 = 96 \qquad s_1 = 4 \cdot 0 \qquad n_1 = 6$$
$$\bar{x}_2 = 92 \qquad s_2 = 3 \cdot 5 \qquad n_2 = 5$$

Follow the usual procedure.

1. Null hypothesis.

This states that there is no difference between the two population means, or: $\mu_1 = \mu_2$.

2. Alternative hypothesis.

We are testing whether or not there is any difference between μ_1 and μ_2, without any knowledge as to which of them is the larger. The alternative hypothesis will therefore be: $\mu_1 \neq \mu_2$.

3. Significance level.

We will use the 0·01 level.

4. Identify the rejection area in the appropriate sampling distribution, assuming that the null hypothesis is true. The first sample mean, $\bar{x}_1$, is in effect a random selection from the t-distribution in Figure 4.4 (a) and the second, $\bar{x}_2$, is a random selection from that in Figure 4.4 (b).

We are interested in evaluating the difference $(\bar{x}_1 - \bar{x}_2)$, so the appropriate sampling distribution will be obtained by subtracting these two distributions. The result is shown in Figure 4.4 (c).

The mean of the resulting distribution is $(\mu_1 - \mu_2)$, which under

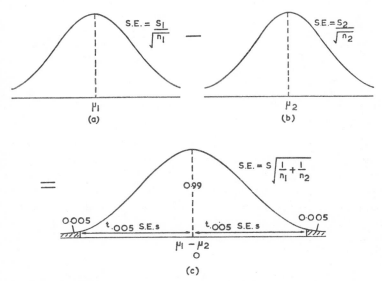

Figure 4.4. Derivation of the t-test for the difference between two means

the null hypothesis is zero. Notice the rather different form of the standard error. It requires that s_1 and s_2 be pooled in a rather complicated-looking way to form a joint estimate s. The formula for doing this is:

$$s = \sqrt{\frac{(n_1 - 1)s_1^2 + (n_2 - 1)s_2^2}{n_1 + n_2 - 2}} \qquad \ldots (4.4)$$

In fact this is nothing more than a weighted average of the sample variances (the variance being the square of the standard deviation). The appropriate weights to use are the degrees of freedom on which each is based, that is, $(n_1 - 1)$ and $(n_2 - 1)$ respectively.

Pooling our sample variances in this way carries the implicit assumption that the populations from which our samples come have the same variance. In the example which we are currently discussing, this means that we must assume the variability in operator performances to be the same in both departments. If this is not the case, the test cannot be used. Where any doubt exists, the sample variances may be tested for compatibility by means of the test described on page 105.

Substituting our sample values in formula (4.4):

$$s = \sqrt{\frac{(5 \times 16) + (4 \times 12 \cdot 25)}{9}} = 3 \cdot 78$$

The standard error is now found by substituting in the formula:

$$\text{S.E.} = s\sqrt{\left(\frac{1}{n_1} + \frac{1}{n_2}\right)} \qquad \ldots (4.5)$$

$$= 3 \cdot 78\sqrt{\left(\frac{1}{6} + \frac{1}{5}\right)} = 2 \cdot 30$$

We must now consider the rejection area. The alternative hypothesis indicates that a two-tail test is appropriate; we are interested in both positive and negative values for $(\bar{x}_1 - \bar{x}_2)$.

As we have decided to use the 0·01 significance level, the rejection area will consist of the extreme $\frac{1}{2}\%$ of each tail of the distribution, as indicated in Figure 4.4 (c). In order to fall in the rejection area, therefore, $(\bar{x}_1 - \bar{x}_2)$ must be more than $t_{.005}$ standard errors away from the mean, zero. We must now get the appropriate value of $t_{.005}$ from Table III. To do so, we require to know the number of degrees of freedom on which the s in formula (4.5) is based. This was calculated as a weighted average of 2 estimates, one having 5 degrees of freedom and the other 4. The composite estimate s is therefore based on 9 degrees of freedom.

In general terms, the number of degrees of freedom for s will be $(n_1 - 1) + (n_2 - 1) = n_1 + n_2 - 2$. Entering Table III with 9 degrees of freedom gives $t_{.005} = 3.250$.

5.   Find the position of the sample result in the sampling distribution. If it falls in the rejection area, the null hypothesis may be rejected.

To establish if $(\bar{x}_1 - \bar{x}_2)$ does fall in the rejection area, we must find how many standard errors away from the mean it lies. The appropriate formula is:

$$t = \frac{(\bar{x}_1 - \bar{x}_2) - 0}{\text{S.E.}} = \frac{\bar{x}_1 - \bar{x}_2}{s\sqrt{\left(\dfrac{1}{n_1} + \dfrac{1}{n_2}\right)}} \qquad \ldots (4.6)$$

Substituting our sample data in this formula:

$$t = \frac{96 - 92}{2.30} = 1.74$$

This is smaller than 3.250, the value required to enable the null hypothesis to be rejected. We are therefore unable to say that these samples establish a difference in average performance between the two departments.

Exercises

4.1.   In a time study, 12 timings of a particular element were as follows. The times are in hundredths of a minute:

16	19	15	17
14	18	17	16
18	15	16	15

(a) Calculate 95% confidence limits for the true average time for this element.

(b) How many more timings must be taken to be 99% certain that the resulting estimate is not more than 0.5 away from the true value?

4.2.   In a textile finishing process, the average time taken is 6·4 hours. A series of 8 trials is made with a modified process in an attempt to reduce this time. The following results are obtained:

6·1	5·9	6·3	6·5
6·2	6·0	6·4	6·2

Has the modification succeeded in reducing average process time?

4.3.   An agricultural experiment is conducted to determine which of two varieties of grain produces the heavier crop. Type 1 is planted on 8 test plots and the resulting crop averages 40 cwt per acre with a standard deviation of 4·0. Type 2 is planted on 8 matching plots and has an average yield of 45 cwt per acre with a standard deviation of 4·8. Does this test establish, at the 0·01 significance level, that there is a difference between the two varieties?

Summary of Small Sample Formulae

1.   Calculation of confidence limits for an unknown mean μ.

$$\mu \text{ lies between } \bar{x} \pm \frac{ts}{\sqrt{n}}$$

where $\bar{x}$ = sample mean,
s = sample standard deviation,
n = sample size.

For 95% confidence limits, use the $t_{.025}$ value with $(n-1)$ degrees of freedom. For 99% confidence limits, use the $t_{.005}$ value with $(n-1)$ degrees of freedom.

2.   Estimation of sample size required for a specified degree of accuracy in the estimate of an unknown mean μ.

$$n = \left(\frac{ts}{L} \right)^2$$

where n = required sample size,
s = sample standard deviation,
L = specified degree of accuracy.

Before n may be calculated, it is thus necessary to take a small initial sample to obtain an estimate of the standard deviation. If this initial sample is of size m, the t value in the formula has $(m-1)$ degrees of freedom. A sample of the size calculated will then provide an estimate of μ which is almost certainly not in error by more than the specified amount L.

'Almost certainly' means $\begin{cases} 95\% \text{ certain if } t_{.025} \text{ is used,} \\ 99\% \text{ certain if } t_{.005} \text{ is used.} \end{cases}$

3. Testing a specified population mean μ.

(a) Null hypothesis: the specified value of μ is correct.

(b) Alternative hypothesis: this could be any one of the following.

  (i) $\mu \neq$ the specified value.

  (ii) $\mu >$ the specified value.

  (iii) $\mu <$ the specified value.

If it is (i), a two-tail test will be appropriate. If it is (ii) or (iii), a one-tail test will be appropriate.

(c) Significance level: usually either 0·05 or 0·01, depending on the consequences of wrongly rejecting the null hypothesis.

(d) Calculate t from the formula:

$$t = \frac{\bar{x} - \mu}{\dfrac{s}{\sqrt{n}}}$$

where $\bar{x}$ = sample mean,

μ = specified population mean,

s = sample standard deviation,

n = sample size.

(e) Interpret t for significance.

The null hypothesis may be rejected if t exceeds the appropriate value from the following table:

Significance level

		0·05	0·01	
	(i)	$\pm t_{.025}$	$\pm t_{.005}$	two-tail test
Alternative hypothesis	(ii)	$+ t_{.05}$	$+ t_{.01}$	one-tail tests
	(iii)	$- t_{.05}$	$- t_{.01}$	

The numerical value of these is found by consulting Table III with $(n-1)$ degrees of freedom.

4.   Comparing two sample means, $\bar{x}_1$ and $\bar{x}_2$.

(*a*) Null hypothesis: $\mu_1 = \mu_2$.

(*b*) Alternative hypothesis: this could be any one of the following.

    (i) $\mu_1 \neq \mu_2$.

    (ii) $\mu_1 > \mu_2$.

    (iii) $\mu_1 < \mu_2$.

If it is (i), a two-tail test will be appropriate. If it is (ii) or (iii), a one-tail test will be appropriate.

(*c*) Significance level: usually either 0·05 or 0·01, depending on the consequences of wrongly rejecting the null hypothesis.

(*d*) Calculate s from the formula:

$$s = \sqrt{\frac{(n_1 - 1)s_1^2 + (n_2 - 1)s_2^2}{n_1 + n_2 - 2}}$$

where n_1 and n_2 = sample sizes,

           s_1 and s_2 = sample standard deviations.

If s_1 and s_2 differ substantially, they should first be tested for compatibility by means of the F-test described on page 104.

(*e*) Calculate t from the formula:

$$t = \frac{\bar{x}_1 - \bar{x}_2}{s\sqrt{\left(\dfrac{1}{n_1} + \dfrac{1}{n_2}\right)}}$$

(*f*) Interpret t for significance.

The null hypothesis may be rejected if t exceeds the appropriate value from the following table:

Significance level

		0·05	0·01	
	(i)	$\pm t_{.025}$	$\pm t_{.005}$	two-tail test
Alternative hypothesis	(ii)	$+ t_{.05}$	$+ t_{.01}$	one-tail tests
	(iii)	$- t_{.05}$	$- t_{.01}$	

The numerical value of these is found by consulting Table III with $(n_1 + n_2 - 2)$ degrees of freedom.

The F-distribution

It is sometimes useful to be able to compare the variability of two samples rather than, or as well as, their mean values. Suppose we manufacture a certain chemical by a batch process. We require the density of the product to be as consistent as possible from batch to batch. The more consistent our process is, the smaller will be the standard deviation of density. There are two processes available for manufacturing this chemical, and a series of 10 trials is made with each one. Process 1 has a standard deviation in density of 4·1 units and Process 2 a standard deviation of 2·0 units. Do these tests indicate that Process 2 has a smaller standard deviation (is more consistent) than Process 1?

The appropriate sampling distribution for evaluating situations of this kind is known as the **F-distribution**. It has been derived in terms of sample variances (squared standard deviations). Figure 4.5 illustrates its derivation. Suppose we take a sample of n_1 items from

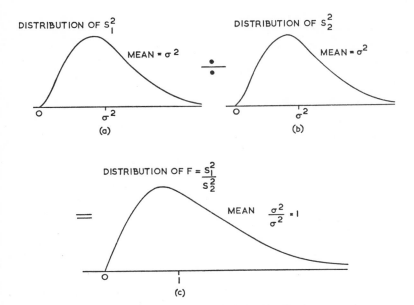

Figure 4.5. Derivation of the F-distribution

a population and work out s_1^2, the sample variance. We then take another sample of the same size and work out s_1^2 again. It will not be the same as the first sample variance, although both are estimates of σ^2, the population variance. In other words, s_1^2 has a sampling distribution. This distribution for samples of size n_1 is shown in Figure 4.5 (a). Any particular value of s_1^2 which arises is in effect a random selection from this distribution. The distribution for samples of size n_2 is shown in Figure 4.5 (b). In each case the average of the distribution is σ^2, the true population variance. Notice that these distributions are not normal in shape, they are skewed.

The F-distribution is now formed as the *ratio* of these two distributions, $\dfrac{s_1^2}{s_2^2}$. The average value of F is 1, because the average of each of its component distributions is σ^2. This distribution is shown in Figure 4.5 (c).

Using the F-distribution

Let us now see how this distribution may be used to develop a significance test to evaluate our two chemical processes. Once again we follow the formal procedure on page 61. Our sample results are:

$$n_1 = 10 \qquad\qquad n_2 = 10$$
$$s_1^2 = 16 \cdot 8 \qquad\qquad s_2^2 = 4$$

1.   Null hypothesis.
As usual, this states that there is no difference in the variances of the populations from which our samples come, or: $\sigma_1^2 = \sigma_2^2$.

2.   Alternative hypothesis.
It is worth mentioning again at this point that the alternative hypothesis must be formulated before the sample results are known. Let us assume that, from technical considerations, Process 2 is expected to be more consistent than Process 1. Our alternative hypothesis will then be: $\sigma_1^2 > \sigma_2^2$.

3.   Significance level.
We will use the 0·05 significance level.

4.   Identify the rejection area of the appropriate sampling distribution under the assumption that the null hypothesis is true.

The appropriate distribution is an F-distribution. If the null hypothesis is true, the average value of $\dfrac{s_1^2}{s_2^2}$ will be 1. The further away from 1 this ratio is, the less likely it is that s_1^2 and s_2^2 are estimates of the same σ^2. Because of our alternative hypothesis, we are only interested in unusually large values of this ratio, that is, the upper tail of the distribution in Figure 4.6. We are using a significance level of 0·05, so our rejection area will be the upper 5% of the distribution. There is then a probability of 0·05 that the ratio $F = \dfrac{s_1^2}{s_2^2}$ will fall in the rejection area even if σ_1^2 and σ_2^2 are equal.

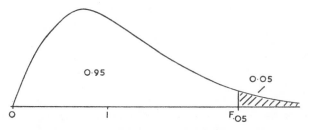

Figure 4.6. The rejection area for a one-tail F-test

It now remains to find the value of F which corresponds to the boundary of the rejection area; that is, the value which only has a 5% chance of being exceeded if the null hypothesis is true. Following previously used notation, this is denoted by $F_{.05}$. This critical value of F will depend on the degrees of freedom on which s_1^2 and s_2^2 are based. These are $(n_1 - 1)$ and $(n_2 - 1)$ respectively. In our example both of these are 9.

Critical values of F for varying combinations of degrees of freedom for s_1^2 and s_2^2 are given in Table IV at the end of the book. Degrees of freedom for s_1^2 (the numerator in the ratio) are tabulated horizontally and those for s_2^2 (the denominator) are shown vertically. Separate tables are included for $F_{.05}$, $F_{.025}$, $F_{.01}$ and $F_{.005}$. Looking at the one for $F_{.05}$, with 9 degrees of freedom for the numerator and 9 for the denominator gives: $F_{.05} = 3·18$.

5. Calculate the position of the sample result in the sampling distribution. If it falls in the rejection area, the null hypothesis may be rejected and the alternative accepted.

This is simply a matter of calculating F from the formula:

$$F = \frac{s_1^2}{s_2^2} = \frac{16 \cdot 8}{4} = 4 \cdot 2$$

This exceeds the $F_{\cdot 05}$ value of $3 \cdot 18$ and we may therefore reject the null hypothesis and claim that Process 2 is more consistent (has a smaller variance) than Process 1.

Two-tail Significance Tests

Suppose that in the example just discussed, we have no prior knowledge about the variability of our two processes. The alternative hypothesis then becomes: $\sigma_1^2 \neq \sigma_2^2$.

This means that we are interested in both unusually large and unusually small values of the F ratio. In other words, a two-tail test is required. To keep the significance level at $0 \cdot 05$, our rejection area will consist of the extreme $2\frac{1}{2}\%$ of both tails, as in Figure 4.7. There are now two critical values of F; one larger than 1 and the other smaller than 1. The smaller one is, however, the reciprocal of the larger, as Figure 4.7 shows. It is not therefore necessary to tabulate both tails.

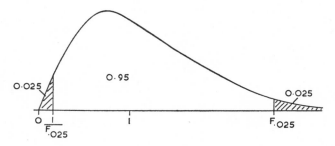

Figure 4.7. The rejection area for a two-tail F-test

The upper critical value, $F_{\cdot 025}$, may be obtained from Table IV with 9 degrees of freedom for both the numerator and denominator. It is $4 \cdot 03$. There is thus a $2\frac{1}{2}\%$ chance that F will be greater than $4 \cdot 03$, and a $2\frac{1}{2}\%$ chance that it will be smaller than $\frac{1}{4 \cdot 03} = 0 \cdot 25$, if $\sigma_1^2 = \sigma_2^2$.

We have an F value of $4 \cdot 2$ from our sample data, which therefore lies in the rejection area, thus enabling us to reject the null hypothesis. We could also have rejected the null hypothesis if the ratio had worked out at less than 0·25.

The calculation is made slightly easier if, when working out the F value, the larger sample variance is always called s_1^2. This ensures that F will always be greater than 1, so we need only concern ourselves with the critical value in the upper tail of the distribution. If the ratio calculated in this way exceeds the $F_{.025}$ value, a significant difference has been established between the two variances at the 0·05 level.

When we were developing a test for comparing two small sample means, it was necessary to pool the sample variances to calculate the appropriate standard error. This involves the implicit assumption that $\sigma_1^2 = \sigma_2^2$ as was mentioned on page 96. Strictly speaking, this assumption should be tested by means of a two-tail F-test before the variances are pooled.

The two sample variances concerned in the example on page 94 were $s_1^2 = 16$ and $s_2^2 = 12·25$, and the sample sizes were $n_1 = 6$ and $n_2 = 5$. The F ratio is therefore:

$$F = \frac{s_1^2}{s_2^2} = \frac{16}{12·25} = 1·31$$

The $F_{.025}$ value, with 5 degrees of freedom for the numerator and 4 for the denominator, is 9·36. These two sample variances are therefore consistent with the hypothesis $\sigma_1^2 = \sigma_2^2$ and may be pooled to calculate the standard error required for the t-test. Had a significantly high value of F been obtained, the t-test could not have been carried out.

Exercises

4.4. A textile company is trying to develop a green dye which will produce a consistent shade of green in cotton material. Two different formulations are tried out, the first on 10 test squares of cotton and the second on 8 test squares. The depth of colour of each square of material is then assessed on a points scale. The standard deviation of the 10 squares on which the first dye was used is 3·0 and that of the 8 squares treated with the second dye is 6·4. Does this test establish that the first dye produces more consistent results than the second? No prior knowledge concerning the two dyes was available.

4.5.   A machine produces metal washers, the standard deviation of their thickness being 1·5 mm. A modification is made to the machine to try to reduce this variability in thickness, and a sample of 21 washers produced by the modified machine have a standard deviation of 1·0 mm. Has the modification been successful?

4.6.   A sample of 9 pieces of yarn made with a synthetic fibre has an average breaking strength of 10 lb with a standard deviation of 0·5 lb. A sample of 16 pieces made with animal fibre has an average breaking strength of 7 lb with a standard deviation of 1·2 lb.

(a) Is the synthetic fibre more consistent in its strength than the animal fibre?

(b) Is the synthetic fibre stronger on average than the animal fibre?

Summary of Procedure for Comparing Two Variances

1.   Null hypothesis: $\sigma_1^2 = \sigma_2^2$.
2.   Alternative hypothesis: this could be either of the following.
    (i) $\sigma_1^2 \neq \sigma_2^2$.
    (ii) One variance is larger than the other. In this case, the larger one is always numbered σ_1^2, giving the alternative hypothesis as: $\sigma_1^2 > \sigma_2^2$.

    Case (i) will require a two-tail test. Case (ii) will require a one-tail test.

3.   Significance level: usually either 0·05 or 0·01, depending on the consequences of wrongly rejecting the null hypothesis.

4.   Calculate F from the formula:

$$F = \frac{s_1^2}{s_2^2}$$

5.   Interpret F for significance.

The null hypothesis may be rejected if F exceeds the appropriate value from the following table:

Significance level

		0·05	0·01	
Alternative	(i)	$F_{.025}$	$F_{.005}$	two-tail test
hypothesis	(ii)	$F_{.05}$	$F_{.01}$	one-tail test

The numerical value of these is found by consulting Table IV with $(n_1 - 1)$ degrees of freedom for the numerator, and $(n_2 - 1)$ degrees of freedom for the denominator.

The Chi Squared Distribution

In Example 2.6 on page 40, we used the normal distribution to represent the way in which chest size is distributed among the adult male population. Before we do this, we must be sure that it provides a reasonable approximation to the true distribution. Again, in Example 2.3 on page 27, we wanted to see how closely the distribution of knots appearing in balls of knitting wool corresponded with that expected if the knots were randomly distributed.

Situations like these may be examined by making use of a sampling distribution known as the **chi squared distribution**. It is so called because it is denoted by the symbol χ^2, which is the Greek letter chi (pronounced 'kye') squared.

The basic approach is always the same. We compare an observed set of frequencies with those expected if some theoretical distribution applies. The χ^2 distribution then enables us to decide how well the theoretical model 'fits' the observed data. Because of the way in which these tests are carried out, they are known as **goodness of fit** tests.

Example 4.1

The distribution shown overleaf is of the chest measurements of 200 adult males. Do these data support the assumption that chest size is normally distributed with a mean of 37·5 in and standard deviation of 2 in?

The first step is to calculate the theoretical frequencies for each class, assuming that the distribution is normal and has the specified

Chest measurement	Observed frequency
32–34	6
34–36	40
36–38	68
38–40	66
40–42	18
42–44	2
	200

parameters. This is done by calculating the proportions of the normal distribution which fall in each class, as in Example 2.6 on page 40. These proportions of the total number in the sample (in this case 200) will then give the theoretical frequencies which would be expected to arise in each class if the distribution were normal. The results are summarized in Table 4.1. The observed frequencies and the differences between observed and expected frequencies are also included in the table.

TABLE 4.1

Class	Expected proportion in class	Expected frequency (E)	Observed frequency (O)	Difference $O - E$
32–34	0·0371	7·42	6	− 1·42
34–36	0·1865	37·30	40	+ 2·70
36–38	0·3721	74·42	68	− 6·42
38–40	0·2957	59·14	66	+ 6·86
40–42	0·0934	18·68	18	− 0·68
42–44	0·0122	2·44	2	− 0·44

The calculation for the expected proportion in the class 42–44 was not made in Example 2.6. The z value corresponding to 44 is:

$$z = \frac{x - \mu}{\sigma} = \frac{44 - 37 \cdot 5}{2 \cdot 0} = 3 \cdot 25$$

Table II only gives the areas corresponding to z values up to 3·09. For all practical purposes, any z value larger than this may be regarded as having an associated area of 0·5000. This will give the expected proportion in the class 42–44 as $0 \cdot 5000 - 0 \cdot 4878 = 0 \cdot 0122$.

Notice that the expected frequencies are not whole numbers. That is because they represent the *average* number of men who would be in each class out of a sample of 200. In any particular sample, the number must of course be an integer.

Also, the sum of the expected frequencies is not exactly 200, because of the small proportion of the theoretical distribution which is outside the range covered by the observed data.

The closer the correspondence between expected and observed frequencies, the more likely it is that the observed data come from the specified distribution. At the same time, knowing that samples from the same population vary, we would not expect the observed and expected frequencies to be identical. Indeed, they could not possibly be, since the observed frequencies must be whole numbers, whereas the expected frequencies are not. The important question is, are the differences between the two sets of frequencies small enough to be due to sampling fluctuations? If so, the theoretical distribution provides a good fit to the observed data.

Some way of evaluating the magnitude of the differences is thus required. To do this, we first need a single measurement which represents the total difference between the two sets of frequencies. We cannot simply add up all the individual class differences; the positive and negative ones will cancel each other out. If, however, we square the differences, they will all become positive.

Also, we must 'standardize' the differences in some way. The difference of 2 between an observed frequency of 110 and an expected one of 108 obviously indicates a closer correspondence than does the same difference of 2 between an observed frequency of 7 and an expected one of 5. This standardization is achieved by simply dividing each squared difference by the expected frequency. These standardized differences are then added up to provide the required measurement of total discrepancy between observed and expected frequencies.

Notationally, this may be expressed as:

$$\sum \frac{(O - E)^2}{E}$$

where Σ is the Greek capital letter S, meaning 'sum of', and O and E are the observed and expected frequencies for each class. For the data in Table 4.1 we have:

$$\sum \frac{(O-E)^2}{E} = \frac{(-1\cdot42)^2}{7\cdot42} + \frac{(2\cdot70)^2}{37\cdot30} + \frac{(-6\cdot42)^2}{74\cdot42} + \frac{(6\cdot86)^2}{59\cdot14} +$$

$$\frac{(-0\cdot68)^2}{18\cdot68} + \frac{(-0\cdot44)^2}{2\cdot44}$$

$$= 0\cdot271 + 0\cdot195 + 0\cdot553 + 0\cdot795 + 0\cdot024 + 0\cdot079$$
$$= 1\cdot917$$

If we were now to take another sample of 200 men, the observed frequencies in this second sample would differ from those in Table 4.1, because of natural sampling fluctuations. In turn this would then give us a different value for $\sum \frac{(O-E)^2}{E}$. A third sample would give yet another value, and so on.

In other words, the statistic $\sum \frac{(O-E)^2}{E}$ has a sampling distribution. Under the assumption that the sample is from the specified population, this sampling distribution may be approximated closely by a χ^2 distribution provided that none of the expected class frequencies is less than 5. For the time being, we will ignore the fact that one of the expected frequencies in Table 4.1 is only 2·44. We will see how to adjust for it later.

Values of χ^2 are tabulated in the same way as values of t and F. Thus $\chi^2_{0\cdot05}$ is the value of χ^2 which has a probability of 0·05 of being exceeded. Figure 4.8 illustrates this. Again like t and F, the value of χ^2 depends on the number of degrees of freedom with which it is calculated. In the example we are considering, for instance, we should expect a larger value for $\sum \frac{(O-E)^2}{E}$ if we had 20 classes in the distribution instead of only 6.

The larger our calculated value of $\sum \frac{(O-E)^2}{E}$, the less likely it is that the sample is from the specified population. We may thus set up a significance test, based on the χ^2 distribution.

Our null hypothesis is that the sample is from a normal population with a mean of 37·5 and a standard deviation of 2·0. Under this hypothesis, the sampling distribution of the statistic $\sum \frac{(O-E)^2}{E}$ is a χ^2 distribution. For a 0·05 significance test, the rejection area will be the upper 5% of the distribution, as indicated in Figure 4.8. A

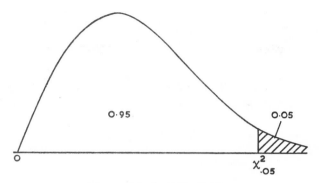

Figure 4.8. A χ^2 distribution

value of $\sum \dfrac{(O-E)^2}{E}$ which exceeds the appropriate value will fall in this rejection area and enable us to reject the null hypothesis. In other words, it will establish that the sample data do not come from the specified population.

A non-significant result, on the other hand, does not prove that the specified distribution does apply, merely that the sample data could have come from such a distribution. In practice, of course, we usually take a non-significant result as sufficient justification for assuming that the specified distribution does apply.

It now only remains to find the critical value of $\chi^2_{.05}$ against which to compare our sample value of $\chi^2 = \sum \dfrac{(O-E)^2}{E}$. To do this, we need to know the number of degrees of freedom on which our sample χ^2 is based. The formula for calculating this is:

$$\text{d.f.} = k - 1 - d \qquad \qquad \ldots (4.7)$$

In this formula, k stands for the number of classes in the distribution, which in our example is 6. The 1 in the formula is the degree of freedom which is lost by making the total of the expected frequencies equal the total of the observed frequencies. The letter d stands for the number of parameters which were *estimated from the sample data* and used to calculate the theoretical frequencies. In our example, d would be 2 if the mean and standard deviation were estimated from the sample. If they were calculated independently from some other data, then d would be zero.

It more often happens that they must be estimated from the sample data, so assuming that to be the case, our degrees of freedom for χ^2 will be: $6 - 1 - 2 = 3$. From Table V (at the end of the book), we find the value of $\chi^2_{.05}$ with 3 d.f. to be 7·815.

Our sample value of χ^2 was only 1·917, which is quite clearly not significant. The data are therefore consistent with having come from a normal population with a mean of 37·5 and a standard deviation of 2·0.

Adjusting for Frequencies Less Than 5

The test which we have just carried out requires a minimum expected frequency of 5 in each class. The expected frequency in the final class is only 2·44 (see Table 4.1) so the calculation is not strictly accurate. In such cases, adjoining classes may be amalgamated until the expected frequency exceeds 5. This will of course mean a corresponding reduction in the number of degrees of freedom.

Amalgamating the last 2 classes in the distribution leads to the following results:

Class	Expected frequency	Observed frequency	$O - E$
32–34	7·42	6	−1·42
34–36	37·30	40	+2·70
36–38	74·42	68	−6·42
38–40	59·14	66	+6·86
40–42 / 42–44	21·12	20	−1·12

χ^2 now becomes:

$$\frac{(-1\cdot42)^2}{7\cdot42} + \frac{(2\cdot70)^2}{37\cdot30} + \frac{(-6\cdot42)^2}{74\cdot42} + \frac{(6\cdot86)^2}{59\cdot14} + \frac{(-1\cdot12)^2}{21\cdot12}$$
$$= 0\cdot271 + 0\cdot195 + 0\cdot553 + 0\cdot795 + 0\cdot059$$
$$= 1\cdot873$$

We now have only 5 classes, so the degrees of freedom will be $5 - 1 - 2 = 2$. From Table V, the value of $\chi^2_{.05}$ with 2 d.f. is 5·991.

Thus the more accurate calculation leads to the same conclusion as before.

Example 4.2

A spinning frame consists of a large number of bobbins on to which the spun yarn is wound automatically. Periodically the yarn breaks and the break has to be repaired by the machine minder (an operation known as 'piecening').

The time taken to fill a set of bobbins is 4 hours, and it is thought that the incidence of breakages varies throughout the filling cycle (the 'doff' cycle). To test this theory, a record is kept of the number of breaks occurring during each half-hour of the doff cycle. The results are as follows:

Half-hour number	1	2	3	4	5	6	7	8
Number of breaks	15	12	8	9	10	7	12	7

Do these data show that the incidence of breakages varies through the doff cycle?

Our null hypothesis is that the incidence of breakages does not vary. We have had a total of 80 breakages during the cycle, so under the null hypothesis, the expected number per half-hour is 10. We therefore have:

$$\chi^2 = \frac{(15-10)^2}{10} + \frac{(12-10)^2}{10} + \frac{(8-10)^2}{10} + \frac{(9-10)^2}{10} + \frac{(10-10)^2}{10} +$$
$$\frac{(7-10)^2}{10} + \frac{(12-10)^2}{10} + \frac{(7-10)^2}{10}$$

$$= 2\cdot5 + 0\cdot4 + 0\cdot4 + 0\cdot1 + 0 + 0\cdot9 + 0\cdot4 + 0\cdot9$$
$$= 5\cdot6$$

We must now find the appropriate value of $\chi^2_{.05}$. We have not estimated any population parameters from the data; we have merely shared the total number of breaks out evenly between the 8 classes. In formula (4.7), therefore, d will be zero, giving us $8 - 1 = 7$ degrees of freedom. Consulting Table V with 7 degrees of freedom, we find: $\chi^2_{.05} = 14\cdot067$.

Our sample value for χ^2 is only 5·6, so we are not able to reject the null hypothesis. In other words, the data do not suggest that the incidence of breakages varies through the doff cycle.

Exercises

4.7. Using the data of Exercise 2.14, test the hypothesis that goals in football matches occur at random.

4.8. The following distribution is of the weights of 100 8 oz boxes of chocolates. Can they reasonably be assumed to come from a normally distributed population?

Weight in oz	Frequency
7·80–7·89	4
7·90–7·99	12
8·00–8·09	30
8·10–8·19	36
8·20–8·29	15
8·30–8·39	3

Contingency Tables

So far we have only considered situations in which we wished to compare one set of observed frequencies against those expected to arise under some assumption about the distribution. It is possible to extend the χ^2 test to compare several sets of frequencies simultaneously. To carry out the test in this extended form, the data are expressed in what is known as a **contingency table**.

As an example, look at the figures in Table 4.2. They were compiled by a personnel manager, and relate to 150 boys who have been through his company's apprentice training scheme. The performance of the boys during training is compared with their final school report before joining the company. Is there any connection between a boy's school report and his performance in training?

TABLE 4.2

	Good report	Average report	Poor report	ROW TOTALS
Good performance	20	10	5	35
Average performance	30	35	10	75
Poor performance	10	15	15	40
COLUMN TOTALS	60	60	30	150

To evaluate the results in a contingency table of this nature, we invariably assume as our null hypothesis that there is no connection between the two factors. This enables us to calculate the expected frequencies for each compartment (usually called a **cell**) of the table.

The row totals may be used to estimate the overall proportion of boys in each training category. We have, out of a grand total of 150 boys, 35 in the 'Good' category. We thus have $\frac{35}{150} \times 100\%$ $=23\cdot3\%$ of boys in this category.

Now 60 of the boys had good school reports (see first column total), so on a straight percentage basis we would expect to get $23\cdot3\%$ of these with a good training performance. The expected frequency for the first cell of the table is therefore $23\cdot3\%$ of 60, which is 14. This is to be compared with the observed frequency of 20.

The calculation of expected frequency may be reduced to a simple formula:

$$\text{Expected frequency for a cell} = \frac{\text{Row total} \times \text{column total}}{\text{Grand total}} \quad \ldots (4.8)$$

For the first cell of Table 4.2 this gives:

$$\frac{35 \times 60}{150} = 14$$

For the second cell in the first column:

$$\text{Expected frequency} = \frac{75 \times 60}{150} = 30$$

and so on.

The full set of expected frequencies is shown in brackets under the observed frequencies in Table 4.3 (page 116). Notice that row and column totals for both expected and observed frequencies are equal.

We now compute χ^2 as before by calculating $\frac{(O-E)^2}{E}$ for each cell of the table and adding:

$$\chi^2 = \frac{(20-14)^2}{14} + \frac{(10-14)^2}{14} + \frac{(5-7)^2}{7} + \frac{(30-30)^2}{30} + \frac{(35-30)^2}{30} +$$
$$\frac{(10-15)^2}{15} + \frac{(10-16)^2}{16} + \frac{(15-16)^2}{16} + \frac{(15-8)^2}{8}$$

$$= 2\cdot57 + 1\cdot14 + 0\cdot57 + 0 + 0\cdot83 + 1\cdot67 + 2\cdot25 + 0\cdot06 + 6\cdot12$$
$$= 15\cdot21$$

TABLE 4.3

	Good	Average	Poor	TOTALS
Good	20 (14)	10 (14)	5 (7)	35
Average	30 (30)	35 (30)	10 (15)	75
Poor	10 (16)	15 (16)	15 (8)	40
TOTALS	60	60	30	150

Degrees of Freedom for Contingency Tables

To carry out a significance test of our null hypothesis, we must obtain the critical value of $\chi^2_{.05}$ from Table V. Before we can do this, we must know on how many degrees of freedom our sample χ^2 is based.

In Table 4.3 there are 9 cells. However, in order to calculate the expected frequencies, we made use of row and column totals. The fixing of each row total uses up one degree of freedom in that row. In the first row, for instance, once the first two cells have been filled, the third is automatically determined because the row total must be 35. The same remark applies to the columns. The first column total must be 60, which means that only two of the cells in that column are 'free'.

In Table 4.3, then, we have only $2 \times 2 = 4$ degrees of freedom. In general, if the table contains r rows and c columns, the number of degrees of freedom for χ^2 is obtained from the simple formula:

$$\text{d.f.} = (r-1)(c-1) \qquad \ldots (4.9)$$

Looking up Table V, we find that $\chi^2_{.05}$ with 4 d.f. is 9·488. Our sample value for χ^2 was 15·21, which is well above this. We are therefore able to reject the null hypothesis and claim that these data do establish a connection between final school report and training performance.

Example 4.3

In Chapter 3, a method of comparing the difference between two sample percentages was derived. Frequently, however, we are interested in comparing three or more sample percentages. Suppose, for example, that random samples of 450, 500, 600 and 450 house-wives are taken from 4 towns. Of these, 320, 360, 450 and 370 respectively use a certain washing powder. Do these data enable us to say that the percentage of users varies from town to town?

The contingency table approach may be used to answer questions of this nature. The numbers of users and non-users in each sample are set out in tabular form as in Table 4.4.

TABLE 4.4

	Town A	Town B	Town C	Town D	TOTALS
Users	320	360	450	370	1500
Non-users	130	140	150	80	500
TOTALS	450	500	600	450	2000

Our null hypothesis is that the percentage of users is the same in each town. Our estimate of this common percentage is the overall percentage of users in the combined samples, or $\frac{1500}{2000} \times 100\%$, which is 75%. If the null hypothesis is true, we should therefore, on average, expect to get 75% of 450 = 337·5 users in a sample of 450.

Once again these expected frequencies may be obtained more quickly by using formula (4.8). Only the first 3 cells need to be calculated in this way. The rest follow by subtraction from row or column totals. This is another demonstration of the fact that there are only $(r-1)(c-1)$, that is, $3 \times 1 = 3$, degrees of freedom in the table.

The observed frequencies are shown in Table 4.5 with the expected frequencies in brackets underneath them.

TABLE 4.5

	Town A	Town B	Town C	Town D	TOTALS
Users	320 (337·5)	360 (375)	450 (450)	(337·5) 370	1500
Non-users	130 (112·5)	140 (125)	150 (150)	80 (112·5)	500
TOTALS	450	500	600	450	2000

We are now able to compute:

$$\chi^2 = \frac{(17\cdot5)^2}{337\cdot5} + \frac{(15)^2}{375} + \frac{(0)^2}{450} + \frac{(32\cdot5)^2}{337\cdot5} + \frac{(17\cdot5)^2}{112\cdot5} + \frac{(15)^2}{125} + \frac{(0)^2}{150} + \frac{(32\cdot5)^2}{112\cdot5}$$

$$= 0\cdot90 + 0\cdot60 + 0 + 3\cdot12 + 2\cdot72 + 1\cdot80 + 0 + 9\cdot38$$

$$= 18\cdot52$$

The $\chi^2_{\cdot05}$ value with 3 d.f. is 7·815. The null hypothesis may therefore be rejected. These data do establish, at the 0·05 significance level, that the percentage of users varies from town to town.

The fact that we have a significant result does not necessarily mean that all the towns have different percentages of users. The percentage in Town D is clearly higher than the others, and this would be sufficient to provide a significant result. Significant differences between Towns A, B and C may be tested for by leaving out Town D and re-calculating χ^2 for the remaining 3 towns (see Exercise 4.11).

Exercises

4.9. Articles made of 3 different kinds of plastic are subjected to a series of tests to compare the relative strengths of the materials. The results are shown in the following table. Is the true percentage of items falling into each category the same for all 3 plastics?

	1	2	3
Undamaged	30	40	45
Slight damage	50	30	45
Completely smashed	20	10	30

4.10. Is the result of Example 4.3 significant at the 0·01 significance level?

4.11. Re-calculate χ^2 for Example 4.3, leaving out Town D. Is there a significant difference in the percentage of users in Towns A, B and C?

4.12. In the marketing of cosmetics, packaging is an important consideration. One particular company has to decide which of 4 suggested packages is to be used for a new product. 4 random samples of 200 customers each are offered the new product, a different package being used for each sample. Do the following results indicate any difference in sales appeal between the 4 packages?

	Pack 1	Pack 2	Pack 3	Pack 4
Number sold	38	55	45	42

4.13. Random samples of 300 voters in each of 4 towns are asked which political party they support. The results are shown in the table below. Are there any differences in the support enjoyed by each party in the 4 towns?

	Town 1	Town 2	Town 3	Town 4
Conservative	125	150	130	155
Labour	120	100	100	95
Liberal	35	40	55	35
Uncommitted	20	10	15	15

5 REGRESSION AND CORRELATION

So far we have been dealing with the problem of interpreting data concerning a single variable which has a probability distribution. Frequently, however, situations occur where there are two or more associated variables to be considered.

One particularly important group of these is concerned with attempting to predict the unknown value of one variable from the known value of another variable. A large food manufacturing company, for example, uses this approach to help predict future movements in the world price of basic commodities such as cocoa beans. It has been discovered that there is a close relationship between rainfall during the early part of the growing cycle of many crops and the subsequent yield of the crop. Thus, once the rainfall becomes known in any particular year, it may be used to predict the ultimate crop yield. This, taken in conjunction with estimated demand, enables the price to be predicted.

To illustrate the general method, we will use the following fictitious data, which relate to rainfall and subsequent crop yield over a five-year period.

	Year 1	Year 2	Year 3	Year 4	Year 5
Rainfall (in)	2	1	3	5	4
Yield (cwt per acre)	25	23	34	40	35

In practice, of course, we would need more pairs of figures than this, but five will suffice for purposes of illustration.

It is useful to represent the data graphically, as in Figure 5.1. Each pair of numbers provides one point on the diagram, rainfall being measured along the x axis and the corresponding yield along the y axis. The way in which the points group themselves on the diagram enables us to see if any relationship between x and y exists. A haphazard scattering of the points would indicate no relationship. A systematic grouping, on the other hand, indicates that some relationship does exist. Because it indicates the way in which the points are scattered, Figure 5.1 is known as a **scatter diagram.**

There is obviously some connection between x and y in Figure 5.1. As x increases, so does y. The problem is to try to find an equation

120

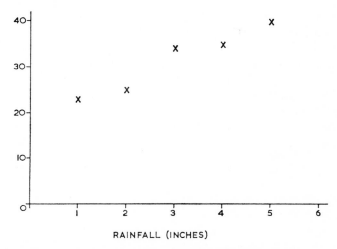

Figure 5.1. Scatter diagram of the rainfall/yield data

which describes this connection so that, given x, predictions may be made about y. The technique of finding the equation which fits the data best is known as **regression analysis.**

Linear Regression

It is possible to fit many different types of equation, but by far the easiest one to calculate is a straight line. The process of fitting such a line is known as **linear regression.** Even where the best relationship may not be strictly linear, a straight line is often fitted as a close approximation to a much more complicated curve.

Any straight line connecting x and y may be expressed as:

$$y = a + bx \qquad \qquad \dots (5.1)$$

When a and b are given numerical values, the line is uniquely specified. The value of a indicates the point on the y axis at which the line crosses it, and the value of b indicates how steeply the line rises or falls. Figure 5.2 illustrates this. The regression problem is to find the values of a and b for the line which provides the best fit to the observed data.

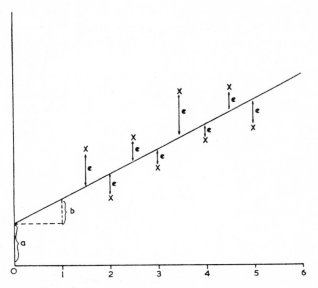

Figure 5.2. Illustrating the meaning of the regression coefficients a and b, and the differences between observed and predicted values

The Method of Least Squares

Before the equation of the best line can be determined, some criterion must be established as to what conditions the best line should satisfy. The condition usually stipulated in regression analysis is that the sum of the squares of the deviations of the observed y values from the fitted line shall be a minimum. This is known as the **least squares** or **minimum squared error** criterion. It can be proved that there is only one line which satisfies this condition. Figure 5.2 shows the problem pictorially. Values of a and b must be found so that the sum of the squares of all the distances like those marked 'e' is as small as possible.

Skipping some not-too-difficult mathematics, the required values of a and b may be found by solving the following pair of simultaneous equations:

$$\left. \begin{array}{l} \sum y = na + b\sum x \\ \sum xy = a\sum x + b\sum x^2 \end{array} \right\} \qquad \ldots (5.2)$$

Everything in these equations except a and b may be calculated from the observed data. The calculations are most conveniently set out in tabular form as follows, using the rainfall and yield data:

Rainfall x	Yield y	xy	x^2
2	25	50	4
1	23	23	1
3	34	102	9
5	40	200	25
4	35	140	16
$\sum x = 15$	$\sum y = 157$	$\sum xy = 515$	$\sum x^2 = 55$

The first two columns are the observed data. Note that the variable which the equation is ultimately going to be used to predict (in this case *yield*) is *always* the y variable. The predictor variable (sometimes called the **independent** variable) is *always* the x variable.

Each entry in the third column is the product of the corresponding entries in the first two columns. The fourth column contains the squares of the entries in the first column. Finally, each column is added up to give the summations required for the pair of equations. The only other quantity in these equations, apart from a and b, is n. This is the number of *pairs* of observations in the data, which in this example is 5.

Substituting all these in the equations gives:

$$157 = 5a + 15b$$
$$515 = 15a + 55b$$

To solve these equations, we must first eliminate one of the variables. This is done by multiplying one or both of the equations by a constant in order to make the coefficient of one of the variables the same in both equations. This is most easily achieved by multiplying the first equation by 3 and leaving the other alone:

$$471 = 15a + 45b$$
$$515 = 15a + 55b$$

Subtracting the first equation from the second now gives:

$$44 = 10b, \text{ or } b = 4\cdot4$$

Substituting this value of b in the first of the original equations:

$$157 = 5a + 66$$
$$91 = 5a$$
$$a = 18\cdot2$$

The required regression equation is therefore:

$$y = 18\cdot2 + 4\cdot4x$$

Using the Regression Equation

This equation may now be used to predict the crop yield which will follow any amount of rainfall which may occur. Suppose that next year there are 3·5 in of rain. The predicted crop yield will be:

$$y = 18\cdot2 + (4\cdot4 \times 3\cdot5)$$
$$= 33\cdot6 \text{ cwt per acre}$$

It is dangerous to extrapolate a regression line outside the range covered by the observed data. We could not put a value of, say, $x = 15$ in of rain into the equation and expect a reasonable estimate of yield. This is because we do not know how far beyond the range covered by our data our assumption of a linear relationship holds. We can test the assumption within the range of observed rainfall by means of a scatter diagram, but it is not reasonable to expect that it will continue to hold for higher or lower values.

Yield will increase with rainfall up to a certain point, but beyond that point more rain would result in a decreased yield because of damage caused by flooding.

Alternative Method of Calculation

The calculation of the regression line may be simplified slightly if we write the equation in the alternative form:

$$y - \bar{y} = b(x - \bar{x}) \qquad \ldots (5.3)$$

where $\bar{x}$ and $\bar{y}$ are the averages of the x and y observations. Instead of having to calculate both a and b, we now have only b to calculate.

The value of a 'comes out in the wash'. The formula for b in this alternative method is:

$$b = \frac{\sum xy - n\bar{x}\bar{y}}{\sum x^2 - n\bar{x}^2}$$

Expressions of the form $\sum xy - n\bar{x}\bar{y}$ occur frequently in statistical analysis, and a simple notation has been devised to represent them. It is:

$$Cxy = \sum xy - n\bar{x}\bar{y}$$
$$Cxx = \sum x^2 - n\bar{x}^2$$
$$Cyy = \sum y^2 - n\bar{y}^2$$

We can now express the formula for b very simply in this new notation:

$$b = \frac{Cxy}{Cxx} \qquad \qquad \ldots (5.4)$$

Re-calculating the above example using this method, we have:

$$\sum x = 15 \quad \therefore \quad \bar{x} = 3$$
$$\sum y = 157 \quad \therefore \quad \bar{y} = 31 \cdot 4$$
$$\sum xy = 515$$
$$\sum x^2 = 55$$

$$Cxy = \sum xy - n\bar{x}\bar{y} = 515 - (5 \times 3 \times 31 \cdot 4) = 44$$
$$Cxx = \sum x^2 - n\bar{x}^2 = 55 - (5 \times 9) = 10$$
$$b = \frac{Cxy}{Cxx} = \frac{44}{10} = 4 \cdot 4$$

The regression line is:

$$y - \bar{y} = b(x - \bar{x})$$
$$y - 31 \cdot 4 = 4 \cdot 4 \ (x - 3)$$
$$y = 31 \cdot 4 - 13 \cdot 2 + 4 \cdot 4x$$
$$= 18 \cdot 2 + 4 \cdot 4x, \text{ as before}$$

Correlation

So far we have not considered how accurate predictions made from a regression equation are likely to be. If the data cluster very closely around the regression line, then the line is a very good fit and quite accurate predictions may be expected. On the other hand, if the data are widely spread, the line is not a very good fit, and predictions made from it might be very inaccurate.

How well the regression line fits the observed data depends on the degree of association or **correlation** between the two variables. This is measured by the **correlation coefficient**. The correlation co-efficient is denoted by the letter r and is calculated from the formula:

$$r = \frac{Cxy}{\sqrt{(Cxx \cdot Cyy)}} \qquad \ldots (5.5)$$

If all the observed pairs of values lie on the fitted line, there is perfect correlation between the two variables; one is predictable exactly from the other. This is reflected in the value of r, which is either $+1$ or -1 in such cases. The sign of r shows the slope of the regression line. If y decreases as x increases, the slope will be negative and r will also be negative. If y increases as x increases, the slope is positive and r is also positive. To ensure that the sign of r behaves in this way, the positive value of the square root in formula (5.5) is always taken.

If there is no correlation between the two variables, the value of r is zero. Thus if the fit is poor, r will be close to zero and if it is good, r will be close to ± 1.

Significance of r

If two completely unrelated sets of data are taken, a certain degree of correlation will exist between them purely by chance. Some method of testing whether or not a calculated value of r is high enough to show a significant correlation is therefore required.

Table VI at the end of the book enables us to carry out such a test very simply. If the calculated value of r exceeds the appropriate value from the table, then a significant correlation between the two variables has been established. Various significance levels, ranging from 0·1 to 0·001, are tabulated.

As in most of the other tables, we also need to know the number of degrees of freedom on which r is based. The rule is:

Degrees of freedom for $r = n - 2$

where n is the number of pairs of data used to calculate r.

Suppose, for example, that a sample of 20 pairs of values produced a correlation coefficient of 0·50. Is this significant at the 0·01 significance level?

Consulting the 0·01 column of Table VI with $(20 - 2) = 18$ d.f., we find a value of 0·5614. Our sample value is not as large as this, so we have failed to establish any correlation between our two variables at the 0·01 significance level. In other words, there is a greater than 1% chance that a correlation coefficient of 0·5 could arise in a sample of 20 pairs of data, even if there is no correlation between the two populations from which our data come.

Spurious Correlation

It is important to realize that, although a significant correlation may exist between two variables, changes in one do not necessarily cause changes in the other. Before any conclusions are drawn from a correlation coefficient, the situation must be examined from a practical point of view, and the reasonableness of a connection established.

An often-quoted example of a so-called **spurious** correlation is that which exists between teachers' salaries and the sales of liquor. This does not mean that teachers spend every rise they get on drink. The correlation arises because both are affected by a common factor, the standard of living.

Accuracy of Prediction

The larger the correlation coefficient, the closer is the association between the two variables. This means that increasing accuracy of prediction is obtained as r gets closer to $+1$ or -1. However, a much more meaningful way of assessing the likely accuracy of predictions made from the regression equation is available.

This consists of finding the standard deviation of the observed y values *around the regression line*. This is known as the **residual** standard deviation, since it measures the amount of variation left in the observed y values after allowing for the effect of the x variable.

We can use the residual standard deviation to calculate tentative confidence limits for our predictions. Assuming the errors to be normally distributed, we can expect our predictions to be within 1 residual standard deviation of the true figure 68% of the time, within 2 about 95% of the time, and so on. The formula from which the residual standard deviation is calculated may be expressed in the form:

$$\text{Residual S.D.} = \sqrt{\frac{Cyy - bCxy}{n-2}} \qquad \ldots (5.6)$$

$(n-2)$ occurs in place of the $(n-1)$ in the ordinary standard deviation calculation because another parameter, b, must be estimated from the data. This uses up another degree of freedom.

An alternative way of writing this formula is of interest because it shows the relationship between the residual standard deviation and the correlation coefficient. It is:

$$\sqrt{\frac{Cyy(1-r^2)}{n-2}}$$

Notice the effect on the size of this as r increases. It becomes gradually smaller as r gets bigger, until by the time $r = 1$, it reduces to zero. This is to be expected, because when $r = 1$, all the observed points lie on the regression line.

Computational Scheme for Linear Regression

The computational work involved in regression and correlation analysis is rather heavy, and a calculating machine is virtually essential. However, all the relevant formulae, (5.4), (5.5) and (5.6), are expressed in terms of Cxx, Cxy and Cyy. This enables the calculation to be set out in a convenient, compact way.

The first stage is to calculate the required sums of x, y, xy, x^2 and y^2 from the observed data. These may be found automatically on a desk calculator. For the rainfall and yield example, they are:

$$\sum x = 15 \quad \therefore \ \bar{x} = 3 \qquad \sum x^2 = 55 \qquad \sum xy = 515$$
$$\sum y = 157 \quad \therefore \ \bar{y} = 31 \cdot 4 \qquad \sum y^2 = 5135$$

Next we find:

$$Cxx = \sum x^2 - n\bar{x}^2$$
$$Cxy = \sum xy - n\bar{x}\bar{y}$$
$$Cyy = \sum y^2 - n\bar{y}^2$$

Errors due to rounding may be reduced by calculating the second part of each of these expressions in a slightly different way.

$$\bar{x} = \frac{\sum x}{n} \quad \therefore \quad n\bar{x}^2 = \frac{(\sum x)^2}{n}$$

Similarly:

$$n\bar{y}^2 = \frac{(\sum y)^2}{n} \quad \text{and} \quad n\bar{x}\bar{y} = \frac{(\sum x)(\sum y)}{n}$$

Using this modification:

$$Cxx = 55 - \frac{15 \times 15}{5} \qquad = 55 - 45 \qquad = 10$$

$$Cxy = 515 - \frac{15 \times 157}{5} \qquad = 515 - 471 \qquad = 44$$

$$Cyy = 5135 - \frac{157 \times 157}{5} = 5135 - 4929 \cdot 8 = 205 \cdot 2$$

These may now be used to calculate b, r and the residual standard deviation.

$$b = \frac{Cxy}{Cxx} = \frac{44}{10} = 4 \cdot 4$$

$$r = \frac{Cxy}{\sqrt{(Cxx \cdot Cyy)}} = \frac{44}{\sqrt{(10 \times 205 \cdot 2)}} = \frac{44}{45 \cdot 3} = 0 \cdot 971$$

$$\text{Residual S.D.} = \sqrt{\frac{Cyy - bCxy}{n - 2}} = \sqrt{\frac{205 \cdot 2 - (4 \cdot 4 \times 44)}{3}}$$

$$= \sqrt{\frac{11 \cdot 6}{3}} \qquad = 1 \cdot 96$$

We now have all that we require to:

(a) Test the correlation between the two variables for significance.

This is done by referring to **Table VI** on page 257, with $(n - 2)$ degrees of freedom. Normally a 0·05 significance level is used. In our example, the critical value of r, with 3 degrees of freedom, is 0·8783. The calculated value of r exceeds this, so a significant degree of correlation has been established.

(b) Calculate the regression equation.

This is done by substituting for $\bar{x}$, $\bar{y}$ and b in the equation:

$$y - \bar{y} = b(x - \bar{x})$$

In our example, this gives:

$$y - 31 \cdot 4 = 4 \cdot 4(x - 3)$$
$$y = 18 \cdot 2 + 4 \cdot 4x$$

This equation may now be used to predict the value of y for any given value of x.

(c) Estimate the magnitude of the likely errors in prediction. The residual standard deviation provides the means of doing this. We can expect with reasonable certainty that our estimate will be within 2 standard deviations of the true figure. In our example, this means that our predictions will be accurate to within about 4 cwt per acre. Most of the time, of course, they will be considerably more accurate than this.

Example 5.1

The calculation of standard times for variable elements of work is a common problem in Time Study. This problem can be resolved by using regression analysis. One such variable element occurred in the order-packing department of a wholesale warehouse. An order could consist of any number of items from 1 to 40. All the items were in small boxes, but the shape and size of the boxes varied.

When making up an order into a parcel, the packer had first to manipulate the boxes into a neat rectangular pile. This manipulation is the variable element which we are going to consider. The time taken was found to vary from virtually zero when only 1 or 2 boxes were to be parcelled, up to over a minute when 30 or more boxes had to be manipulated.

A total of 30 parcels was studied, and the manipulation time for each parcel recorded. The 30 parcels covered the entire range of 1 to 40 boxes as comprehensively as was possible. The resulting data are shown in Table 5.1. The times are expressed in hundredths of a minute.

TABLE 5.1

Number of boxes (x)	Time (y)	Number of boxes (x)	Time (y)
1	0	18	70
2	9	20	81
3	12	22	72
4	32	23	90
5	16	24	89
6	45	25	95
7	30	27	110
8	44	28	96
9	51	29	110
10	49	32	141
11	38	33	141
13	68	35	130
15	50	37	161
16	70	38	140
17	61	40	148

The scatter diagram is shown in Figure 5.3 (page 132). From this we can see that a straight line will describe the relationship between number of boxes and time quite well.

We wish to predict time from number of boxes, so time will be the y variable and number of boxes will be the x variable as in the scatter diagram. From the basic data in Table 5.1, we calculate:

$$\sum x = 558 \quad \therefore \quad \bar{x} = 18.60 \qquad \sum x^2 = 14\ 488 \qquad \sum xy = 57\ 057$$
$$\sum y = 2249 \quad \therefore \quad \bar{y} = 74.97 \qquad \sum y^2 = 227\ 751$$

Next we require:

$$Cxx = \sum x^2 - \frac{(\sum x)^2}{n} \qquad = 14\ 488 - 10\ 378.8 \quad = 4109.2$$

$$Cxy = \sum xy - \frac{(\sum x)(\sum y)}{n} = 57\ 057 - 41\ 831.4 \quad = 15\ 225.6$$

$$Cyy = \sum y^2 - \frac{(\sum y)^2}{n} \qquad = 227\ 751 - 168\ 600.0 = 59\ 151.0$$

We now use these to get b, r and the residual standard deviation:

$$b = \frac{Cxy}{Cxx} = \frac{15\ 225.6}{4109.2} = 3.7$$

$$r = \frac{Cxy}{\sqrt{(Cxx \cdot Cyy)}} = \frac{15\ 225.6}{64.1 \times 243.2} = \frac{15\ 225.6}{15\ 589.1} = 0.97$$

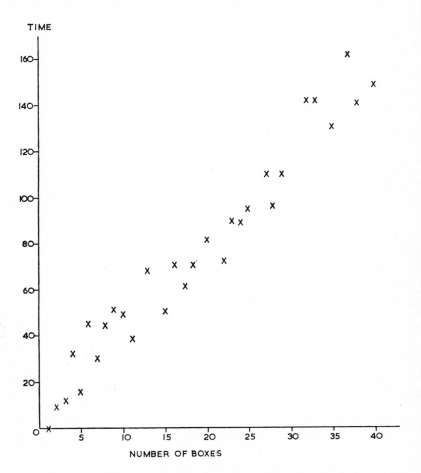

Figure 5.3. Scatter diagram of time study data of Example 5.1

The calculation of r is not really necessary in this case. It does, however, bring out another computational point. When Cxx and Cyy are large numbers, it is easier to take the square root of both of them first and then find the product.

The regression line is now obtained by substituting for $\bar{x}$, $\bar{y}$ and b in the equation:

$$y - \bar{y} = b(x - \bar{x})$$
$$y - 74 \cdot 97 = 3 \cdot 7(x - 18 \cdot 60)$$
$$y = 74 \cdot 97 - 68 \cdot 82 + 3 \cdot 7x$$
$$= 6 \cdot 15 + 3 \cdot 7x$$

The time for any number of boxes may now be estimated from this equation. For 20 boxes, for example, we have:

$$y = 6 \cdot 15 + (3 \cdot 7 \times 20) = 80 \cdot 15$$

which is 0·80 minutes. Figure 5.4 (page 134) shows the scatter diagram with the regression line drawn in.

To assess the likely accuracy of estimates made by using the equation, we need the residual standard deviation:

$$\text{Residual S.D.} = \sqrt{\frac{Cyy - bCxy}{n - 2}}$$
$$= \sqrt{\frac{59\ 151 \cdot 0 - (3 \cdot 7 \times 15\ 225 \cdot 6)}{28}}$$
$$= \sqrt{100 \cdot 58}$$
$$= 10 \cdot 03$$

We can be reasonably certain that an estimate will not be in error by more than 2 residual deviations, that is ±20, which is 0·20 minutes. Thus the estimate of 0·80 minutes which we calculated for a parcel of 20 boxes could be up to $\frac{0 \cdot 20}{0 \cdot 80} \times 100 \% = 25 \%$ in error.

This seems too inaccurate to be of much use, and if we required accurate individual estimates for parcels, it might well be unsatisfactory. However, in a day's work the packer will perform this element many times. The average percentage error over a number of parcels will be much less than 25%.

Suppose that 36 parcels are packed in the day. The standard deviation of the average error will be $\frac{10}{\sqrt{36}} = 1 \cdot 67$. We can therefore be reasonably certain that over 36 parcels the average error will not be more than $\frac{2 \times 1 \cdot 67}{0 \cdot 80} = 4 \cdot 17 \%$, which is a satisfactory degree of

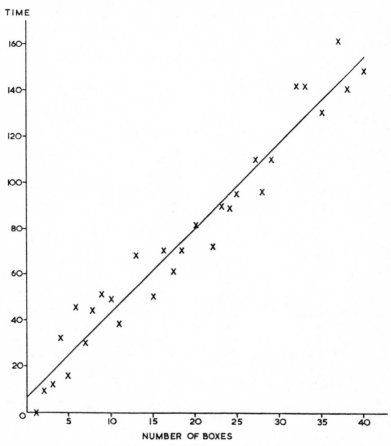

Figure 5.4. A regression line fitted to the data of Figure 5.3

accuracy. This point is discussed more fully in my paper on time study.*

Example 5.2

Regression methods are also used to fit trend lines to sales and other data in order to forecast future developments. The following

* 'The accuracy of time study'. *Work Study and Management Services*, February 1967.

data relate to the amount of electricity used in this country and were taken from *The Monthly Digest of Statistics* (C.S.O.). The figures are in 1 000 000 MWh.

Assuming a linear trend in electricity usage, estimate the requirements for 1970, 1971 and 1972.

x	y electricity used
1961	122·4
1962	134·7
1963	145·8
1964	153·6
1965	165·1
1966	171·0
1967	176·9

Whenever we have equally spaced values of the x variable, the calculations may be simplified by choosing the scale of x in such a way that $\Sigma x = 0$. This in turn means that $\bar{x} = 0$, which reduces the amount of computation quite substantially. To achieve this, the centre value is put equal to zero, as in the modified data below.

We may also 'code' the y variable by subtracting a constant amount. This helps to keep the numbers in the calculations small. A convenient amount to subtract in our present example would be 120.

Our coded values then become:

x	y
−3	2·4
−2	14·7
−1	25·8
0	33·6
1	45·1
2	51·0
3	56·9

Following the standard computations, we have:

$$\sum x = 0 \quad \therefore \quad \bar{x} = 0 \qquad \sum x^2 = 28\cdot0 \qquad \sum xy = 255\cdot40$$
$$\sum y = 229\cdot5 \quad \therefore \quad \bar{y} = 32\cdot79 \qquad \sum y^2 = 9889\cdot07$$

$$Cxx = \sum x^2 - \frac{(\sum x)^2}{n} \qquad = 28\cdot0$$

$$Cxy = \sum xy - \frac{(\sum x)(\sum y)}{n} = 255\cdot40$$

$$Cyy = \sum y^2 - \frac{(\sum y)^2}{n} \qquad = 9889\cdot07 - 7524\cdot32 = 2364\cdot75$$

$$b = \frac{Cxy}{Cxx} = \frac{255\cdot4}{28\cdot0} = 9\cdot12$$

$$r = \frac{Cxy}{\sqrt{(Cxx \cdot Cyy)}} = \frac{255\cdot40}{\sqrt{(28\cdot0 \times 2364\cdot75)}} = \frac{255\cdot40}{257\cdot31} = 0\cdot992$$

The regression equation is:

$$y - \bar{y} = b(x - \bar{x})$$
$$y - 32\cdot79 = 9\cdot12(x - 0)$$
$$y = 32\cdot8 + 9\cdot12x$$

The equation in this form will forecast coded values of y. What we have called y in our calculations is in reality $(y - 120)$. We can easily convert the equation to give forecasts in terms of the true y by putting $(y - 120)$ in place of y. Doing this, we get:

$$y - 120 = 32\cdot8 + 9\cdot12x$$
$$y = 152\cdot8 + 9\cdot12x$$

The data are plotted in Figure 5.5 with the regression line drawn through them.

To obtain forecasts for 1970, 1971 and 1972, we must substitute in the regression equation the appropriate values of x on the arbitrary scale which we have used. These will be 6, 7 and 8 respectively. The forecasts will then be:

For 1970: $y = 152\cdot8 + (9\cdot12 \times 6) = 207\cdot5$
For 1971: $y = 152\cdot8 + (9\cdot12 \times 7) = 216\cdot6$
For 1972: $y = 152\cdot8 + (9\cdot12 \times 8) = 225\cdot8$

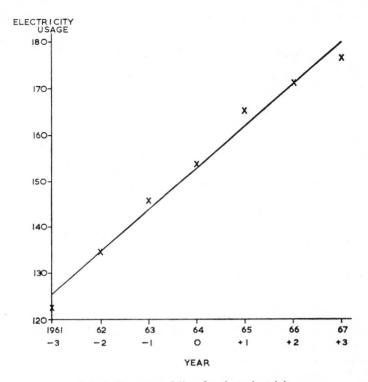

Figure 5.5. A linear trend line fitted to electricity usage

We have used this regression equation in a very different way from previous examples. For the first time, we have extrapolated the line beyond the range of x values over which it was calculated. This implicitly assumes that the linear trend over the seven years to which the data apply will continue into the future, at least for the next five years. Whether or not it will do so is anybody's guess. Accordingly, it is rather meaningless in this situation to calculate the residual standard deviation. To pretend that it will give a reasonable estimate of the likely accuracy of the forecast is, to say the least, a little naïve.

Another objection is that, even over the seven years covered by the data, a straight line is only an approximation to the true trend. From a subjective examination of the points in Figure 5.5, it looks as though some kind of slight curve would fit them better. Even if this were done, however, it is unlikely that the same curved trend would continue very far into the future.

It is of course mathematically possible to fit many different types of curve. With seven pairs of data, a curve involving terms up to x^6 could be found which would provide an exact fit, in that all the seven points would lie on the fitted line. The projection of that line into the future, however, would in all probability produce hopeless forecasts.

Trend projection for long-term forecasting is thus a very chancy business. A better approach is to try to find some economic variable or set of variables which is closely correlated with the one being forecast. Exercise 5.1 illustrates this approach and some of the problems involved. The subject of Sales Forecasting is a very important one, and many techniques other than regression analysis have been developed. The book by Battersby* is a very readable introduction to the subject.

Exercises

5.1. Industry is the prime user of electricity, and the Index of Industrial Production is a measure of the level of industrial activity. Accordingly, therefore, one would expect to find a correlation between the average value of the Index over a year and the amount of electricity used during that year. Calculate the correlation coefficient between the Index and electricity usage for the following data. Calculate also the linear regression equation to estimate electricity requirements from the Index. What is the main drawback to the use of this equation as a predictor?

	Index of Industrial Production	Electricity used
1961	113·9	122·4
1962	115·1	134·7
1963	119·0	145·8
1964	128·2	153·6
1965	131·9	165·1
1966	133·4	171·0
1967	133·3	176·9

* A. Battersby, *Sales Forecasting*. Cassell, 1968.

5.2. Books are printed as large sheets with a number of pages laid out on each sheet. These large sheets are then folded to produce sections of the book which are then bound together. It is the policy of a printing company to keep an intermediate stock of printed sheets for all books which they produce. This is known as **quire stock**. The company is concerned at the rate at which quire stock is building up.

The following data show the number of new books printed each month over a period of a year, together with the total size of quire stock at the end of each month. If, during the next year, an average of 24 new books a month is expected, what will be the size of the quire stock at the end of that year, assuming the company's stock policy remains unchanged?

Month	1	2	3	4	5	6	7	8	9	10	11	12
New books printed	18	20	23	26	15	33	18	19	18	23	26	25
Quire stock (*1000 sheets*)	217	249	265	269	273	341	356	397	378	391	413	450

Multiple Regression

In the previous section, we developed a method which enabled us to estimate crop yield from rainfall figures. Rainfall, however, is by no means the only factor which affects yield. The amount of sunshine during the growing period is also likely to have an effect. No doubt we could think of several other possible factors. It seems intuitively reasonable that if we could take several of these factors into account instead of just one, our estimate of yield would be improved. The technique which enables us to do this is known as **multiple regression** and is a simple extension of the ideas already developed.

Let us suppose that, in the crop yield example, we have sunshine figures available as well as rainfall. We will denote rainfall (in inches) by x_1 and sunshine (in hours) by x_2.

	Year 1	Year 2	Year 3	Year 4	Year 5
x_1 *rainfall*	2	1	3	5	4
x_2 *sunshine*	50	60	60	48	55
y yield	25	23	34	40	35

The regression equation must be extended to include a term for each of the factors being considered and becomes:

$$y - \bar{y} = b_1(x_1 - \bar{x}_1) + b_2(x_2 - \bar{x}_2) \qquad \ldots (5.7)$$

This contains two coefficients, b_1 and b_2, and we therefore require two equations from which to calculate them. It can be shown that the required equations are:

$$\left. \begin{array}{l} Cx_1y = b_1Cx_1x_1 + b_2Cx_2x_1 \\ Cx_2y = b_1Cx_1x_2 + b_2Cx_2x_2 \end{array} \right\} \qquad \ldots (5.8)$$

Everything in these two equations except b_1 and b_2 may be calculated from the basic data. We must first calculate:

$$\sum x_1 = 15 \quad \therefore \quad \bar{x}_1 = 3 \qquad \sum x_1^2 = 55 \qquad \sum x_1y = 515$$
$$\sum x_2 = 273 \quad \therefore \quad \bar{x}_2 = 54 \cdot 6 \qquad \sum x_2^2 = 15\,029 \qquad \sum x_2y = 8515$$
$$\sum y = 157 \quad \therefore \quad \bar{y} = 31 \cdot 4 \qquad \sum y^2 = 5135 \qquad \sum x_1x_2 = 800$$

These basic quantities enable us to calculate:

$$Cx_1y = \sum x_1y - \frac{(\sum x_1)(\sum y)}{n} \quad = 515 - \frac{(15 \times 157)}{5} \quad = 44$$

$$Cx_2y = \sum x_2y - \frac{(\sum x_2)(\sum y)}{n} \quad = 8515 - \frac{(273 \times 157)}{5} = -57 \cdot 2$$

$$Cx_1x_1 = \sum x_1^2 - \frac{(\sum x_1)^2}{n} \quad = 55 - \frac{(15)^2}{5} \quad = 10$$

$$Cx_2x_2 = \sum x_2^2 - \frac{(\sum x_2)^2}{n} \quad = 15\,029 - \frac{(273)^2}{5} \quad = 123 \cdot 2$$

$$Cx_1x_2 = \sum x_1x_2 - \frac{(\sum x_1)(\sum x_2)}{n} = 800 - \frac{(15 \times 273)}{5} \quad = -19$$

$$Cx_2x_1 = Cx_1x_2 \qquad\qquad\qquad = -19$$

$$Cyy = \sum y^2 - \frac{(\sum y)^2}{n} \qquad = 5135 - \frac{(157)^2}{5} \quad = 205 \cdot 2$$

We now substitute these figures into the pair of equations (5.8) and solve them to get the values of b_1 and b_2.

$$44 = 10b_1 - 19b_2$$
$$-57 \cdot 2 = -19b_1 + 123 \cdot 2b_2$$

Multiplying the first equation by 19 and the second by 10 gives:

$$836 = 190b_1 - 361b_2$$
$$-572 = -190b_1 + 1232b_2$$

Adding the equations together, we have:

$$264 = 871b_2$$
$$b_2 = 0.303$$

Substituting this value for b_2 in the first of the original equations:

$$44 = 10b_1 - (19 \times 0.303)$$
$$10b_1 = 49.757$$
$$b_1 = 4.976$$

The regression equation is therefore:

$$y - \bar{y} = b_1(x_1 - \bar{x}_1) + b_2(x_2 - \bar{x}_2)$$
$$y - 31.4 = 4.976(x_1 - 3) + 0.303(x_2 - 54.6)$$
$$y = 31.4 - 14.928 - 16.544 + 4.976x_1 + 0.303x_2$$
$$= -0.072 + 4.976x_1 + 0.303x_2$$

This equation may now be used to predict crop yield by substituting the actual rainfall and sunshine figures which occur. Suppose, for example, that we had 3·5 in of rain and 50 hours of sunshine in a particular year. Our forecast of crop yield would be:

$$y = -0.072 + (4.976 \times 3.5) + (0.303 \times 50)$$
$$= 32.5 \text{ cwt per acre}$$

Partial Correlation Coefficients

We may calculate the correlation coefficients between yield (y) and rainfall (x_1) and between yield and sunshine (x_2) in precisely the same way as before. Calling these r_{y1} and r_{y2} respectively, the formulae are:

$$r_{y1} = \frac{Cx_1y}{\sqrt{(Cx_1x_1 \cdot Cyy)}} = \frac{44}{\sqrt{(10 \times 205.2)}} = \frac{44}{45.3} = 0.971$$

$$r_{y2} = \frac{Cx_2y}{\sqrt{(Cx_2x_2 \cdot Cyy)}} = \frac{-57.2}{\sqrt{(123.2 \times 205.2)}} = \frac{-57.2}{159.0} = -0.359$$

This tells us that there is a high positive correlation between rainfall and yield and a low negative correlation between sunshine and yield, apparently suggesting that sunshine has a harmful effect on yield! This negative correlation is misleading, however, because rainfall and sunshine are themselves negatively correlated. The more rain there is in a month, the less sunshine there will be.

Let us suppose that rainfall and sunshine both have beneficial effects, but that the effect of rainfall is more marked. Rainfall will then be the main factor in determining yield, and so years with high rainfall will have high yield. Because of the negative correlation between rainfall and sunshine, however, these will be years with low sunshine figures. High yield years will therefore correspond with low sunshine years, giving rise to a negative correlation between the two. This negative correlation is in reality caused by the negative correlation between sunshine and rainfall.

It is clear from the above that in order to assess the effects of our two factors properly, we must remove the effect of the correlation between the two factors themselves. This is done by calculating what are known as the **partial correlation coefficients**.

We will denote the partial correlation coefficient between y and x_1, having removed the effect of x_2, by $r_{y1.2}$. Similarly, the partial correlation coefficient between y and x_2, having removed the effect of x_1, will be $r_{y2.1}$. The appropriate formulae for calculating these coefficients are:

$$r_{y1.2} = \frac{r_{y1} - r_{y2}r_{12}}{\sqrt{\{(1 - r_{y2}^2)(1 - r_{12}^2)\}}}$$

$$r_{y2.1} = \frac{r_{y2} - r_{y1}r_{12}}{\sqrt{\{(1 - r_{y1}^2)(1 - r_{12}^2)\}}}$$

We have already calculated $r_{y1} = 0.971$ and $r_{y2} = -0.359$. The only other quantity required for the evaluation of these partial coefficients is r_{12}, that is, the correlation between x_1 and x_2. This will be given by the usual formula:

$$r_{12} = \frac{Cx_1x_2}{\sqrt{(Cx_1x_1 . Cx_2x_2)}} = \frac{-19}{\sqrt{(10 \times 123.2)}} = \frac{-19}{35.1} = -0.541$$

Substituting the values of r_{y1}, r_{y2} and r_{12} in the formulae for the partial correlation coefficients gives:

$$r_{y1.2} = \frac{0.971 - (-0.359 \times -0.541)}{\sqrt{(0.871 \times 0.707)}} = \frac{0.777}{0.785} = 0.989$$

$$r_{y2.1} = \frac{-0.359 - (0.971 \times -0.541)}{\sqrt{(0.057 \times 0.707)}} = \frac{0.166}{0.200} = 0.830$$

These partial correlation coefficients now tell us the correlations between yield and rainfall, having allowed for sunshine, and between yield and sunshine, having allowed for rainfall.

They may be tested for significance in the same way as ordinary coefficients by consulting Table VI with $(n-3)$ degrees of freedom. The test is rather meaningless in this example, as n is only equal to 5. Very large values of the coefficients are necessary to establish significance when only 2 degrees of freedom are available for the estimates. For a 0·05 significance level test, for example, they must exceed 0·95.

If we had a more realistically sized set of data, both would be significant instead of only $r_{y1.2}$. This would mean that both sunshine and rainfall figures contributed usefully to our estimate of yield. If one of these were very low, for example $r_{y2.1} = 0·05$, it would mean that, having taken rainfall figures into account, no great improvement could be made by also considering sunshine figures. This factor could then be eliminated, and the regression equation would contain only one factor.

This illustrates how partial correlation coefficients may be used to determine which of several possible factors can usefully be applied in the regression equation, and which need not be included. Suppose that we had a third factor to consider in our yield example. We would need a partial correlation coefficient of the form $r_{y3.12}$, that is, the correlation between y and x_3, having allowed for the effect of both x_1 and x_2.

The successive calculation of partial correlation coefficients in this way enables a large number of possible factors to be considered. Usually it is found that after, at most, 6 variables have been selected, all further partial coefficients are virtually zero. This means that it is pointless to complicate the equation further by including more variables. A detailed analysis of this kind involves a tremendously heavy computational load and is virtually impossible to handle without a computer. However, standard computer programs for carrying out the work are readily available.

The Multiple Correlation Coefficient

The partial correlation coefficients measure the individual value of each variable in the regression equation, but a measure of total correlation between the observed results and the predictions made by the equation is also required. This measure is provided by the **multiple correlation coefficient**. It is denoted by R, and when there are only two x variables in the regression equation, it is calculated from the formula:

$$R = \sqrt{1 - (1 - r_{y1}^2)(1 - r_{y2 \cdot 1}^2)}$$

In our rainfall and sunshine example, therefore, the multiple correlation coefficient is:

$$R = \sqrt{1 - (0 \cdot 057 \times 0 \cdot 311)} = \sqrt{0 \cdot 982} = 0 \cdot 991$$

The Residual Standard Deviation

As in the simple linear case, a more meaningful assessment of the likely accuracy of predictions made from the equation is obtained by calculating the residual standard deviation. To show the relationship between the multiple correlation coefficient and residual standard deviation, the formula may be expressed as:

$$\text{Residual S.D.} = \sqrt{\frac{Cyy(1 - R^2)}{n - 3}}$$

This is directly comparable with the simple case, having R in place of r. Also, a further degree of freedom has been lost, because two b coefficients have been estimated from the data instead of only one.

For purposes of calculation, however, the formula is expressed in the form:

$$\text{Residual S.D.} = \sqrt{\frac{Cyy - b_1 Cx_1 y - b_2 Cx_2 y}{n - 3}}$$

Substituting the appropriate values, we have:

$$\text{Residual S.D.} = \sqrt{\frac{205 \cdot 2 - (4 \cdot 976 \times 44) - (0 \cdot 303 \times - 57 \cdot 2)}{2}}$$

$$= \sqrt{1 \cdot 794} = 1 \cdot 34$$

This compares with a residual standard deviation of $1 \cdot 96$ for the equation containing only the one variable, rainfall, which we calculated on page 129.

More Than Two Factors

The foregoing methods can readily be extended to allow for any number of factors, although the amount of calculation to be done increases rapidly as more factors are added. The general regression equation, with w factors, is:

$$y - \bar{y} = b_1(x_1 - \bar{x}_1) + b_2(x_2 - \bar{x}_2) + \ldots + b_w(x_w - \bar{x}_w)$$

This contains w coefficients, which can be found from the w equations:

$$Cx_1y = b_1Cx_1x_1 + b_2Cx_2x_1 + \ldots + b_wCx_wx_1$$
$$Cx_2y = b_1Cx_1x_2 + b_2Cx_2x_2 + \ldots + b_wCx_wx_2$$
$$\vdots \qquad \vdots \qquad \vdots \qquad \vdots$$
$$Cx_wy = b_1Cx_1x_w + b_2Cx_2x_w + \ldots + b_wCx_wx_w$$

The general formula for the multiple correlation coefficient is:

$$R = \sqrt{1 - (1 - r_{y1}^2)(1 - r_{y2.1}^2)(1 - r_{y3.12}^2) \ldots \{1 - r_{yw.123 \ldots (w-1)}^2\}}$$

The general formula for the residual standard deviation is:

$$\text{Residual S.D.} = \sqrt{\frac{Cyy - b_1Cx_1y - b_2Cx_2y - \ldots - b_wCx_wy}{n - 1 - w}}$$

Example 5.3

The general store supplying a factory was to be time studied. The store contained about 1000 different stock items. Instead of following orthodox methods, an approach based on regression analysis was tried. Over a period of several days, a complete study was made of the storeman's activities and his total time on stores issue work for each day was recorded. These are the figures in the first column of Table 5.2.

TABLE 5.2

| | Time taken in minutes y | Number of items issued each day from: | | |
		Section 1 x_1	Section 2 x_2	Section 3 x_3
Day 1	282	40	25	10
2	312	30	20	20
3	306	37	28	12
4	296	39	22	14
5	304	32	26	17
6	276	41	24	9

One of the main factors governing the length of time required to get an item out of stores was the location of the bin in which it was kept. The store was arbitrarily divided into three sections, Section 1 containing the bins nearest to the service hatch, Section 2 the intermediate ones, and Section 3 those furthest away. The total number of items issued each day from each section was also recorded. This information is contained in columns 2, 3 and 4 of Table 5.2.

These data were then used to derive a regression equation to predict the daily amount of time spent on stores issue work, using the number of items issued from Sections 1, 2 and 3 as the x_1, x_2 and x_3 variables.

The required equation is of the form:

$$y - \bar{y} = b_1(x_1 - \bar{x}_1) + b_2(x_2 - \bar{x}_2) + b_3(x_3 - \bar{x}_3)$$

and b_1, b_2 and b_3 are found by solving the equations:

$$Cx_1y = b_1Cx_1x_1 + b_2Cx_2x_1 + b_3Cx_3x_1$$
$$Cx_2y = b_1Cx_1x_2 + b_2Cx_2x_2 + b_3Cx_3x_2$$
$$Cx_3y = b_1Cx_1x_3 + b_2Cx_2x_3 + b_3Cx_3x_3$$

From the data, we first find the sums of all the individual values, squares and cross products. These enable us to calculate:

$$Cx_1x_1 = 101 \cdot 500 \qquad Cx_2x_2 = 40 \cdot 833 \qquad Cx_1y = -274 \cdot 000$$
$$Cx_1x_2 = 17 \cdot 500 \qquad Cx_2x_3 = -29 \cdot 667 \qquad Cx_2y = -22 \cdot 000$$
$$Cx_1x_3 = -90 \cdot 000 \qquad Cx_3x_3 = 89 \cdot 333 \qquad Cx_3y = 256 \cdot 000$$
$$Cyy = 1016 \cdot 000$$

The three simultaneous equations then become:

$$-274 \cdot 000 = 101 \cdot 500 b_1 + 17 \cdot 500 b_2 - 90 \cdot 000 b_3$$
$$-22 \cdot 000 = 17 \cdot 500 b_1 + 40 \cdot 833 b_2 - 29 \cdot 667 b_3$$
$$+256 \cdot 000 = -90 \cdot 000 b_1 - 29 \cdot 667 b_2 + 89 \cdot 333 b_3$$

The solution of these equations is:

$$b_1 = 1 \cdot 55$$
$$b_2 = 2 \cdot 65$$
$$b_3 = 5 \cdot 31$$

The regression equation is therefore:

$$y - \bar{y} = b_1(x_1 - \bar{x}_1) + b_2(x_2 - \bar{x}_2) + b_3(x_3 - \bar{x}_3)$$
$$y - 289 \cdot 17 = 1 \cdot 55(x_1 - 36 \cdot 5) + 2 \cdot 65(x_2 - 24 \cdot 17) + 5 \cdot 31(x_3 - 13 \cdot 67)$$
$$y = 95 \cdot 95 + 1 \cdot 55 x_1 + 2 \cdot 65 x_2 + 5 \cdot 31 x_3$$

All that now need be done to estimate the amount of work done each day by the storeman is to feed into this equation the number of items which he has issued from each of the three sections. Suppose that on one particular day he issues the following:

40 items from Section 1 (x_1)
30 items from Section 2 (x_2)
15 items from Section 3 (x_3)

The work done is estimated at:

$$y = 95 \cdot 95 + (1 \cdot 55 \times 40) + (2 \cdot 65 \times 30) + (5 \cdot 31 \times 15) = 317 \cdot 1$$

It is interesting to note the way in which b_1, b_2 and b_3 vary in size. They are in effect estimates of the length of time taken to get an item from each of the three sections. As we should expect, b_1 is the smallest and b_3 the largest.

Estimate of Likely Errors

The regression equation will not be of much use if the estimates made from it are likely to be a long way out. The residual standard deviation will tell us the likely magnitude of the errors.

$$\text{Residual S.D.} = \sqrt{\frac{Cyy - b_1 Cx_1 y - b_2 Cx_2 y - b_3 Cx_3 y}{n - 1 - 3}}$$

$$= \sqrt{69 \cdot 82} = 8 \cdot 4$$

We can thus be almost certain that an estimate made from the equation will not be in error by more than about 16 minutes. The average value ($\bar{y}$) of estimates will be about 290, so the possible error of 16 is a percentage error of $\frac{16}{290} \times 100\% = 5 \cdot 5\%$, which is just about acceptable.

Exercise

5.3. In Exercise 5.1, we calculated a linear regression equation to predict electricity requirements from the Index of Industrial Production. Perhaps a more accurate forecast could be obtained if the equation were extended to include a second factor which is linked to domestic electricity usage. It is suggested that the total amount of

Personal Disposable Income available annually might be suitable for this purpose.

This additional information is included in the table below. Calculate the multiple regression equation including both these factors. Calculate also both partial correlation coefficients and the residual standard deviation. What do you conclude about the value of including the second variable?

	Index	Personal income
1961	113·9	19·1
1962	115·1	20·5
1963	119·0	21·8
1964	128·2	23·4
1965	131·9	25·0
1966	133·4	26·4
1967	133·3	27·4

APPENDIX A CALCULATION OF MEAN AND STANDARD DEVIATION

The normal curve is completely identified by its mean and standard deviation. Consequently, these two parameters must be known before any calculations based on the normal curve may be made. Almost invariably, their exact value is not known. Estimates calculated from samples must be used. This appendix gives a number of methods by which these calculations may be carried out.

Mean

The **arithmetic mean,** or average, indicates the centre of the distribution. An estimate of the population mean is obtained from a sample by adding up all the sample values and dividing by the number of items in the sample.

This may be represented briefly by using Σ (the Greek capital letter S or sigma) as shorthand for 'the sum of', and x for any item in the sample. Σx therefore means 'the sum of all the x's', that is, the sum of all the sample values. If we denote the number of items in the sample by n, the method of calculating the mean is then $\frac{\Sigma x}{n}$.

The population mean is conventionally denoted by μ (the Greek letter m or mu) and a sample estimate of it by the symbol $\bar{x}$ (called x-bar). We thus have the formula for the mean:

$$\bar{x} = \frac{\Sigma x}{n} \qquad \ldots (A.1)$$

Standard Deviation

The **standard deviation** is a measure of variability. The wider the distribution is spread around the mean, the larger the standard deviation will be. If a population contains N items and has a mean of μ, the standard deviation (denoted by the Greek letter σ) is defined by the formula:

$$\sigma = \sqrt{\frac{\Sigma(x - \mu)^2}{N}}$$

149

In practice, N is usually so large (perhaps even infinitely large) that calculation of the exact value of σ is impracticable. We are only able to estimate it from a sample. Before we can do so, we must first make an estimate of μ. This is done by calculating $\bar{x}$, as we have already seen. The formula for the sample estimate (denoted by s) of σ then becomes:

$$s = \sqrt{\frac{\sum(x - \bar{x})^2}{n - 1}} \qquad \ldots \text{(A.2)}$$

It is rather surprising to see $(n - 1)$ in the denominator of this formula instead of n. The reason is that the sample mean $\bar{x}$ is used in the calculation. This uses up 1 **degree of freedom**. It is not possible to give a detailed account of exactly what this means without using some fairly advanced mathematics. However, the matter is discussed in a little more detail on page 90.

Example A.1

Calculate estimates of the mean and standard deviation of the population from which the following sample comes: 10, 8, 12, 7, 13.

$$\bar{x} = \frac{\sum x}{n} = \frac{10 + 8 + 12 + 7 + 13}{5} = 10$$

The stages in the calculation of the standard deviation are best illustrated in tabular form:

x	$(x - \bar{x})$	$(x - \bar{x})^2$
10	0	0
8	-2	4
12	2	4
7	-3	9
13	3	9
		$26 = \sum(x - \bar{x})^2$

$$s = \sqrt{\frac{\sum(x - \bar{x})^2}{n - 1}} = \sqrt{\frac{26}{4}} = \sqrt{6 \cdot 5} = 2 \cdot 55$$

The quantity $\dfrac{\sum(x - \bar{x})^2}{n - 1}$ is also frequently used as a measure of variability, particularly in more advanced statistical work. It is known as the **variance**. In the example which we have just calculated, the variance is 6·5. The standard deviation, therefore, is the square root of the variance.

Exercise

A.1. Calculate $\bar{x}$ and s for the following sample data:

11	12	11	9	7
13	8	11	7	11

Short-cut Methods

Very often, particularly with large samples of variable data, calculation of the standard deviation in the manner just described involves a great deal of work, even if a desk calculator is available. Consider, for example, the data in Table A.1 which represent the chest measurements of 50 men.

TABLE A.1

37·14	38·72	38·73	37·12	39·74
38·34	37·15	36·30	41·23	38·50
37·92	35·30	38·35	37·46	38·85
34·30	40·65	39·16	36·21	34·80
40·93	40·77	36·22	35·20	35·31
36·88	37·36	35·65	40·71	37·32
37·66	33·58	39·96	39·98	37·69
35·95	38·38	39·37	37·32	35·60
38·78	40·22	34·02	36·98	37·21
33·86	39·12	39·48	37·04	36·84

Calculation of the mean would be a fairly simple matter with a desk calculator, but it is something of an understatement to say that calculation of the standard deviation from formula (A.2) would be tedious.

There are two ways in which the volume of computation may be reduced. The first of these is to change the expression in formula (A.2) into a form which enables the calculations to be done much more easily on a desk calculator. The second, essentially a manual method, is to form the data into a grouped frequency distribution. We will discuss each of these in turn.

Machine Calculation

Formula (A.2) may be manipulated algebraically to give:

$$s = \sqrt{\left(\frac{\sum x^2}{n-1} - \frac{(\sum x)^2}{n(n-1)}\right)} \qquad \ldots (A.3)$$

This looks more complicated than (A.2), but in fact is much easier to work with. It requires us to find the sum of the sample values ($\sum x$) and the sum of the squared sample values ($\sum x^2$). These are readily obtained simultaneously on a desk calculator.

It is sometimes possible to simplify the calculation further by subtracting a constant amount from each sample item. This often considerably reduces the size of the numbers to be handled. Subtracting 30 from each item in Table A.1, we then find:

$$\sum x = 381 \cdot 36$$
$$\sum x^2 = 3101 \cdot 044$$
$$\frac{\sum x}{n} = \frac{381 \cdot 36}{50} = 7 \cdot 63$$

To find $\bar{x}$, we must add to this the constant which we subtracted from all the data. This gives:

$$\bar{x} = 30 + 7 \cdot 63 = 37 \cdot 63$$

To find s, we substitute for $\sum x^2$ and $\sum x$ in formula (A.3). It is not necessary to make any adjustment for the constant which was subtracted.

$$s = \sqrt{\left(\frac{3101 \cdot 044}{49} - \frac{(381 \cdot 36)^2}{50 \times 49}\right)}$$
$$= \sqrt{(63 \cdot 2866 - 59 \cdot 3614)}$$
$$= \sqrt{3 \cdot 9252}$$
$$= 1 \cdot 98$$

Grouped Distribution Method

The first step in this method is to form the data into a grouped frequency distribution. This is done by dividing the range of values covered by the data into a number of **classes** and counting the number of items which fall into each class. All the classes must be the same width.

This immediately raises the question of how many classes to use. Unlike the previous method, this one only gives the approximate mean and standard deviation of the data. The smaller the number of classes, the more inaccurate the calculation is likely to be. However, as the number of classes increases, so does the amount of work to be done.

A rough guide to the minimum number which will give a reasonably accurate answer is provided by Sturge's rule. This says that the number of classes should be about $1 + 3.3 \log n$, where n is sample size. Applying this rule to the data of Table A.1, we get:

$$1 + 3.3 \log 50 = 1 + (3.3 \times 1.699) = 6.6$$

We should, therefore, aim for about 6 or 7 classes in the distribution. 6 is usually regarded as being the smallest permissible number of classes to take.

The range of our sample data is from 33·58 (the smallest measurement) to 41·23 (the largest). We therefore have to cover the interval from about 33 to about 42. There is no need to start our first class at 33·58; it is much easier to choose convenient numbers for our class limits. This range may conveniently be covered by 6 classes as follows:

$$33.00–34.49$$
$$34.50–35.99$$
$$36.00–37.49$$
$$37.50–38.99$$
$$39.00–40.49$$
$$40.50–41.99$$

Note that the classes do not go from 33·00–34·50, 34·50–36·00, etc. The first class includes values from 33·00 up to *but not including* 34·50. Because our data are rounded to two decimal places, therefore, the largest number which this class could contain is 34·49. It is an important rule that the upper and lower limits of a class are the highest and lowest numbers which could be in that class. If, for example, the data had been rounded to 1 decimal place, the upper limit of the first class would be 34·4. The importance of this will be seen later when the calculation of the mean is carried out.

Having defined our classes, the next step is to find out how many items lie in each class. The easiest way to do this is to work through the data putting a tally mark against the appropriate class for each item in the well-known 'five-barred gate' style:

Class	Tally	Class frequency
33·00–34·49	1111	4
34·50–35·99	⊞ 11	7
36·00–37·49	⊞ ⊞ ⊞	15
37·50–38·99	⊞ ⊞ 1	11
39·00–40·49	⊞ 111	8
40·50–41·99	⊞	5

Once a set of data has been grouped in this way, each individual item has lost its identity. From the frequency distribution, all we can say is that there are, for instance, 15 items with a value between 36·00 and 37·49. However, if we assume that those 15 items are spread evenly across the class, their average value will be the mid-point of the class.

This assumption is made in the method which we are developing, and is responsible for the fact that it only produces the approximate mean and standard deviation of the data.

The mid-points of the classes in our example are:

Class	Class mid-point	Frequency
33·00–34·49	33·745	4
34·50–35·99	35·245	7
36·00–37·49	36·745	15
37·50–38·99	38·245	11
39·00–40·49	39·745	8
40·50–41·99	41·245	5

We could now calculate the mean and standard deviation by using the formula already given. Σx, for example, would be $(4 \times 33·745) + (7 \times 35·245) + \ldots$

Although greatly simplified, the work involved in doing this is still rather tedious. Further simplifications (which do not introduce any further approximation) may be made by taking an assumed mean and working in class intervals. Simplifying the calculation of the true mean by first taking an assumed mean is a short-cut method which is widely known. In effect, this is what we did when we subtracted 30 from the data in Table A.1.

As a further example, the calculation of the mean of 101, 99, 100, 103, 98 is greatly simplified by guessing that it is about 100. We then take 100 away from each value, giving 1, -1, 0, 3, -2. The average of these is 0·2. Adding back our assumed mean then gives the true mean as 100·2.

A similar device is adopted in the calculation of the standard deviation. It is first found in terms of class intervals away from the assumed mean. Multiplying this by the class interval then gives the true standard deviation.

All this will become clear if we carry out the calculations for our chest size data. They are best laid out in tabular form as follows:

Class	Class mid-point	f	u	uf	u^2f
33·00–34·49		4	-2	-8	16
34·50–35·99		7	-1	-7	7
$A\rightarrow$36·00–37·49	36·745	15	0	0	0
37·50–38·99		11	1	11	11
39·00–40·49		8	2	16	32
40·50–41·99		5	3	15	45
		$\sum f = 50$		$\sum uf = 27$	$\sum u^2f = 111$

We first fill in the 'class' and 'frequency' columns of the table. Next we select the class which is most likely to contain the mean. This is usually near the centre of the distribution. The third class has been chosen in our example and marked 'A'. The mid-point of this class is now calculated and put into the second column. This is the only class for which the mid-point need be determined.

Next the column headed 'u' is completed. This is the number of classes away from the assumed mean. To fill it in, we first number the assumed mean class zero, and number each class consecutively away from this. Note that classes containing smaller values than the assumed mean class are numbered negatively.

The remaining columns 'uf' and 'u^2f' now follow automatically, uf being the product of the u and f (frequency) columns (being careful about signs) and u^2f the product of the u and uf columns.

The f, uf and u^2f columns are now totalled to give Σf, Σuf and Σu^2f. The mean and standard deviation are now calculated by substituting in the following formulae:

$$\bar{x} = A + C\left(\frac{\Sigma uf}{\Sigma f}\right) \qquad \ldots \text{(A.4)}$$

$$s = C\sqrt{\frac{\Sigma u^2f}{\Sigma f} - \left(\frac{\Sigma uf}{\Sigma f}\right)^2} \qquad \ldots \text{(A.5)}$$

where A is the mid-point of the assumed mean class,

C is the class interval, that is, the distance between class mid-points. This is the same as the distance between consecutive lower class limits, which in our example is 1·5.

Substituting the appropriate values for our example, we have:

$$\bar{x} = 36{\cdot}745 + \frac{1{\cdot}5 \times 27}{50} = 37{\cdot}555$$

$$s = 1{\cdot}5\sqrt{\frac{111}{50} - \left(\frac{27}{50}\right)^2}$$

$$= 1{\cdot}5\sqrt{(2{\cdot}220 - 0{\cdot}292)}$$

$$= 2{\cdot}08$$

Strictly speaking, this value of s requires a slight adjustment. What we have calculated is $\sqrt{\dfrac{\Sigma(x-\bar{x})^2}{n}}$ instead of $\sqrt{\dfrac{\Sigma(x-\bar{x})^2}{n-1}}$. We should therefore now multiply by $\sqrt{\dfrac{n}{n-1}}$.

However, this grouped frequency method is only worth while for large samples, which makes the adjustment scarcely worth bothering about. As n increases, the correction factor approaches nearer and nearer to 1. In our example it is only 1·01.

The approximate values of $\bar{x} = 37{\cdot}555$ and $s = 2{\cdot}08$ correspond quite closely to the exact values of 37·63 and 1·98 calculated by the machine method.

Exercises

A.2.   Calculate the mean and standard deviation of the journey time data of Chapter 1, repeated below:

Journey time	Frequency
17	6
18	8
19	9
20	12
21	9
22	4
23	2

A.3.   The following are times in minutes during which a machine operating as part of an assembly line was idle. Calculate the average idle time and its standard deviation, comparing the results obtained by the exact method with those obtained by the grouped frequency method.

10	13	14	15	16	17	17	16	13	22
15	17	12	14	14	19	15	14	16	17
19	21	19	17	13	16	16	19	15	14
20	12	23	16	15	16	17	17	19	18

A.4.   The following data are the weights in ounces of 50 packages selected at random from the output of the margarine-packing machine in Example 2.7 with the machine set to produce a pack weight of 8·00 oz. Calculate the mean and standard deviation.

7·96	7·97	8·04	8·06	7·96
7·79	7·94	8·04	8·01	7·90
8·14	7·92	7·98	7·88	7·93
8·07	7·95	7·84	7·92	8·02
7·98	8·01	7·92	7·92	8·04
7·99	7·72	7·97	8·05	8·06
7·93	7·80	8·10	8·17	7·90
7·98	8·08	7·94	7·95	7·97
8·11	7·96	7·89	7·93	7·85
7·95	7·84	8·00	8·03	8·05

APPENDIX B SUMMARY OF NOTATION

This appendix contains all the symbols used in the book and what they represent. They are given in the order in which they appear in the text.

$P(A)$	The probability that event A will occur.
$P(AB)$	The probability that both A and B will occur.
$P(B\mid A)$	The probability that B will occur, given that A has occurred.
$x!$	Factorial x, which is $1 \times 2 \times 3 \times \ldots \times x$.
n	Sample size.
p	Used in connection with the binomial distribution, it is the probability that an item picked at random will possess the characteristic of interest, for example that it will be a defective component.
e	A mathematical constant, equal to approximately 2·7183.
m	The mean of a Poisson distribution.
μ	The mean of a normal distribution.
σ	The standard deviation (S.D.) of a normal distribution.
z	The number of standard deviations or standard errors away from the mean which a given point in a normal distribution lies.
π	The true population percentage having a specified characteristic.
P	A sample estimate of π.
L	A specified limit of accuracy for an estimate of a percentage or mean.
S.E.	Standard error of an estimate of a percentage or mean.
$\therefore$	Therefore
$<$	Is less than.
$\neq$	Is not equal to.
$>$	Is greater than.
$\bar{x}$	A sample estimate of the population mean, μ.
s	A sample estimate of the population standard deviation, σ.
W.L.	The warning limits on a quality control chart.
A.L.	The action limits on a quality control chart.
t	The number of standard errors away from the mean which a given point in a Student-t distribution lies.

159

$t._{05}$	The value of t corresponding to the point in a Student-t distribution which has 5% of the distribution above it. Similarly for $t._{01}$, $t._{025}$, etc.
d.f.	Degrees of freedom.
s^2	A sample estimate of the population variance, σ^2.
F	The sampling distribution of the ratio of two sample variances.
$F._{05}$	The point in an F-distribution which has 5% of the distribution above it. Similarly for $F._{01}$, $F._{025}$, etc.
χ^2	The variable in the chi squared distribution.
E	Expected frequency in a χ^2 test.
O	Observed frequency in a χ^2 test.
$\chi^2._{05}$	The value of χ^2 which has 5% of the distribution above it. Similarly for $\chi^2._{01}$, $\chi^2._{025}$, etc.
k	The number of classes in a frequency distribution.
d	The number of parameters estimated from the sample data when fitting a theoretical distribution to observed data.
r	The number of rows in a contingency table.
c	The number of columns in a contingency table.
a	The point at which a regression line crosses the y axis.
b	The slope of a regression line.
Σ	The sum of.
Cxy	$\Sigma xy - n\bar{x}\bar{y}$
Cxx	$\Sigma x^2 - n\bar{x}^2$
Cyy	$\Sigma y^2 - n\bar{y}^2$
r	The correlation coefficient.
r_{y1}	The correlation between y and x_1.
$r_{y2.1}$	The partial correlation between y and x_2 having allowed for the effect of x_1.
$r_{y3.12}$	The partial correlation between y and x_3 having allowed for x_1 and x_2.
R	The multiple correlation coefficient.

APPENDIX C ADDITIONAL PROBLEMS ON PROBABILITY AND BASIC DISTRIBUTIONS

C.1. Accidents occur at random in a certain factory, with an average of 3·0 per week.

(a) Calculate the probability that more than 6 will occur in a given week.

(b) How many weeks a year will, on average, be free of accidents?

C.2. The following data are the diameters (in inches) of a random sample of 50 apples from a certain crop.

1·5	4·0	3·4	3·1	2·8	3·4	3·1	2·1	4·1	3·6
2·5	2·9	1·7	2·6	2·3	3·7	3·5	2·5	3·3	4·6
2·0	4·3	3·0	1·8	3·1	3·3	3·8	4·4	2·6	2·2
3·0	2·4	3·2	3·8	3·3	4·2	4·3	2·8	3·0	2·7
3·6	3·9	3·4	4·1	3·7	2·7	3·2	4·8	3·2	2·9

(a) Calculate the mean and standard deviation.

(b) The crop is to be graded by diameter into 5 sizes so that 10% of the crop shall be in the largest grade A, 20% in B, 30% in C, 20% in D and 20% in E. Assuming that apple diameter is normally distributed, calculate the sizes of the necessary holes in the grading sieves.

C.3 A telephone call on S.T.D. must travel over 5 sections of cable. If the probability that the call fails at any section is 0·05, what is the probability that the call will get through?

C.4 On a journey through a town, a motorist passes through 5 sets of traffic lights. The timing of all the lights is the same, being 40 seconds green, 10 seconds amber, 40 seconds red and 10 seconds red and amber.

Assuming that the lights operate independently of each other:

(a) What is the probability that the motorist will encounter no red lights? (Do not include amber or red and amber.)

(b) What is the probability of encountering more than 3 red lights?

161

C.5. The times which elapsed between 100 successive customers arriving at a supermarket check-out was recorded. Compare this distribution with that expected if customers arrive in a random fashion.

Time between successive arrivals (minutes)	Frequency
0·0–0·5	54
0·5–1·0	23
1·0–1·5	13
1·5–2·0	5
2·0–2·5	3
> 2·5	2

C.6. 5% of metal plates produced for an addressing machine contain errors. Find the probability that in a sample of 20 chosen at random, exactly 2 will contain errors by using:

(*a*) the binomial distribution,
(*b*) the Poisson approximation.

C.7. A machine produces components with an average length of 4·00 in and a standard deviation of 0·01 in. What proportion of the components will be:

(*a*) between 3·98 in and 4·01 in long,
(*b*) outside tolerance limits of 4·00 in ±0·02 in?

If the machine 'drifts' so that an average bolt length of 4·01 in is being produced, what proportion of the production will now be outside the required tolerance limits?

C.8. The demand for a certain type of biscuit in a grocer's shop is randomly distributed with an average of 5 boxes per week.

(*a*) What is the probability of being asked for 5 boxes in a particular week?
(*b*) At the beginning of each week, the grocer replenishes his stock to 9 boxes. How many times a year will he run out of stock, on average?

C.9.   The probability that a man will be alive in 25 years is 3/5 and the probability that his wife will be alive in 25 years is 2/3. Find the probability that:

   (a) both will be alive,
   (b) only the man will be alive,
   (c) only the wife will be alive,
   (d) at least one will be alive.

C.10.   Three components in a sub-assembly in a radar set must all function if the sub-assembly is to work efficiently. The effective life of the components follows the negative exponential distribution with means of 1000 hours, 2000 hours and 3000 hours respectively.

   What is the probability that the sub-assembly will function effectively for at least:

   (a) 1000 hours,
   (b) 2000 hours,
   (c) 3000 hours?

C.11.   A small hotel has 10 rooms, and the owner is considering buying television sets to rent to guests. He estimates that 50% of his guests will be willing to rent a set, so he buys 5 sets.

   Assuming that his estimate is correct and that all rooms are always occupied:

   (a) What proportion of evenings will there be more requests than sets?
   (b) If a set costs £50 and lasts for 1000 days, whether it is used or not, what rental should be charged in order to break even?

C.12.   Plungers are produced with a mean diameter of 98·4 mm and a standard deviation 0·3 mm to mate with cylinder bores produced with a mean diameter of 100 mm and a standard deviation 0·5 mm.

   If pairs of plunger and cylinder bore are selected at random:

   (a) What proportion will not fit together at all?
   (b) What proportion will have a clearance of more than 1·5 mm?

C.13. The following distribution is of the number of car accidents per day for a 50-day period in a certain city. Assuming that accidents occur at random, fit the appropriate theoretical distribution.

No. of accidents (x)	No. of days with x accidents
0	21
1	18
2	7
3	3
4	1

C.14. The probability that A hits a target is 1/4 and the probability that B hits it is 1/3.

(a) If each fires twice, what is the probability that the target will be hit at least once?

(b) If A only fires twice, how many times must B fire so that there is a probability of at least 0·90 that the target will be hit?

C.15. If a machine produces components which are 10% defective, find the probability that a random sample of 400 contains:

(a) Not more than 30 defectives,

(b) Between 30 and 40 defectives.

C.16. In a test consisting of 10 questions, the answers are restricted to 'Yes' and 'No'. What is the probability of getting 5 or more correct answers purely by chance?

How is this probability affected if there are four choices of answer to each question?

C.17. There is a probability of 0·001 that an individual injected with a certain vaccine will suffer a reaction. What is the probability that, out of 2000 individuals:

(a) more than 2,

(b) 3 or less,

(c) at least 1,

(d) just 1,

will suffer a reaction?

C.18.   The ABC company produces widgets. The process used produces a distribution with an average length of 6·00 in and a standard deviation of 0·30 in. To be usable, a widget must be between 5·60 and 6·50 inches long.

Using the most appropriate theoretical distribution, find:

(a) What proportion of widgets are too short,
(b) What proportion are too long,
(c) What proportion are satisfactory.

C.19.   If a bridge player and his partner have 9 trumps between them, what is the probability that the 4 trumps held by their opponents will be:

(a) 2 in each hand,
(b) 3 in one hand and 1 in the other?

C.20.   Find the probability that in a family of 4 children there will be:

(a) at least one boy,
(b) at least one boy and one girl.

Assume that the probability of a male birth is 0·5.

C.21.   The mean inside diameter of a large sample of washers produced by a machine is 0·502 in and the standard deviation is 0·005 in. The purpose for which the washers are made allows for a maximum tolerance in the diameter of 0·496 in to 0·508 in. Determine the percentage of defective washers assuming the diameters are distributed normally.

C.22.   40% of the customers buying suits at a tailor's shop purchase additional items such as shirts or ties. During a particular day, 20 customers buy suits. Calculate the probability that ten of them make an additional purchase, using the normal approximation. Compare the result with the probability calculated by using the correct distribution.

C.23.   A 1 gallon tin of paint will cover an average area of 1000 sq. ft, with a standard deviation of 20 sq. ft. An area of 24 850 sq. ft is to be painted, and 25 tins of paint are provided. What is the probability that this will be enough to finish the job?

C.24. Of a certain make of car, 1 in every 100 has a faulty gearbox. A company buys a fleet of 50 of these cars for its sales force. What is the probability that none of them has a faulty gearbox?

C.25. The average weight of male students at a certain college is 151 lb with a standard deviation of 15 lb. If there are 2000 students altogether, find how many of them are likely to be:

(*a*) between 120 lb and 150 lb,
(*b*) more than 185 lb,
(*c*) less than 128 lb.

APPENDIX D ADDITIONAL PROBLEMS ON SAMPLING DISTRIBUTIONS

D.1.   A personnel manager claims that 60% of all single women hired for secretarial jobs leave to get married within 2 years. An analysis shows that of a random sample of 120 women, 64 left to be married. Is this sample consistent with the manager's claim?

D.2.   (a) The following values are taken from the construction costs per square foot for a number of buildings of the same type, completed in the same year. Calculate 95% and 99% confidence limits for the average building cost for this type of building.

£5·66, £6·05, £5·68, £4·46, £6·56, £6·06, £6·61, £6·27, £5·80, £4·36.

(b) A sample taken the previous year had the following costs per square foot. To what extent is the conclusion that costs have risen justified?

£5·71, £4·80, £3·78, £4·73, £5·41, £4·88, £4·49.

D.3.   A sample survey was carried out to discover the opinions of businessmen in various fields about prospects for the coming year. A sample of 500 was taken, with the following results. Do these data indicate that there are differences of opinion about the future in the different fields of activity?

	Bankers	Industrialists	Farmers
Poor prospects	40	50	30
Average prospects	80	120	60
Good prospects	30	80	10

D.4.   Past records on a process show that the average production rate is 50 per hour per operator. Modifications to the process are made to try to increase the average production rate. This new method is tried with 9 operators, whose production rates are 51, 48, 50, 56, 52, 55, 54, 53, 49. Does this trial establish that the new method has a higher average production rate than the old?

How many more trials must be made to be 95% certain of getting an estimate of the new average production rate which is not in error by more than 1 unit?

167

D.5.   A machine produces parts with a SD of 2·8 mm. A modification to reduce the variability of the machine is carried out, and a sample of 20 now has $s = 1·7$ mm. Has the conversion successfully reduced variability?

D.6.   For expenses purposes, a representative receives 500 miles per week car allowance. Over a nine-week period his actual mileages are:

$$495, 535, 505, 490, 495, 505, 515, 500, 550$$

Is it likely that the allowance is inadequate?

How many more weeks should be included in the sample to give an estimate of his average mileage which is accurate to within 5 miles, at the 95% confidence level?

D.7.   A large chain of grocery stores wishes to know whether a projected new store should be self-service or not. 600 women shoppers in the area are interviewed, and 340 state a preference for self-service. Is it likely that a majority of all the shoppers prefer self-service?

D.8.   In a random sample of 36 men from Town A, an average income of £1500 p.a. with a standard deviation of £600 was observed. A random sample of 49 men from Town B had an average of £1800 p.a. with a standard deviation of £700. Would you conclude that there is a real difference in average income between the two towns?

D.9.   The management of a firm wants to know how its employees feel about working conditions in the factory, particularly whether there are differences of opinion between various departments.

Random samples are taken from each of the four departments, with the following results. Do these data indicate that such differences of opinion exist?

		Department			
		A	*B*	*C*	*D*
	Good	65	112	85	80
Conditions:	Average	27	67	60	44
	Poor	8	21	15	16

D.10.   From a large consignment of nuts, a sample of 400 showed 80 not tapped.

(a) Within what limits does the true percentage defective lie, at the 95% confidence level?

(b) A sample of 500 from a different supplier had 70 not tapped. Is there a significant difference between the two suppliers?

D.11. The following table gives data on the hardness of wood stored inside and outside. Is hardness affected by weathering?

	Inside	Outside
Sample size	30	40
Mean hardness	126	120
SD	15	12

D.12. A manufacturer of transistors estimates that the defective rate in production is about 15%. How large a sample would be needed to establish this to within $\pm 1\%$ at the 95% confidence level?

D.13. An investigation into two brands of flashlight batteries showed that a random sample of 50 batteries of Brand A had an average lifetime of 24·2 hours with a standard deviation of 1·5, and 40 batteries of Brand B had an average lifetime of 22·8 hours with a standard deviation of 2·0 hours. Do these data indicate that there is a significant difference between the average life of the two brands?

D.14. In 360 throws of a pair of dice, the following frequency distribution was obtained. Are the dice biased?

Score	Frequency
2	8
3	18
4	28
5	41
6	50
7	68
8	54
9	39
10	28
11	19
12	7

D.15. A detergent company is considering which of two new-style plastic bottles to adopt for its product. The two bottles are put on sale side by side, the customer being free to choose between them.

Over a trial period of 12 weeks the following sales figures are obtained. Is there a significant difference (at the 0·05 level) between the sales of the two bottles?

	Bottle A	Bottle B
Average weekly sales:	152	160
Standard deviation:	15	12

D.16. A random sample of 500 students contained 200 who smoked. Calculate 95% and 99% confidence limits for the percentage of smokers in the entire student body.

How many more students would need to be included in the sample to get an estimate which was accurate to within $\pm 2\%$, at the 95% confidence level?

D.17. A tyre manufacturer claims an average life of 20 000 miles for his product. A sample of 30 tyres are tested and have an average life of 19 000 miles with a standard deviation of 2000. Is this consistent with the manufacturer's claim?

D.18. In a political survey, a sample of 1000 electors in constituency A contained 450 Conservative supporters, and a sample of 800 in constituency B contained 320 Conservative supporters. Do these results indicate that there is any difference in support for the Conservative party in the two constituencies?

D.19. In a test to compare two varieties of grain, 6 test plots planted with Variety A yielded an average of 85·3 bushels per acre with a standard deviation of 5·8. Variety B (also planted on 6 test plots) averaged 92·7 bushels per acre with a standard deviation of 6·1. Is there a significant difference in yield between the two varieties, at the 5% significance level?

D.20. The manufacturer in example D.12 took a sample of 1000 from one production unit and found that it contained 130 defectives. A sample of 1000 from another unit, which was suspected of being inferior to the first, contained 160 defectives. Does this support the view that the second is inferior?

D.21. Three coins were tossed a total of 240 times, and each time the number of heads turning up was recorded. Test the hypothesis that the coins are unbiased.

No. of Heads	Frequency
0	22
1	105
2	92
3	21

D.22. The life of 6 machine tools was measured, with the following results:

$$4\cdot5, \ 4\cdot9, \ 4\cdot7, \ 4\cdot8, \ 4\cdot6, \ 4\cdot9$$

A sample from a different manufacturer, who claims a longer life for his product, gave the following results:

$$4\cdot7, \ 4\cdot9, \ 4\cdot9, \ 5\cdot0, \ 5\cdot2$$

Do these data support the second manufacturer's claim?

D.23.   A car manufacturer claims that 30% of all cars built by his firm in 1963 were still running in 1973. A random sample of 800 cars made in 1963 showed that 200 were still running in 1973. Does this disprove the manufacturer's claim?

D.24.   An advertising agency claims that an attractive picture display on a vending machine will increase sales. Over a 30-day period, sales from the machine without the display averaged £25 per day with a standard deviation of £5. With the display, sales averaged £30 per day with a standard deviation of £6, over a similar period. Do these data justify the agency's claim?

D.25. The results of a survey made to determine whether the age of a driver has any effect on the number of car accidents in which he is involved per year are indicated in the table below. Is the number of accidents per year associated with age?

No. of accidents	Age of Driver				
	21–30	31–40	41–50	51–60	61–70
0	748	821	786	720	672
1	74	60	51	66	50
2	31	25	22	16	15
more than 2	9	10	6	5	7

SOLUTIONS TO EXERCISES

Exercise 1.1

There are 36 different ways in which the two dice may fall. They are:

1st die	111111	222222	333333	444444	555555	666666
2nd die	123456	123456	123456	123456	123456	123456

(*a*) Only 2 of these will give a total score of 3, therefore:

$$P(\text{score of } 3) = \frac{2}{36} = \frac{1}{18}$$

(*b*) 6 of them will give a total score of 7, therefore:

$$P(\text{score of } 7) = \frac{6}{36} = \frac{1}{6}$$

(*c*) 2 of them will give a total score of 11, therefore:

$$P(\text{score of } 11) = \frac{2}{36} = \frac{1}{18}$$

Exercise 1.2

(*a*) The probability that the first valve selected is defective is $\frac{3}{30}$. Having obtained a defective, the conditional probability that the second is also defective is $\frac{2}{29}$. Hence, by the multiplication rule, the probability that both are defective is $\frac{3}{30} \times \frac{2}{29} = \frac{1}{145}$.

(*b*) There are two ways in which just one defective may arise; it could be obtained at either the first or second pick.

The probability of getting the sequence 'good, defective' will be $\frac{27}{30} \times \frac{3}{29} = \frac{27}{290}$.

The probability of getting the sequence 'defective, good' will be $\frac{3}{30} \times \frac{27}{29} = \frac{27}{290}$.

Either of these will produce one defective, so by the addition rule,

$$P(1 \text{ defective}) = \frac{27}{290} + \frac{27}{290} = \frac{27}{145}$$

(c) The probability that neither is defective, by the multiplication rule is $\frac{27}{30} \times \frac{26}{29} = \frac{117}{145}$.

Exercise 1.3

(a) $\frac{4}{52} \times \frac{3}{51} \times \frac{2}{50} \times \frac{1}{49} = \frac{1}{270\ 725}$

(b) $\frac{1}{52} \times \frac{1}{51} \times \frac{1}{50} \times \frac{1}{49} = \frac{1}{6\ 497\ 400}$

Exercise 1.4

If the clerk's claim is true, the probability that one record selected at random is misfiled is 0·01. By the multiplication rule, therefore, the probability that two will be misfiled is $(0·01)^2 = 0·0001$. The odds are thus 9999 to 1 against his claim being true.

Exercise 1.5

The probability that an individual will not leave is 0·60. The probability that all 3 will not leave is therefore $(0·60)^3 = 0·216$.

Exercise 1.6

In order to calculate these probabilities exactly, the number of bolts in the batch should be known. Suppose, for example, that this were 1000. Of these, 10% (that is 100) have faulty threads. The probability that the first bolt of the 5 selected will be faulty is thus $\frac{100}{1000}$, the conditional probability that the second is also faulty will be $\frac{99}{999}$, that the third is faulty $\frac{98}{998}$, and so on.

However, so long as the sample which we are considering is small relative to the size of the batch, these conditional probabilities will differ very little from 0·1. It will simplify the calculation enormously if we assume that the probability of picking a faulty bolt remains constant at 0·1 and the probability of picking a good one remains constant at 0·9. This point is referred to again in the discussion of the binomial distribution in Chapter 2.

An alternative way to ensure that these probabilities do remain constant is to sample **with replacement**. That is, each bolt is returned to the batch before the next one is selected.

Assuming that these probabilities do remain constant, the following calculations may be made:

(a) If no faulty bolts are to occur in the sample, all must be good. The probability of this happening, using the multiplication rule, is:

$$0·9 \times 0·9 \times 0·9 \times 0·9 \times 0·9 = (0·9)^5 = 0·590$$

(b) One faulty bolt may arise in 5 different ways. It could occur as the first, second, third, fourth or fifth member of the sample:

F	G	G	G	G
G	F	G	G	G
G	G	F	G	G
G	G	G	F	G
G	G	G	G	F

The probability that a faulty bolt will be picked first, followed by 4 good ones is:

$$0·1 \times 0·9 \times 0·9 \times 0·9 \times 0·9 = (0·1)(0·9)^4 = 0·0656$$

This is also the probability that the faulty bolt will occur in any other specified position. The probability that it will occur somewhere in the sample is therefore, by the addition rule:

$$0·0656 + 0·0656 + 0·0656 + 0·0656 + 0·0656 = 5 \times 0·0656 = 0·3280$$

Exercise 1.7

It is easier to find the probability that all 25 men have different birthdays. The probability that at least 2 have the same birthday will then be 1 minus this probability.

Let us number the men from 1 to 25. The probability that number 2 does not have the same birthday as number 1 is $\frac{364}{365}$, because there is only one day which he may not have. The probability that number 3 does not have the same birthday as either number 2 or number 1 is $\frac{363}{365}$ because there are 2 days which he may not have. Similarly, the corresponding probabilities for numbers 4, 5, 6 . . . 25 will be: $\frac{362}{365}, \frac{361}{365}, \frac{360}{365}, \cdots \frac{341}{365}$.

We are interested in the joint probability of all these events. By the multiplication rule, this will be:

$$\frac{364}{365} \times \frac{363}{365} \times \cdots \times \frac{342}{365} \times \frac{341}{365} = 0.431$$

The probability that at least 2 do have the same birthday will therefore be $1 - 0.431 = 0.569$. In other words, there is a rather better than even chance that at least 2 of them have the same birthday. This is far higher than one would guess intuitively.

The calculation is only approximate, in that all days have been assumed equi-probable for birthdays and the complication of leap year has been ignored.

Exercise 2.1

A typical set of experimental results is shown in Figure S.1.

The theoretical expected frequencies will be 48 times the probabilities in the distribution shown in Figure 2.2.

Number of heads	Experimental frequency	Expected frequency
0	5	6
1	20	18
2	16	18
3	7	6

Exercise 2.2

The probabilities of getting a score of 2, 3, 4 . . . 11, 12 may be calculated as shown for 3, 7, and 11 in the solution to Exercise 1.1. The resulting probability distribution is shown in Figure S.2.

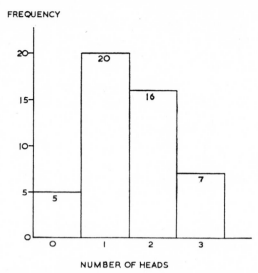

Figure S.1. Experimental results obtained when three coins were tossed

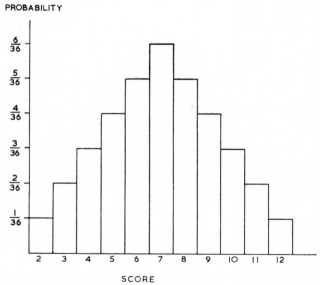

Figure S.2. Probability distribution of the score obtained when two dice
are thrown

The theoretical expected frequencies for 72 throws will be 72 times the probabilities in Figure S.2. These are given below, together with a typical set of experimental results.

Score	Experimental frequency	Expected frequency
2	1	2
3	5	4
4	6	6
5	6	8
6	11	10
7	14	12
8	9	10
9	7	8
10	8	6
11	3	4
12	3	2

Exercise 2.3

The number of ways in which 0 defectives can arrange themselves is always 1, whatever the size of n. Substituting $x = 0$ and $n = 6$ in the combinations formula, we have: $\dfrac{6!}{0!\,6!}$.

Since $0! = 1$, this expression works out to 1, as it should. It is a little difficult to see why $0!$ should equal 1. However, the fact that it does may be demonstrated by putting $n = 1$ in the equation $n! = n(n - 1)!$

The number of ways in which 1 defective may occur $= \dfrac{6!}{1!\,5!} = 6$

,, ,, ,, ,, ,, 2 defectives ,, ,, $= \dfrac{6!}{2!\,4!} = 15$

,, ,, ,, ,, ,, 3 ,, ,, ,, $= \dfrac{6!}{3!\,3!} = 20$

,, ,, ,, ,, ,, 4 ,, ,, ,, $= \dfrac{6!}{4!\,2!} = 15$

The number of ways in which 5 defectives may occur $= \dfrac{6!}{5!\,1!} = 6$

„   „   „   „   „ 6 „   „   „ $= \dfrac{6!}{6!\,0!} = 1$

Exercise 2.4

If the operator is of average standard, 5% of the cards which she punches will contain errors. The 4 cards selected will then be from a population in which the proportion p containing errors is $0\cdot05$.

The probability that 2 of the 4 will contain errors is therefore given by:

$$P(2 \text{ errors}) = \frac{4!}{2!\,2!}\,(0\cdot05)^2(0\cdot95)^2$$
$$= 6 \times 0\cdot0025 \times 0\cdot9025$$
$$= 0\cdot014$$

It would thus be rather unusual to find 2 errors in 4 cards, if the operator were up to standard. Whether or not you consider odds of about 70 to 1 against 'convincing' is up to you.

Strictly speaking, we should not base our decision on the probability of getting *exactly* 2 errors, but on the probability of getting 2 *or more*. It would be a good idea to reconsider this exercise after reading the procedure for significance testing on page 61.

Exercise 2.5

In effect, we have a sample of $n = 5$ from a population containing a proportion $p = 0\cdot4$ possessing the characteristic 'leave within 12 months'.

The required probabilities may therefore be found by substituting these values for n and p in formula (2.1).

(*a*) $P(0 \text{ leavers}) = \dfrac{5!}{0!\,5!}\,(0\cdot4)^0(0\cdot6)^5 = 0\cdot0778$

(*b*) $P(1 \text{ leaver}) = \dfrac{5!}{1!\,4!}\,(0\cdot4)^1(0\cdot6)^4 = 0\cdot2592$

(c) 'At least 1' means 1 or 2 or 3 or 4 or 5. We could find all these probabilities separately and add them up. However, it is much easier to find $1 - P(0)$. This will lead to the same answer, because:

$$P(0) + P(1) + P(2) + P(3) + P(4) + P(5) = 1$$

We have just calculated $P(0) = 0.0778$, so:

$$P \text{ (at least 1 leaver)} = 1 - 0.0778 = 0.9222.$$

Exercise 2.6

Substituting in formula (2.1) the values $n = 6$ and $p = \frac{1}{6}$, we find:

(a) $P(0) = \dfrac{6!}{0! \, 6!} \left(\dfrac{1}{6}\right)^0 \left(\dfrac{5}{6}\right)^6 = 0.3348$

(b) $P(1) = \dfrac{6!}{1! \, 5!} \left(\dfrac{1}{6}\right)^1 \left(\dfrac{5}{6}\right)^5 = 0.4018$

(c) $P(\text{more than } 1) = 1 - \{P(0) + P(1)\}$
$$= 1 - 0.7366$$
$$= 0.2634$$

Exercise 2.7

The probabilities of 0, 1, 2 ... 20 Kreemy-Krunch centres per $\frac{1}{4}$ lb will follow the binomial distribution with $n = 20$ and $p = 0.10$. The required probability is:

$$P(1) + P(2) + \ldots + P(20)$$

Instead of evaluating each of these separately and adding them up, it is much easier to calculate $P(0)$ and subtract it from 1.

$$P(0) = (0.9)^{20} = 0.1216$$

The probability of at least one Kreemy-Krunch in $\frac{1}{4}$ lb is therefore $1 - 0.1216 = 0.8784$.

Exercise 2.8

(a) $P(0) = \dfrac{5!}{0! \, 5!} (0.1)^0 (0.9)^5 = 0.5905$

$$P(1) = \frac{5!}{1!\,4!}\,(0\cdot1)^1(0\cdot9)^4 = 0\cdot3280$$

$$P(2) = \frac{5!}{2!\,3!}\,(0\cdot1)^2(0\cdot9)^3 = 0\cdot0729$$

$$P(3) = \frac{5!}{3!\,2!}\,(0\cdot1)^3(0\cdot9)^2 = 0\cdot0081$$

$$P(4) = \frac{5!}{4!\,1!}\,(0\cdot1)^4(0\cdot9)^1 = 0\cdot0005$$

$$P(5) = \frac{5!}{5!\,0!}\,(0\cdot1)^5(0\cdot9)^0 = 0\cdot0000$$

To 4 decimal place accuracy, $P(5) = 0$. It is in fact $0\cdot000\,01$.

(b) $\quad P(0) = \dfrac{5!}{0!\,5!}\,(0\cdot5)^0(0\cdot5)^5 = 0\cdot0312$

$$P(1) = \frac{5!}{1!\,4!}\,(0\cdot5)^1(0\cdot5)^4 = 0\cdot1563$$

$$P(2) = \frac{5!}{2!\,3!}\,(0\cdot5)^2(0\cdot5)^3 = 0\cdot3125$$

$$P(3) = \frac{5!}{3!\,2!}\,(0\cdot5)^3(0\cdot5)^2 = 0\cdot3125$$

$$P(4) = \frac{5!}{4!\,1!}\,(0\cdot5)^4(0\cdot5)^1 = 0\cdot1563$$

$$P(5) = \frac{5!}{5!\,0!}\,(0\cdot5)^5(0\cdot5)^0 = 0\cdot0312$$

Exercise 2.9

The histogram for $n = 5$, $p = 0\cdot1$ is shown in Figure S.3 (*a*) and for $n = 5$, $p = 0\cdot5$ in Figure S.3 (*b*) (page 181). The distribution with $p = 0\cdot1$ is markedly skew. As p approaches nearer and nearer to $0\cdot5$, the distribution becomes less and less skew. When $p = 0\cdot5$, it becomes perfectly symmetrical.

Exercise 2.10

The probability that demand during the week will exceed any specified number of motors may be obtained by adding together the appropriate probabilities from Table I. Average demand is 6 per week, so we consult the table for $m = 6$.

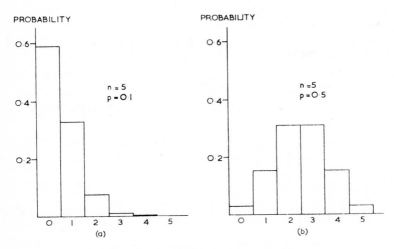

Figure S.3. Binomial distributions of Exercise 2.9

Suppose 12 motors are in stock at the beginning of the week. The probability that more than this will be asked for during the week will be $P(13) + P(14) + \ldots$ From Table I, we find that this is:

$$0{\cdot}0052 + 0{\cdot}0022 + 0{\cdot}0009 + 0{\cdot}0003 + 0{\cdot}0001$$
$$= 0{\cdot}0087$$

If the storekeeper re-ordered when his stock had fallen to 12, therefore, he would be 99·13% certain that he could meet requirements.

By reducing the re-order level to 11, he would increase the probability of being unable to meet requirements to $0{\cdot}0087 + 0{\cdot}0113 = 0{\cdot}0200$, that is, he would now only be 98·00% certain of meeting demand. He would, however, be reducing his average stockholding by 1 motor. The resulting saving might well more than offset the slight increase in the risk of running out of stock.

This is one of the central problems in stock control. A balance must be struck between the savings which accrue from reducing stock levels and the costs which are incurred by running short of essential materials. The book by Battersby* provides a good elementary, non-mathematical introduction to the general subject of stock

* A. Battersby, *A Guide to Stock Control.* Pitman, 1962.

control. The one by Magee and Boodman* provides a more formal treatment.

In the example which we are discussing, a risk level of 5% has been decided upon. The nearest we can get to this without exceeding it is to have a re-order level of 10. The probability of being asked for more than 10 is $P(11) + P(12) + \ldots$, which is:

$$0 \cdot 0225 + 0 \cdot 0113 + 0 \cdot 0052 + 0 \cdot 0022 + 0 \cdot 0009 + 0 \cdot 0003 + 0 \cdot 0001$$
$$= 0 \cdot 0425$$

If the storekeeper re-orders when his stock has fallen to 10, he is 95·75% certain of being able to meet requirements.

Exercise 2.11

The probability that the switchboard will be overloaded is the probability that more than 20 calls will be received when the average is 10. We therefore require to find $P(21) + P(22) + \ldots$ from Table I, with $m = 10$. This is:

$$0 \cdot 0009 + 0 \cdot 0004 + 0 \cdot 0002 + 0 \cdot 0001$$
$$= 0 \cdot 0016$$

Exercise 2.12

(a) During a one-minute interval, the average number of arrivals is 4. From Table I, with $m = 4$:

$$P(0 \text{ arrivals}) = 0 \cdot 0183$$

(b) During a two-minute period, the average number of arrivals is 8. We require to find the number which has a probability of not more than 0·05 of being exceeded.

This is found to be 13 by using Table I. The probability of exceeding 13 is $P(14) + P(15) + \ldots$, which is 0·0341. The probability of exceeding 12 is $0 \cdot 0341 + P(13)$, which comes to more than 0·05. It is in fact 0·0637.

Exercise 2.13

The expected, or average number of calls is 6. From Table I, with $m = 6$, we require the number that has a probability of not more than

---

* J. Magee and D. M. Boodman, *Production Planning and Inventory Control.* 2nd revised edition. McGraw-Hill, 1967.

0·01 of being exceeded. This is found to be 12. The probability of exceeding 12 is:

$$0·0001 + 0·0003 + 0·0009 + 0·0022 + 0·0052$$
$$= 0·0087$$

This is as close to 0·01 as we can go without exceeding it.

Exercise 2.14

The total number of goals scored is:
$$(0 \times 32) + (1 \times 52) + (2 \times 44) + (3 \times 29) + (4 \times 13) + (5 \times 6) + (6 \times 2)$$
$$= 321$$

The number of teams is:

$$(32 + 52 + 44 + 29 + 13 + 6 + 2)$$
$$= 178$$

The average number of goals per team is therefore: $\dfrac{321}{178} = 1·80$.

The probabilities that a team will score 0, 1, 2, . . . goals may now be read from Table I, with $m = 1·8$. Multiplying these probabilities by 178 then gives the theoretical frequencies. The results may be tabulated as follows:

Number of goals (x)	Probability	Theoretical frequency	Observed frequency
0	0·1653	29·4	32
1	0·2975	53·0	52
2	0·2678	47·7	44
3	0·1607	28·6	29
4	0·0723	12·9	13
5	0·0260	4·6	6
6	0·0078	1·4	2
7	0·0020	0·4	0

The histogram of observed frequencies is shown in Figure S.4, with the theoretical frequencies superimposed.

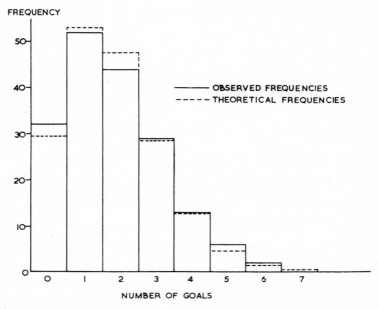

Figure S.4. The theoretical and observed frequencies of Exercise 2.14
compared

Exercise 2.15

(a) $z = \dfrac{x - \mu}{\sigma} = \dfrac{23 - 20}{4} = 0.75$

From Table II, the corresponding area is found to be 0·2734.

(b) Here we require to find the area of a strip similar to that in Figure 2.7 (*b*), but on the other side of the mean. The *z* values for the boundaries of the strip are:

$$z_1 = \frac{17 - 20}{4} = -0.75$$

$$z_2 = \frac{19 - 20}{4} = -0.25$$

The associated areas are 0·2734 and 0·0987 respectively. The area of the required strip is the difference between these, which is 0·2734 − 0·0987 = 0·1747.

(c) The boundaries of the required area lie on either side of the mean, as in Figure 2.7 (c).

$$z_1 = \frac{18 - 20}{4} = -0.5$$

$$z_2 = \frac{23 - 20}{4} = 0.75$$

The required area is therefore $0.1915 + 0.2734 = 0.4649$.

(d)
$$z = \frac{15 - 20}{4} = -1.25$$

The area between the mean and 15 is therefore 0.3944. The area below 15 is thus $0.5000 - 0.3944 = 0.1056$.

(e)
$$z = \frac{26 - 20}{4} = 1.50$$

The area between the mean and 26 is therefore 0.4332. The area above 26 is thus $0.5000 - 0.4332 = 0.0668$. Similarly, the area below 14 is also 0.0668.
The area outside the range 20 ± 6 is therefore $2 \times 0.0668 = 0.1336$.

Exercise 2.16

First we find the z values corresponding to the grade boundaries. The top 10% of the candidates will go into Grade 1. Using Table II, we find that the z value corresponding to the point in the normal curve which has 10% of the distribution above it is about 1.28. This point therefore defines the boundary between Grade 1 and Grade 2.

Similarly, the boundary between Grades 2 and 3 will be the point which has 30% of the distribution above it. The z value for this point is about 0.52. The boundary between Grades 3 and 4 has 70% of the distribution above it. The corresponding z value is -0.52. Finally, the boundary between Grades 4 and 5 has a z value of -1.28.

These z values now require converting into actual marks. The boundary between Grades 1 and 2 is 1.28 standard deviations above the mean. The mean is 60 and the standard deviation 15, so the boundary mark is:

$$60 + (1.28 \times 15) = 79.2$$

All the others may be found in a similar manner. They are:

Grade 2/3 boundary $= 60 + (0.52 \times 15) = 67.8$
Grade 3/4 boundary $= 60 - (0.52 \times 15) = 52.2$
Grade 4/5 boundary $= 60 - (1.28 \times 15) = 40.8$

Exercise 2.17

The distribution of difference in diameter between piston and cylinder will have the parameters:

$$\mu = 3.010 - 3.000 \qquad = 0.010$$
$$\sigma = \sqrt{(0.004^2 + 0.006^2)} = 0.0072$$

This distribution is shown in Figure S.5.

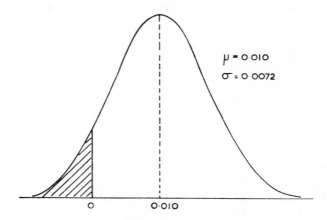

Figure S.5. Distribution of cylinder/piston fit

(*a*) The proportion of cylinder/piston pairs in which the piston is larger than the cylinder will be the shaded portion of Figure S.5. The z value corresponding to the upper boundary of this area will be:

$$z = \frac{0 - 0.010}{0.0072} = -1.39$$

From Table II, the associated area is 0.4177. The shaded portion of the distribution is therefore: $0.5000 - 0.4177 = 0.0823$.

(b) The proportion within the specified tolerance limits will be the proportion of the distribution in Figure S.5. which lies between 0·003 and 0·020. The z values for these two points are:

$$z_1 = \frac{0·003 - 0·010}{0·0072} = -0·97$$

$$z_2 = \frac{0·020 - 0·010}{0·0072} = 1·39$$

The corresponding areas from Table II are 0·3340 and 0·4177 respectively. The area between the two tolerance limits is thus $0·3340 + 0·4177 = 0·7517$.

This in turn means that the proportion which will not meet the tolerance requirements is $1·0000 - 0·7517 = 0·2483$.

Exercise 2.18

The distribution of the time taken to complete the entire job is the sum of 10 elemental distributions, each with a mean of 0·5 and a standard deviation of 0·05. The mean of the overall distribution will therefore be $10 \times 0·5 = 5·0$ minutes, and the standard deviation will be $\sqrt{(10 \times 0·05^2)} = 0·158$.

It is interesting to compare the relative variation of the elemental time with that of the job time. In the elemental time distribution, the standard deviation is $\frac{0·05}{0·5} \times 100\% = 10\%$ of the mean value. In the job time distribution, however, the standard deviation is only $\frac{0·158}{5·0} \times 100\% = 3·16\%$ of the mean value. The job time thus exhibits much less relative variation than the element time.

The measurement $\frac{\text{S.D.}}{\text{Mean}} \times 100\%$ is a useful way to compare relative variation. It is known as the **coefficient of variation.**

Exercise 2.19

(a) The point in the normal curve with only 5% of the distribution above it has a z value of 1·64. We may thus be 95% certain that during any particular week, the maximum demand will be:

$$100 + (1·64 \times 10) = 116·4$$

On average, of course, weekly demand will only be 100. The additional 16·4 provides a **buffer stock** to allow for unpredictable variations in demand.

(b) Average demand for a four-week period will be 400, with a standard deviation of $\sqrt{(4 \times 10^2)} = 20$. We may thus be 95% certain that during a given four-week period, the maximum demand will be:

$$400 + (1·64 \times 20) = 432·8$$

The buffer stock for a four-week period is thus only twice that required for a one-week period. In general, the buffer stock for an *n*-week period is $\sqrt{n}$ times that required for a one-week period.

Exercise 2.20

$$\frac{1}{m} = 3, \qquad \therefore m = \frac{1}{3}$$

(a) If $t = 10$, $mt = 3·33$
    $P(> 10 \text{ minutes}) = e^{-3·33} = 0·0360$

(b) $t_1 = 1$ minute, $\therefore mt_1 = 0·33$
    $t_2 = 2$ minutes, $\therefore mt_2 = 0·67$

$P(> 1 \text{ minute}) = e^{-0·33} = 0·7189$
$P(> 2 \text{ minutes}) = e^{-0·67} = 0·5117$

$\therefore$ P(between 1 and 2 minutes) $= 0·7189 - 0·5117 = 0·2072$

Exercise 2.21

$$\frac{1}{m} = 2000, \qquad \therefore m = \frac{1}{2000}$$

Life (hours)	t	mt	$P(> t)$	Class probability
	0	0	1·0000	
0–1000				0·3935
	1000	0·5	0·6065	
1000–2000				0·2386
	2000	1·0	0·3679	

Life (hours)	t	mt	$P(>t)$	Class probability
2000–3000				0·1448
	3000	1·5	0·2231	
3000–4000				0·0878
	4000	2·0	0·1353	
4000–5000				0·0532
	5000	2·5	0·0821	
5000–6000				0·0323
	6000	3·0	0·0498	
> 6000				0·0498
	∞	∞	0	

Exercise 3.1

(*a*) The appropriate formula for calculating sample size is:

$$n = \frac{4P(100 - P)}{L^2}$$

Putting $P = 30$ and $L = 2$ gives:

$$n = \frac{4 \times 30 \times 70}{4}$$
$$= 2100$$

(*b*) The original estimate of P (30%) is nearer to 50% than is the revised estimate (25%). The sample will therefore not need to be enlarged to ensure the required accuracy.

Exercise 3.2

(*a*) Activity	Estimated %	95% confidence limits
Working	70%	$\pm 2\sqrt{\dfrac{70 \times 30}{1000}} = \pm 2 \cdot 90\%$
Idle	20%	$\pm 2\sqrt{\dfrac{20 \times 80}{1000}} = \pm 2 \cdot 53\%$
Setting up	10%	$\pm 2\sqrt{\dfrac{10 \times 90}{1000}} = \pm 1 \cdot 90\%$

(*b*) The sample size must be based on the activity with the nearest percentage to 50%. This is the 'working' category, with $P = 70\%$.

$$n = \frac{4 \times 70 \times 30}{4} = 2100$$

We therefore must take a further 1100 observations.

Exercise 3.3

1. Null hypothesis: $\pi = 80\%$.
2. Alternative hypothesis: $\pi < 80\%$.
3. Significance level: 0·05.
4. Assuming the null hypothesis to be true, the appropriate sampling distribution will have a mean of 80 and a standard error

of $\sqrt{\dfrac{80 \times 20}{400}} = 2\cdot0$.

The rejection area will be the lowest 5% of the distribution. To fall in the rejection area, P must be more than 1·64 standard errors below 80%.

5. $z = \dfrac{P - \pi}{\text{S.E.}} = \dfrac{75 - 80}{2} = -2\cdot5$

Our sample result is therefore 2·5 standard errors below the mean, which enables us to reject the null hypothesis and accept the alternative. We therefore conclude that this machine is not achieving the required standard.

Exercise 3.4

1. Null hypothesis: $\pi = 60\%$.
2. Alternative hypothesis: $\pi \neq 60\%$.
3. Significance level: 0·05.
4. Assuming the null hypothesis to be true, the appropriate sampling distribution will have a mean of 60 and a standard error

of $\sqrt{\dfrac{60 \times 40}{500}} = 2\cdot19$.

The alternative hypothesis indicates that the rejection area will consist of the extreme $2\frac{1}{2}\%$ in each tail of the distribution. To fall in the rejection area, P must therefore be more than 1·96 standard errors away from 60%.

5. $z = \dfrac{P - \pi}{\text{S.E.}} = \dfrac{54 - 60}{2 \cdot 19} = 2 \cdot 74$

This is greater than 1·96, so we may reject the null hypothesis. Our sample result therefore is not consistent with a true percentage of 60%. This would probably indicate that there had been a significant change in the candidate's support between the time the door-to-door canvass was carried out and the sample taken.

Exercise 3.5

$$n_1 = 650 \qquad n_2 = 500$$
$$P_1 = 52\% \qquad P_2 = 46\%$$

1. Null hypothesis: $\pi_1 = \pi_2 = \pi$.
2. Alternative hypothesis: $\pi_1 > \pi_2$.

Formulating the alternative in this way assumes that we had prior grounds for suspecting that the product had lost ground. If this were not so, the alternative would be $\pi_1 \neq \pi_2$.

3. Significance level: 0·01.

4. Assuming the null hypothesis to be true, the appropriate sampling distribution will have a mean of zero and a standard error of:

$$\sqrt{\left(\frac{\pi(100 - \pi)}{n_1} + \frac{\pi(100 - \pi)}{n_2} \right)}$$

To estimate π, we pool both samples. This gives $\pi = \dfrac{568}{1150} \times 100\% = 49 \cdot 4\%$. Substituting this in the standard error formula:

$$\text{S.E.} = \sqrt{\left(\frac{49 \cdot 4 \times 50 \cdot 6}{650} + \frac{49 \cdot 4 \times 50 \cdot 6}{500} \right)}$$
$$= \sqrt{(3 \cdot 846 + 4 \cdot 999)}$$
$$= 2 \cdot 97$$

The rejection area will consist of unusually large positive values of the difference $(P_1 - P_2)$. As we are using a 0·01 significance level, therefore, z must be greater than 2·33 to enable the null hypothesis to be rejected.

5. $z = \dfrac{P_1 - P_2}{\text{S.E.}} = \dfrac{52 - 46}{2 \cdot 97} = 2 \cdot 02$

This is less than 2·33. We are therefore unable to reject the null hypothesis. These data do not establish, at the 0·01 significance level, that the product has lost ground.

Exercise 3.6

$$n_1 = 1000 \qquad n_2 = 1200$$
$$P_1 = 18\% \qquad P_2 = 20 \cdot 8\%$$

1.   Null hypothesis: $\pi_1 = \pi_2 = \pi$.
2.   Alternative hypothesis: $\pi_1 \neq \pi_2$.
3.   Significance level: 0·01
4.   To estimate π, we pool both samples: $\pi = \dfrac{430}{2200} \times 100\% = 19 \cdot 5\%$.

The appropriate standard error will therefore be:

$$\text{S.E.} = \sqrt{\left(\frac{19 \cdot 5 \times 80 \cdot 5}{1000} + \frac{19 \cdot 5 \times 80 \cdot 5}{1200} \right)}$$
$$= 1 \cdot 70$$

The alternative hypothesis indicates that we are interested in both tails of the distribution. As we are using a 0·01 significance level, therefore, z must exceed 2·58 to establish a significant difference between P_1 and P_2.

5. $z = \dfrac{P_1 - P_2}{\text{S.E.}} = \dfrac{2 \cdot 8}{1 \cdot 7} = 1 \cdot 65$

This is not large enough to enable us to reject the null hypothesis. There is thus no significant difference in labour turnover between the two factories.

Exercise 3.7

$$\bar{x} = 30 \qquad s = 4 \qquad n = 36$$

For 95% confidence limits:

$$\mu \text{ lies between } \bar{x} \pm \frac{2\sigma}{\sqrt{n}}$$

We do not know σ, but s may be used instead as we have a large sample.

$$\mu \text{ lies between } 30 \pm \frac{2 \times 4}{\sqrt{36}}$$

$$= 30 \pm 1.33, \text{ or between } 28.67 \text{ and } 31.33.$$

For 99% confidence limits:

$$\mu \text{ lies between } \bar{x} \pm \frac{2.58\sigma}{\sqrt{n}}$$

$$= 30 \pm \frac{2.58 \times 4}{\sqrt{36}}$$

$$= 30 \pm 1.72, \text{ or between } 28.28 \text{ and } 31.72$$

Very often the z value of 2.58 in this calculation is rounded off to 3 for convenience.

Exercise 3.8

$$\sigma = 0.05 \qquad L = 0.01$$

Substituting these values in formula (3.6):

$$n = \frac{4\sigma^2}{L^2} = \frac{4 \times 0.0025}{0.0001} = 100$$

Exercise 3.9

$$\bar{x} = 120 \qquad s = 10 \qquad n = 30$$

With 95% confidence:

$$\mu \text{ lies between } \bar{x} \pm \frac{2\sigma}{\sqrt{n}}$$

Using s in place of σ:

$$\mu \text{ lies between } 120 \pm \frac{2 \times 10}{\sqrt{30}}$$

$$= 120 \pm 3.65$$

We require an estimate which is not more than 2 points out, with 99% confidence. We must therefore have a sample large enough to ensure that:

$$\frac{2 \cdot 58\sigma}{\sqrt{n}} = 2$$

$$n = (1 \cdot 29\sigma)^2 = (1 \cdot 29 \times 10)^2 = 166 \cdot 4, \text{ say } 167$$

Another 137 students must therefore be tested to ensure that the estimate of average I.Q. has the required accuracy.

Exercise 3.10

$$\bar{x} = 85 \qquad \sigma = 8 \qquad n = 36$$

1. Null hypothesis: $\mu = 90$.
2. Alternative hypothesis: $\mu < 90$.
3. Significance level: 0·05.
4. The appropriate standard error is:

$$\text{S.E.} = \frac{\sigma}{\sqrt{n}} = \frac{8}{6} = 1 \cdot 33$$

The alternative hypothesis indicates that a one-tail test is appropriate. As we are using a 0·05 significance level, this means that $\bar{x}$ must be at least 1·64 standard errors below $\mu = 90$.

5. $z = \dfrac{\bar{x} - \mu}{\text{S.E.}} = \dfrac{85 - 90}{1.33} = -3 \cdot 76$

This is large enough for the null hypothesis to be rejected. This sample establishes that the department in question is below average.

It should be noted that we have assumed the suspect department's standard deviation to be the same as the overall factory standard deviation. This may well not be so. We could test this assumption by means of the F-test described on page 106.

Exercise 3.11

$$\bar{x} = 38 \qquad \sigma = 4 \qquad n = 30$$

1. Null hypothesis: $\mu = 35$.
2. Alternative hypothesis: $\mu \neq 35$.

This assumes that we had no pre-knowledge of the way in which the new ingredient might affect reaction time.

3. Significance level: 0·01.

4. The alternative hypothesis indicates that we are interested in both tails of the sampling distribution. We are using a 0·01 significance level, so $\bar{x} = 38$ must be at least 2·58 standard errors away from $\mu = 35$ for us to be able to reject the null hypothesis.

The standard error is:

$$\text{S.E.} = \frac{\sigma}{\sqrt{n}} = \frac{4}{\sqrt{30}} = 0\cdot73$$

5. $z = \dfrac{\bar{x} - \mu}{\text{S.E.}} = \dfrac{38 - 35}{0\cdot73} = 4\cdot11$

We have thus established that the new ingredient does affect reaction time. The reaction takes longer with the new ingredient than it does without it.

It has been assumed in this test that *variability* of process time has not been affected. This assumption should be tested by comparing the standard deviation of the sample data with that of the established process. The appropriate test is described on page 106.

Exercise 3.12

$n_1 = 30$	$n_2 = 30$
$\bar{x}_1 = 35$	$\bar{x}_2 = 38$
$s_1 = 3$	$s_2 = 3$

1. Null hypothesis: $\mu_1 = \mu_2$.
2. Alternative hypothesis: $\mu_1 < \mu_2$.
3. Significance level: 0·01.
4. The standard error of $(\bar{x}_1 - \bar{x}_2)$ is:

$$\text{S.E.} = \sqrt{\left(\frac{\sigma_1^2}{n_1} + \frac{\sigma_2^2}{n_2} \right)}$$

Using s_1 and s_2 in place of σ_1 and σ_2:

$$\text{S.E.} = \sqrt{\left(\frac{9}{30} + \frac{9}{30} \right)} = 0\cdot77$$

A one-tail test is indicated by the alternative hypothesis. We are using a 0·01 significance level, so this means that the z value must be less than $-2 \cdot 33$ if the sample result is to fall in the rejection area.

5. $z = \dfrac{\bar{x}_1 - \bar{x}_2}{\text{S.E.}} = \dfrac{35 - 38}{0 \cdot 77} = -3 \cdot 90$

The test has thus established that the additive does increase m.p.g.

Exercise 3.13

$$
\begin{array}{ll}
n_1 = 40 & n_2 = 30 \\
\bar{x}_1 = 50 & \bar{x}_2 = 45 \\
s_1 = 10 & s_2 = 8
\end{array}
$$

1. Null hypothesis: $\mu_1 = \mu_2$.
2. Alternative hypothesis: $\mu_1 \neq \mu_2$.
3. Significance level: $0 \cdot 05$.
4. The standard error is:

$$
\text{S.E.} = \sqrt{\left(\frac{100}{40} + \frac{64}{30} \right)} = 2 \cdot 15
$$

This is a two-tail test at the $0 \cdot 05$ significance level. A z value in excess of $1 \cdot 96$ is thus required to enable the null hypothesis to be rejected.

5. $z = \dfrac{\bar{x}_1 - \bar{x}_2}{\text{S.E.}} = \dfrac{50 - 45}{2 \cdot 15} = 2 \cdot 33$

There is therefore a significant difference in appeal between the two recipes, the first being the more popular.

Exercise 4.1

We must first calculate the mean and standard deviation of the sample data. Using formulae (A.1) and (A.3) from Appendix A:

$$
\bar{x} = \frac{\sum x}{n} = \frac{196}{12} = 16 \cdot 33
$$

$$
s = \sqrt{\left(\frac{\sum x^2}{n-1} - \frac{(\sum x)^2}{n(n-1)} \right)}
$$

$$
= \sqrt{\left(\frac{3226}{11} - \frac{38\,416}{132} \right)} = \sqrt{2 \cdot 242} = 1 \cdot 5
$$

(a) $\bar{x} = 16\cdot33$ $s = 1\cdot5$ $n = 12$

With 95% confidence:

$$\mu \text{ lies between } \bar{x} \pm t_{\cdot025} \frac{s}{\sqrt{n}}$$

The value of $t_{\cdot025}$ with $(n-1) = 11$ d.f. is $2\cdot201$.

$$\mu \text{ lies between } 16\cdot33 \pm \frac{2\cdot201 \times 1\cdot5}{\sqrt{12}}$$

$$= 16\cdot33 \pm 0\cdot95$$

(b) To be 99% certain that the resulting estimate is not more than 0·5 away from the true value:

$$t_{\cdot005} \frac{s}{\sqrt{n}} = 0\cdot5$$

$$n = 4(t_{\cdot005}s)^2$$

The $t_{\cdot005}$ value with 11 d.f. $= 3\cdot106$, therefore:

$$n = 4(3\cdot106 \times 1\cdot5)^2$$
$$= 87$$

A further 75 timings are thus required.

Exercise 4.2

The sample mean and standard deviation are:

$$\bar{x} = \frac{49\cdot6}{8} = 6\cdot2$$

$$s = \sqrt{\left(\frac{307\cdot8}{7} - \frac{2460\cdot16}{56}\right)} = 0\cdot2$$

1. Null hypothesis: $\mu = 6\cdot4$.
2. Alternative hypothesis: $\mu < 6\cdot4$.
3. Significance level: 0·05.
4. The standard error is:

$$\text{S.E.} = \frac{s}{\sqrt{n}} = \frac{0\cdot2}{\sqrt{8}} = 0\cdot07$$

This is a one-tail test at the 0·05 significance level. The sample $\bar{x} = 6\cdot2$ must therefore be more than $t_{\cdot05}$ standard errors below $\mu = 6\cdot4$ to enable the null hypothesis to be rejected.

The appropriate value of $t_{.05}$ with 7 d.f. is found from Table III to be 1·895.

5. $t = \dfrac{\bar{x} - \mu}{\text{S.E}} \quad \dfrac{6\cdot2 - 6\cdot4}{0\cdot07} = -2\cdot86$

This sample therefore establishes that average process time has been reduced.

Exercise 4.3

$$
\begin{array}{ll}
n_1 = 8 & n_2 = 8 \\
\bar{x}_1 = 40 & \bar{x}_2 = 45 \\
s_1 = 4 & s_2 = 4\cdot8
\end{array}
$$

1. Null hypothesis: $\mu_1 = \mu_2$.
2. Alternative hypothesis: $\mu_1 \neq \mu_2$.
3. Significance level: 0·01.
4. To calculate the appropriate standard error, we must first pool the sample variances by using formula (4.4):

$$s = \sqrt{\frac{(7 \times 16) + (7 \times 23\cdot04)}{14}}$$

$$= 4\cdot42$$

The standard error is now obtained from formula (4.5):

$$\text{S.E.} = 4\cdot42\sqrt{(\tfrac{1}{8} + \tfrac{1}{8})}$$
$$= 2\cdot21$$

The alternative hypothesis indicates that a two-tail test is appropriate. Because we are using a significance level of 0·01, therefore, a t value in excess of the $t_{.005}$ value is required for the null hypothesis to be rejected. The value of $t_{.005}$ with $(n_1 + n_2 - 2) = 14$ d.f. is 2·977.

5. $t = \dfrac{\bar{x}_1 - \bar{x}_2}{\text{S.E.}} = \dfrac{40 - 45}{2\cdot21} = -2\cdot26$

We are not able to reject the null hypothesis. These data do not establish a difference between the two varieties, at the 0·01 significance level.

Exercise 4.4

$$
\begin{array}{ll}
n_1 = 8 & n_2 = 10 \\
s_1 = 6\cdot4 & s_2 = 3\cdot0
\end{array}
$$

Note that the sample with the larger variance has been numbered 1.

1. Null hypothesis: $\sigma_1^2 = \sigma_2^2$.
2. Alternative hypothesis: $\sigma_1^2 \neq \sigma_2^2$.
3. Significance level: 0·05.
4. The alternative hypothesis indicates that a two-tail test is appropriate. The critical value of F is thus the $F_{.025}$ value, with 7 d.f. for the numerator and 9 for the denominator. This is found from Table IV to be 4·20.
5. $F = \dfrac{s_1^2}{s_2^2} = \dfrac{40·96}{9·0} = 4·55$

We may therefore conclude that there is a difference between the two dyes. The one with the smaller sample variance produces the most consistent results.

Exercise 4.5

This situation is rather different from the previous exercise in that one of the variances is known exactly. In such a case, the F-test assumes that variance estimate to be based on ∞ (infinite) d.f.

1. Null hypothesis: $\sigma_1^2 = \sigma_2^2$.
where $\sigma_1^2 =$ variance before modification,
$\quad\quad \sigma_2^2 =$ variance after modification.
2. Alternative hypothesis: $\sigma_1^2 > \sigma_2^2$.
3. Significance level: 0·05.
4. A one-tail test is indicated by the alternative hypothesis. The critical value of F is therefore the $F_{.05}$ value with ∞ d.f. for the numerator and 20 d.f. for the denominator. This is 1·84.
5. $F = \dfrac{(1·5)^2}{(1·0)^2} = 2·25$

We therefore conclude that the modification has reduced the variability in the thickness of the washers.

Exercise 4.6

$$n_1 = 16 \quad\quad\quad n_2 = 9$$
$$\bar{x}_1 = 7 \quad\quad\quad \bar{x}_2 = 10$$
$$s_1 = 1·2 \quad\quad\quad s_2 = 0·5$$

(a) $F = \dfrac{(1 \cdot 2)^2}{(0 \cdot 5)^2} = 5 \cdot 76$

The $F_{\cdot 01}$ value, with 15 d.f. for the numerator and 8 for the denominator, is $5 \cdot 52$. The synthetic fibre is therefore significantly more consistent in its strength than the animal fibre, at the $0 \cdot 01$ significance level.

(b) The fact that s_1 and s_2 have been shown by the F-test to differ significantly makes a t-test of the sample means invalid.

The best that can be done in such circumstances is to calculate confidence limits for each of the sample means separately. If the two confidence bands do not overlap, we may reasonably claim that there is a difference between the means of the populations from which the samples come.

The 95% confidence limits are:

μ_1 lies between $\bar{x}_1 \pm t_{\cdot 025} \dfrac{s_1}{\sqrt{n_1}}$ ($t_{\cdot 025}$ with 15 d.f.)

$$= 7 \pm \frac{2 \cdot 131 \times 1 \cdot 2}{4}$$

$= 7 \pm 0 \cdot 64$, or between $6 \cdot 36$ and $7 \cdot 64$

μ_2 lies between $\bar{x}_2 \pm t_{\cdot 025} \dfrac{s_2}{\sqrt{n_2}}$ ($t_{\cdot 025}$ with 8 d.f.)

$$= 10 \pm \frac{2 \cdot 306 \times 0 \cdot 5}{3}$$

$= 10 \pm 0 \cdot 38$, or between $9 \cdot 62$ and $10 \cdot 38$

The upper limit for μ_1 is $7 \cdot 64$ and the lower limit for μ_2 is $9 \cdot 62$. We may therefore reasonably conclude that there is a difference in average breaking strength of the two yarns.

Exercise 4.7

In the solution to Exercise 2.14, the following results were calculated:

Number of goals (x)	Expected frequency	Observed frequency
0	29·4	32
1	53·0	52
2	47·7	44
3	28·6	29
4	12·9	13
5	4·6	6
6	1·4	2
7	0·4	0

If goals occur at random, the number of teams scoring x goals will follow the Poisson distribution. The expected frequencies in the above table have been calculated assuming this to be so.

To test this assumption, therefore, we calculate:

$$\chi^2 = \frac{(32-29·4)^2}{29·4} + \frac{(52-53·0)^2}{53·0} + \frac{(44-47·7)^2}{47·7} +$$

$$\frac{(29-28·6)^2}{28·6} + \frac{(13-12·9)^2}{12·9} + \frac{(8-6·4)^2}{6·4}$$

$$= 0·230 + 0·019 + 0·287 + 0·006 + 0·001 + 0·400$$
$$= 0·943$$

In accordance with the rule that no expected class frequency shall be less than 5, the last 3 classes have been amalgamated.

We only have 6 classes in the computation of χ^2, and 1 parameter (the mean) has been estimated from the data in order to calculate the expected frequencies. The degrees of freedom for χ^2 are therefore $(6-1-1)=4$. The $\chi^2_{·05}$ value, with 4 d.f., is 9·488.

The data are therefore quite consistent with the assumption that goals occur at random.

Exercise 4.8

We must first calculate the expected class frequencies, assuming the distribution to be normal. To do this, the mean and standard deviation are required (see Appendix A, pages 149–50, for an explanation of the terms used in the table below).

Weight	f	u	uf	u^2f
7·80–7·89	4	−3	−12	36
7·90–7·99	12	−2	−24	48
8·00–8·09	30	−1	−30	30
$A \rightarrow$ 8·10–8·19	36	0	0	0
8·20–8·29	15	1	15	15
8·30–8·39	3	2	6	12
	$\sum f = 100$		$\sum uf = -45$	$141 = \sum u^2f$

$$\bar{x} = A + C\left(\frac{\sum uf}{\sum f}\right)$$

$$= 8\cdot145 + 0\cdot1\left(\frac{-45}{100}\right) = 8\cdot10$$

$$s = C\sqrt{\frac{\sum u^2f}{\sum f} - \left(\frac{\sum uf}{\sum f}\right)^2} = 0\cdot1\sqrt{\frac{141}{100} - \left(\frac{-45}{100}\right)^2}$$

$$= 0\cdot1\sqrt{1\cdot41 - 0\cdot2025} = 0\cdot110$$

We now use $\bar{x}$ and s as estimates of μ and σ to calculate the expected class frequencies.

We must remember that the data in our sample are rounded to 2 decimal places. This means that the first class in the distribution covers the true range 7·795 to 7·895, the second class 7·895 to 7·995 and so on. These are known as the **class boundaries**.

The calculation may conveniently be set out in tabular form. The first two columns give the classes into which the sample data have been divided, and the class boundaries. The class boundaries are always midway between the upper and lower limits of consecutive classes.

The third column gives the z value for each class boundary, and the fourth column the corresponding area from Table II.

Successive subtraction of these areas gives the class proportions, or probabilities. These are shown in column 5. Note that the areas for the fourth class are *added* because the mean occurs in that class (see Example 2.6).

Finally, the expected frequencies in column 6 are found by

multiplying the class probabilities by 100 (sample size). To make comparison easier, the observed frequencies are shown in the last column.

Class limits	Class boundaries	z	Probability	Class probability	Expected frequency	Observed frequency
	7·795	− 2·77	0·4972			
7·80–7·89				0·0286	2·86	4
	7·895	− 1·86	0·4686			
7·90–7·99				0·1397	13·97	12
	7·995	− 0·95	0·3289			
8·00–8·09				0·3129	31·29	30
	8·095	− 0·04	0·0160			
8·10–8·19				0·3211	32·11	36
	8·195	+ 0·86	0·3051			
8·20–8·29				0·1565	15·65	15
	8·295	+ 1·77	0·4616			
8·30–8·39				0·0347	3·47	3
	8·395	+ 2·68	0·4963			

To calculate χ^2, we must combine the first two classes and the last two to make all class frequencies greater than 5. We then find:

$$\chi^2 = \frac{(16 - 16\cdot83)^2}{16\cdot83} + \frac{(30 - 31\cdot29)^2}{31\cdot29} + \frac{(36 - 32\cdot11)^2}{32\cdot11} + \frac{(18 - 19\cdot12)^2}{19\cdot12}$$

$$= 0\cdot041 + 0\cdot053 + 0\cdot471 + 0\cdot066$$
$$= 0\cdot631$$

We have only 4 classes in the computation of χ^2, and 2 parameters were estimated from the data and used to calculate the expected frequencies. The d.f. for χ^2 is therefore $(4 - 1 - 2) = 1$ d.f. The $\chi^2_{\cdot05}$ value, with 1 d.f., is 3·841. The calculated value is less than this, so the data are consistent with having come from a normal distribution.

Exercise 4.9

The expected frequencies are shown in brackets underneath the observed frequencies in the following table.

	1	2	3	ROW TOTALS
Undamaged	30 (38·3)	40 (30·7)	45 (46)	115
Slight damage	50 (41·7)	30 (33·3)	45 (50)	125
Completely smashed	20 (20)	10 (16·0)	30 (24)	60
COLUMN TOTALS	100	80	120	300

$$\chi^2 = \frac{(8·3)^2}{38·3} + \frac{(9·3)^2}{30·7} + \frac{(1)^2}{46} + \frac{(8·3)^2}{41·7} + \frac{(3·3)^2}{33·3} + \frac{(5)^2}{50} + \frac{(0)^2}{20} + \frac{(6)^2}{16} + \frac{(6)^2}{24}$$

$$= 1·799 + 2·817 + 0·022 + 1·652 + 0·327 + 0·500 + 0 + 2·250 + 1·500$$

$$= 10·867$$

This value of χ^2 is based on $(r-1)(c-1) = 2 \times 2 = 4$ d.f. The $\chi^2_{·05}$ value, with 4 d.f., is 9·488, which is less than the calculated value. These data therefore establish that there are significant differences between the materials.

Exercise 4.10

The $\chi^2_{·01}$ value, with 3 d.f., is 11·345. This is still lower than the calculated value of 18·52. The result is therefore significant at the 0·01 level.

Exercise 4.11

	Town A	*Town B*	*Town C*	TOTALS
Users	320 (328·1)	360 (364·5)	450 (437·4)	1130
Non-users	130 (121·9)	140 (135·5)	150 (162·6)	420
TOTALS	450	500	600	1550

The revised expected frequencies are shown in brackets in the above table.

$$\chi^2 = \frac{(8·1)^2}{328·1} + \frac{(4·5)^2}{364·5} + \frac{(12·6)^2}{437·4} + \frac{(8·1)^2}{121·9} + \frac{(4·5)^2}{135·5} + \frac{(12·6)^2}{162·6}$$

$$= 0·200 + 0·056 + 0·363 + 0·538 + 0·149 + 0·976$$

$$= 2·282$$

The $\chi^2_{.05}$ value, with $(3-1)(2-1)=2$ d.f., is 5·991. We cannot therefore claim that the percentage of users differs in Towns A, B and C.

Exercise 4.12

	Pack 1	Pack 2	Pack 3	Pack 4	TOTALS
Buyers	38 (45)	55 (45)	45 (45)	42 (45)	180
Non-buyers	162 (155)	145 (155)	155 (155)	158 (155)	620
TOTALS	200	200	200	200	800

$$\chi^2 = \frac{7^2 + 10^2 + 0^2 + 3^2}{45} + \frac{7^2 + 10^2 + 0^2 + 3^2}{155}$$

$$= 3·511 + 1·019$$
$$= 4·530$$

$\chi^2_{.05}$ with 3 d.f. $= 7·815$. These data do not therefore establish any significant difference in sales appeal between the 4 packs.

Exercise 4.13

	Town 1	Town 2	Town 3	Town 4	TOTALS
Conservative	125 (140)	150 (140)	130 (140)	155 (140)	560
Labour	120 (103·75)	100 (103·75)	100 (103·75)	95 (103·75)	415
Liberal	35 (41·25)	40 (41·25)	55 (41·25)	35 (41·25)	165
Uncommitted	20 (15)	10 (15)	15 (15)	15 (15)	60
TOTALS	300	300	300	300	1200

$$\chi^2 = \frac{15^2 + 10^2 + 10^2 + 15^2}{140} + \frac{(16·25)^2 + (3·75)^2 + (3·75)^2 + (8·75)^2}{103·75} +$$
$$\frac{(6·25)^2 + (1·25)^2 + (13·75)^2 + (6·25)^2}{41·25} + \frac{5^2 + 5^2 + 0^2 + 0^2}{15}$$

$$= 4·643 + 3·554 + 6·515 + 3·333$$
$$= 18·045$$

The $\chi^2_{.05}$ value, with $(4-1)(4-1)=9$ d.f., is $16\cdot919$. These data therefore indicate that there are differences between the 4 towns in their political affiliations.

Exercise 5.1

	Index of industrial production (x)	Electricity used (y)
1961	113·9	122·4
1962	115·1	134·7
1963	119·0	145·8
1964	128·2	153·6
1965	131·9	165·1
1966	133·4	171·0
1967	133·3	176·9

To simplify the calculations, we will code the data by subtracting 110 from the x values and 120 from the y values, calling these coded variables X and Y.

$x-110=X$	3·9	5·1	9·0	18·2	21·9	23·4	23·3
$y-120=Y$	2·4	14·7	25·8	33·6	45·1	51·0	56·9

$\sum X = 104\cdot8$ $\therefore \bar{X} = 14\cdot97$ $\sum X^2 = 2023\cdot52$ $\sum XY = 4434\cdot91$

$\sum Y = 229\cdot5$ $\therefore \bar{Y} = 32\cdot78$ $\sum Y^2 = 9889\cdot07$

$$C_{XX} = \sum X^2 - \frac{(\sum X)^2}{n} \qquad = 2023\cdot52 - \frac{10\,983\cdot04}{7} = 454\cdot51$$

$$C_{XY} = \sum XY - \frac{(\sum X)(\sum Y)}{n} = 4434\cdot91 - \frac{24\,051\cdot60}{7} = 998\cdot97$$

$$C_{YY} = \sum Y^2 - \frac{(\sum Y)^2}{n} \qquad = 9889\cdot07 - \frac{52\,670\cdot25}{7} = 2364\cdot75$$

$$r = \frac{C_{XY}}{\sqrt{(C_{XX} \cdot C_{YY})}} = \frac{998\cdot97}{\sqrt{(454\cdot51 \times 2364\cdot75)}} = \frac{998\cdot97}{1036\cdot73} = 0\cdot963$$

Thus there is high degree of correlation between the two variables. From Table VI, the $r_{.05}$ value, with $(7-2)=5$ d.f., is $0\cdot7545$.

$$b = \frac{C_{XY}}{C_{XX}} = \frac{998\cdot97}{454\cdot51} = 2\cdot20$$

The regression equation, in terms of X and Y, is:

$$Y - \overline{Y} = b(X - \overline{X})$$
$$Y - 32 \cdot 78 = 2 \cdot 20 \ (X - 14 \cdot 97)$$
$$Y = -0 \cdot 15 + 2 \cdot 20 X$$

Putting $Y = y - 120$ and $X = x - 110$ to remove the effect of the coding:

$$y - 120 = -0 \cdot 15 + 2 \cdot 20 \ (x - 110)$$
$$y = 2 \cdot 20 x - 122 \cdot 15$$

This equation may now be used to predict electricity requirements, provided that a reliable estimate of the Index of Industrial Production is available. Therein lies the snag.

It is not much use knowing that the variable of interest is highly correlated with another variable unless the latter is easy to predict reliably. One way round this difficulty is to try to find as a predictor a variable the value of which will be known in advance. Where this can be done, there is said to be a **lagged** relationship between the variables. Such a relationship exists between rainfall and crop yield, for instance, in the example discussed at the beginning of Chapter 5.

Exercise 5.2

Each new book printed leads to an increase in quire stock. We are therefore looking for the connection between quire stock and *total* number of new books printed:

Total books to date (x)	18	38	61	87	102	135	153	172	190	213	239	264
Quire stock (y)	217	249	265	269	273	341	356	397	378	391	413	450

These data are plotted in the scatter diagram of Figure S.6, from which it may be seen that a straight line will describe the relationship reasonably well (page 208).

We will code the data by subtracting 100 from the x values and 300 from the y values:

$x - 100 = X$	-82	-62	-39	-13	2	35	53	72	90	113	139	164
$y - 300 = Y$	-83	-51	-35	-31	-27	41	56	97	78	91	113	150

$$\sum X = 472 \qquad \therefore \ \overline{X} = 39 \cdot 33 \qquad \sum X^2 = 88 \ 566 \qquad \sum XY = 80 \ 679$$
$$\sum Y = 399 \qquad \therefore \ \overline{Y} = 33 \cdot 25 \qquad \sum Y^2 = 76 \ 265$$

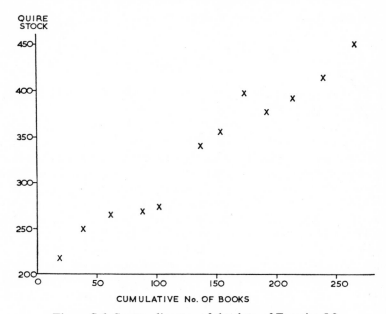

Figure S.6. Scatter diagram of the data of Exercise 5.2

$$C_{XX} = \sum X^2 - \frac{(\sum X)^2}{n} \qquad = 88\ 566 - \frac{222\ 784}{12} = 70\ 000{\cdot}7$$

$$C_{XY} = \sum XY - \frac{(\sum X)(\sum Y)}{n} = 80\ 679 - \frac{188\ 328}{12} = 64\ 985{\cdot}0$$

$$C_{YY} = \sum Y^2 - \frac{(\sum Y)^2}{n} \qquad = 76\ 265 - \frac{159\ 201}{12} = 62\ 998{\cdot}2$$

$$r = \frac{C_{XY}}{\sqrt{(C_{XX} \cdot C_{YY})}} = \frac{64\ 985{\cdot}0}{264{\cdot}6 \times 251{\cdot}0} = 0{\cdot}978$$

$$b = \frac{C_{XY}}{C_{XX}} \qquad = \frac{64\ 985{\cdot}0}{70\ 000{\cdot}7} \qquad = 0{\cdot}93$$

The regression equation, in terms of X and Y, is:

$$Y - \overline{Y} = b(X - \overline{X})$$
$$Y - 33{\cdot}25 = 0{\cdot}93(X - 39{\cdot}33)$$
$$Y = -3{\cdot}33 + 0{\cdot}93X$$

Putting $X = x - 100$ and $Y = y - 300$:

$$y - 300 = -3 \cdot 33 + 0 \cdot 93(x - 100)$$
$$y = 203 \cdot 67 + 0 \cdot 93x$$

The correlation coefficient of 0·978 confirms that a straight line represents the data very well.

The current total of books is 264. If 24 new ones a month are to be printed, the total in a year's time will be: $264 + (12 \times 24) = 552$. Putting $x = 552$ in the regression equation gives the required estimate of quire stock:

$$y = 203 \cdot 67 + (0 \cdot 93 \times 552) = 717$$

The residual standard deviation is:

$$\text{Residual S.D.} = \sqrt{\frac{C_{YY} - bC_{XY}}{n - 2}}$$

$$= \sqrt{\frac{62\,998 \cdot 2 - (0 \cdot 93 \times 64\,985 \cdot 0)}{10}}$$

$$= 16$$

If the linear relationship continues to hold, we may therefore reasonably expect our estimate of 717 to be within about 40 or 50 of the true figure.

Exercise 5.3

Electricity (y)	Index (x_1)	Income (x_2)
122·4	113·9	19·1
134·7	115·1	20·5
145·8	119·0	21·8
153·6	128·2	23·4
165·1	131·9	25·0
171·0	133·4	26·4
176·9	133·3	27·4

We will first code the data as follows:

$y - 120\ (Y)$	$x_1 - 110\ (X_1)$	$x_2 - 20\ (X_2)$
2·4	3·9	−0·9
14·7	5·1	0·5
25·8	9·0	1·8
33·6	18·2	3·4
45·1	21·9	5·0
51·0	23·4	6·4
56·9	23·3	7·4

$\sum X_1 = 104\cdot8 \quad \therefore \bar{X}_1 = 14\cdot97 \quad \sum X_1^2 = 2023\cdot52 \quad \sum X_1 Y = 4434\cdot91$

$\sum X_2 = 23\cdot6 \quad \therefore \bar{X}_2 = 3\cdot37 \quad \sum X_2^2 = 136\cdot58 \quad \sum X_2 Y = 1138\cdot83$

$\sum Y = 229\cdot5 \quad \therefore \bar{Y} = 32\cdot78 \quad \sum Y^2 = 9889\cdot07 \quad \sum X_1 X_2 = 508\cdot80$

$$CX_1 Y = 4434\cdot91 - \frac{(104\cdot8 \times 229\cdot5)}{7} = 998\cdot97$$

$$CX_2 Y = 1138\cdot83 - \frac{(23\cdot6 \times 229\cdot5)}{7} = 365\cdot09$$

$$CX_1 X_1 = 2023\cdot52 - \frac{(104\cdot8)^2}{7} = 454\cdot51$$

$$CX_2 X_2 = 136\cdot58 - \frac{(23\cdot6)^2}{7} = 57\cdot01$$

$$CX_1 X_2 = 508\cdot80 - \frac{(104\cdot8 \times 23\cdot6)}{7} = 155\cdot47$$

$$CYY = 9889\cdot07 - \frac{(229\cdot5)^2}{7} = 2364\cdot75$$

Substituting into the pair of equations (5.8):

$$998\cdot97 = 454\cdot51 b_1 + 155\cdot47 b_2$$
$$365\cdot09 = 155\cdot47 b_1 + 57\cdot01 b_2$$

Solving these equations gives:

$$b_1 = 0\cdot11$$
$$b_2 = 6\cdot10$$

The multiple regression equation, in terms of Y, X_1 and X_2 is:

$$Y - \bar{Y} = b_1(X_1 - \bar{X}_1) + b_2(X_2 - \bar{X}_2)$$
$$Y - 32 \cdot 78 = 0 \cdot 11(X_1 - 14 \cdot 97) + 6 \cdot 10(X_2 - 3 \cdot 37)$$
$$Y = 10 \cdot 58 + 0 \cdot 11 X_1 + 6 \cdot 10 X_2$$

We now remove the effect of the coding:

$$y - 120 = 10 \cdot 58 + 0 \cdot 11(x_1 - 110) + 6 \cdot 10(x_2 - 20)$$
$$y = -3 \cdot 52 + 0 \cdot 11 x_1 + 6 \cdot 10 x_2$$

Partial correlation coefficients

We must first calculate the simple coefficients:

$$r_{y1} = \frac{CX_1Y}{\sqrt{(CX_1X_1 \cdot CYY)}} = \frac{998 \cdot 97}{\sqrt{(454 \cdot 51 \times 2364 \cdot 75)}} = 0 \cdot 963$$

$$r_{y2} = \frac{CX_2Y}{\sqrt{(CX_2X_2 \cdot CYY)}} = \frac{365 \cdot 09}{\sqrt{(57 \cdot 01 \times 2364 \cdot 75)}} = 0 \cdot 994$$

$$r_{12} = \frac{CX_1X_2}{\sqrt{(CX_1X_1 \cdot CX_2X_2)}} = \frac{155 \cdot 47}{\sqrt{(454 \cdot 51 \times 57 \cdot 01)}} = 0 \cdot 965$$

The partial coefficients may now be calculated:

$$r_{y1.2} = \frac{r_{y1} - r_{y2}r_{12}}{\sqrt{\{(1 - r_{y2}^2)(1 - r_{12}^2)\}}} = \frac{0 \cdot 963 - 0 \cdot 959}{\sqrt{(0 \cdot 012 \times 0 \cdot 069)}} = 0 \cdot 14$$

$$r_{y2.1} = \frac{r_{y2} - r_{y1}r_{12}}{\sqrt{\{(1 - r_{y1}^2)(1 - r_{12}^2)\}}} = \frac{0 \cdot 994 - 0 \cdot 929}{\sqrt{(0 \cdot 0726 \times 0 \cdot 069)}} = 0 \cdot 92$$

The first of these, $r_{y1.2}$, tells us that having included x_2 (Income) in the equation there is nothing to be gained by also including x_1. Although the simple coefficient r_{y1} is high, the partial coefficient $r_{y1.2}$ is very low. This is because the two factors Income and Index are themselves highly correlated. This correlation is measured by r_{12}.

However, the coefficient $r_{y2.1}$ is quite high. This tells us that, having included x_1 in the equation, there is still value in including x_2. In other words, although the use of x_2 makes the use of x_1 unnecessary, the converse is not true.

Accordingly, as our predictor, we would use the simple linear equation connecting y with x_2. For this equation:

$$b = \frac{CX_2 Y}{CX_2 X_2} = \frac{365 \cdot 09}{57 \cdot 01} = 6 \cdot 40$$

$$Y - 32 \cdot 78 = 6 \cdot 40(X_2 - 3 \cdot 37)$$
$$Y = 11 \cdot 21 + 6 \cdot 40 Y_2$$
$$y - 120 = 11 \cdot 21 + 6 \cdot 40(x_2 - 20)$$
$$y = 3 \cdot 21 + 6 \cdot 40 x_2$$

Residual standard deviation

The residual standard deviation of the multiple regression equation, including both x variables, is:

$$\sqrt{\frac{CYY - b_1 CX_1 Y - b_2 CX_2 Y}{n - 3}}$$

$$\sqrt{\frac{2364 \cdot 75 - 109 \cdot 89 - 2227 \cdot 05}{4}}$$

$$= 2 \cdot 64$$

It is interesting to compare this with the residual standard deviation for the linear equation containing only x_2:

$$\sqrt{\frac{CYY - bCX_2 Y}{n - 2}}$$

$$= \sqrt{\frac{2364 \cdot 75 - 2336 \cdot 58}{5}}$$

$$= 2 \cdot 37$$

This is in fact slightly smaller than 2·64, but not significantly so. The simple equation is thus just as good a predictor as the more complicated one.

Exercise A.1

$$\bar{x} = \frac{\sum x}{n} = \frac{100}{10} = 10$$

$$s = \sqrt{\frac{\sum (x - \bar{x})^2}{n - 1}} = \sqrt{\frac{40}{9}} = 2 \cdot 11$$

Exercise A.2

Journey time	f	u	uf	u^2f
17	6	-3	-18	54
18	8	-2	-16	32
19	9	-1	-9	9
$A\rightarrow20$	12	0	0	0
21	9	1	9	9
22	4	2	8	16
23	2	3	6	18
	$\sum f = 50$		$\sum uf = -20$	$138 = \sum u^2f$

$$\bar{x} = A + C\left(\frac{\sum uf}{\sum f}\right) = 20 + 1\left(\frac{-20}{50}\right) = 19\cdot6$$

$$s = C\sqrt{\frac{\sum u^2f}{\sum f} - \left(\frac{\sum uf}{\sum f}\right)^2} = 1\sqrt{\frac{138}{50} - \left(\frac{-20}{50}\right)^2}$$

$$= \sqrt{(2\cdot76 - 0\cdot16)} = 1\cdot61$$

Exercise A.3

Exact method:

$$\bar{x} = \frac{\sum x}{n} = \frac{648}{40} = 16\cdot2$$

$$s = \sqrt{\left(\frac{\sum x^2}{n-1} - \frac{(\sum x)^2}{n(n-1)}\right)} = \sqrt{\left(\frac{10\,798}{39} - \frac{419\,904}{1560}\right)}$$

$$= \sqrt{(276\cdot871 - 269\cdot169)} = 2\cdot78$$

Grouped frequency method:

Time	f	u	uf	u^2f
10–11	1	-3	-3	9
12–13	5	-2	-10	20
14–15	10	-1	-10	10
$A{\rightarrow}16$–17	14	0	0	0
18–19	6	1	6	6
20–21	2	2	4	8
22–23	2	3	6	18
	$\sum f = 40$		$\sum uf = -7$	$71 = \sum u^2f$

$$\bar{x} = A + C\left(\frac{\sum uf}{\sum f}\right) = 16{\cdot}5 + 2\left(\frac{-7}{40}\right) = 16{\cdot}15$$

$$s = C\sqrt{\frac{\sum u^2f}{\sum f} - \left(\frac{\sum uf}{\sum f}\right)^2} = 2\sqrt{\frac{71}{40} - \left(\frac{-7}{40}\right)^2}$$

$$= 2\sqrt{(1{\cdot}775 - 0{\cdot}031)} = 2{\cdot}64$$

Exercise A.4

Weight	f	u	uf	u^2f
7·70–7·74	1	− 5	− 5	25
7·75–7·79	1	− 4	− 4	16
7·80–7·84	3	− 3	− 9	27
7·85–7·89	3	− 2	− 6	12
7·90–7·94	11	− 1	− 11	11
$A \rightarrow$ 7·95–7·99	13	0	0	0
8·00–8·04	8	1	8	8
8·05–8·09	6	2	12	24
8·10–8·14	3	3	9	27
8·15–8·19	1	4	4	16
	$\sum f = 50$		$\sum uf = -2$	$166 = \sum u^2f$

$$\bar{x} = A + C\left(\frac{\sum uf}{\sum f}\right) = 7{\cdot}970 + 0{\cdot}05\left(\frac{-2}{50}\right) = 7{\cdot}968$$

$$s = C\sqrt{\frac{\sum u^2f}{\sum f} - \left(\frac{\sum uf}{\sum f}\right)^2} = 0{\cdot}05\sqrt{\frac{166}{50} - \left(\frac{-2}{50}\right)^2}$$

$$= 0{\cdot}05\sqrt{(3{\cdot}3200 - 0{\cdot}0016)} = 0{\cdot}091$$

An exact calculation gives:

$$\bar{x} = \frac{\sum x}{n} = \frac{398{\cdot}41}{50} = 7{\cdot}968$$

$$s = \sqrt{\left(\frac{\sum x^2}{n-1} - \frac{(\sum x)^2}{n(n-1)}\right)} = \sqrt{\left(\frac{3175{\cdot}011}{49} - \frac{158\,730{\cdot}528}{2450}\right)}$$

$$= \sqrt{(64{\cdot}7961 - 64{\cdot}7880)} = 0{\cdot}090$$

Appendix C

C.1. The number of accidents per week will follow the Poisson distribution with $m = 3.0$.

(*a*) P(more than 6) = P(7) + P(8) + ...
$$= 0.0216 + 0.0081 + ...$$
$$= 0.0335$$

(*b*) P(0) = 0.0498
∴ assuming 50 weeks per year, there will be an average of $50 \times 0.0498 = 2.5$ weeks per year free of accidents.

C.2. (*a*) Using the grouped distribution method of Appendix A:

Class	Class mid-point	f	u	uf	u^2f
1·5–1·9		3	−3	−9	27
2·0–2·4		5	−2	−10	20
2·5–2·9		10	−1	−10	10
$A \rightarrow$ 3·0–3·4	3·2	15	0	0	0
3·5–3·9		8	1	8	8
4·0–4·4		7	2	14	28
4·5–4·9		2	3	6	18
		$\Sigma f = 50$		$\Sigma uf = -1$	$\Sigma u^2f = 111$

$$\bar{x} = A + C\left(\frac{\Sigma uf}{\Sigma f}\right) = 3.2 + 0.5\left(\frac{-1}{50}\right) = 3.19$$

$$s = C\sqrt{\frac{\Sigma u^2f}{\Sigma f} - \left(\frac{\Sigma uf}{\Sigma f}\right)^2} = 0.5\sqrt{\frac{111}{50} - \left(\frac{-1}{50}\right)^2} = 0.75$$

An exact calculation gives:

$$\Sigma x = 159.4 \qquad \Sigma x^2 = 537.12 \qquad n = 50$$
$$\bar{x} = \frac{\Sigma x}{n} = \frac{159.4}{50} = 3.19$$

$$s = \sqrt{\left(\frac{\Sigma x^2}{n-1} - \frac{(\Sigma x)^2}{n(n-1)}\right)} = \sqrt{\left(\frac{537.12}{49} - \frac{(159.4)^2}{2450}\right)} = 0.77$$

(b) It is required that 10% of the crop shall be in the largest grade, so the first step is to find the z value corresponding to the point in the normal curve which has 10% of the distribution above it. To use Table II, we require the area between this point and the mean. This is 0·4. From Table II we find that the z value corresponding to 0·3997 (the nearest we can get to 0·4 without interpolation) is 1·28.

The lower boundary of grade A is therefore 1·28 standard deviations above the mean. Using the estimates of the mean and standard deviation calculated above, we have:

$$3·19 + (1·28 \times 0·77) = 4·18$$

Similarly, the lower boundary of grade B will be the point with 30% of the distribution above it. From Table II, the area nearest to 0·2 has a z value of 0·52. The lower boundary of grade B is therefore 0·52 standard deviations above the mean:

$$3·19 + (0·52 \times 0·77) = 3·59$$

The grade C and D lower boundaries have 40% and 20% respectively of the distribution below them. The z values corresponding to these points are 0·25 and 0·84.

The grade C lower boundary is thus:

$$3·19 - (0·25 \times 0·77) = 3·00$$

and the grade D lower boundary is:

$$3·19 - (0·84 \times 0·77) = 2·54$$

C.3.   The probability that the call gets through the first section is 0·95. The probability of getting through the first *and* the second is 0·95 × 0·95 and so on.

The probability of getting through all 5 sections is thus $(0·95)^5 = 0·7738$.

C.4.   Each journey may be regarded as a sample of 5 trials at the event 'encounter a red light'. As the 5 trials are independent of each other and the probability of encountering a red light is constant, the actual number of red lights encountered will vary in accordance with the binomial distribution with $n = 5$ and $p = 0·4$.

(a) $P(0) = (0.6)^5 = 0.0778$
(b) P(more than 3) = P(4) + P(5)

$$P(4) = \frac{5!}{4!1!} (0.4)^4 (0.6) = 0.0768$$

$P(5) = (0.4)^5 = 0.0102$
∴ P(more than 3) = 0.0768 + 0.0102 = 0.0870

C.5. If customers arrive at random, the time between arrivals will vary in accordance with the negative exponential distribution. To calculate the theoretical frequencies to compare with the observed frequencies, the parameter m (average number of arrivals per minute) is required.

We first find the average time between arrivals $1/m$ from the observed data. The data are in summarised form, so an exact calculation is not possible. However, assuming that the average time for each class lies at the centre of the class;

$$\frac{1}{m} = \frac{(54 \times 0.25) + (23 \times 0.75) + (13 \times 1.25) + (5 \times 1.75) +}{100}$$

$$\frac{+ (3 \times 2.25) + (2 \times 2.75)}{100}$$

$$\frac{1}{m} = 0.68$$

$$\therefore \quad m = \frac{1}{0.68} = 1.47$$

The theoretical frequencies may now be calculated as follows, using Table IX to get e^{-mt}.

Time between arrivals	t	mt	e^{-mt}	Class probability	Theoretical frequency	Observed frequency
	0.0	0	1.0000			
0.0–0.5				0.5229	52.59	54
	0.5	0.74	0.4771			
0.5–1.0				0.2472	24.72	23
	1.0	1.47	0.2299			
1.0–1.5				0.1191	11.91	13
	1.5	2.20	0.1108			
1.5–2.0				0.0579	5.79	5

Time between arrivals	t	mt	e^{-mt}	Class probability	Theoretical frequency	Observed frequency
	2·0	2·94	0·0529			
2·0–2·5				0·0275	2·75	3
	2·5	3·68	0·0252			
>2·5				0·0252	2·52	2
	∞	∞	0			

There is a close correspondence between the theoretical and observed frequencies, confirming that the assumption of random arrivals is reasonable.

C.6. (a) $n = 20$, $p = 0.05$

$$P(2) = \frac{20!}{2!18!} (0.05)^2 (0.95)^{18} = 0.1887$$

(b) $m = np = 1.0$

From Table I, $P(2) = 0.1839$

This is very close to the exact binomial calculation, although n is relatively small.

C.7. (a) Assuming that the components follow the normal distribution with $\mu = 4.00$ in and $\sigma = 0.01$ in, the proportion between 3·98 in and 4·01 in may be found by using Table II. The area is similar to that in Figure 2.7(c).

$$z_1 = \frac{3.98 - 4.00}{0.01} = -2.0$$

∴ area between 3·98 and 4·00 in = 0·4772

$$z_2 = \frac{4.01 - 4.00}{0.01} = 1.0$$

∴ area between 4·00 and 4·01 in = 0·3413
∴ area between 3·98 and 4·01 in = 0·8185 or 81·85%.

(b) $z = \frac{4.02 - 4.00}{0.01} = 2.0$

∴ area between 4·02 and 4·00 in = 0·4772
∴ proportion above 4·02 in = 0·0228

Similarly, the proportion below 3·98 in is also 0·0228, giving a total of $2 \times 0.0228 = 0.0456$, or 4·56% outside the required tolerance limits.

If the average drifted to 4·01 in, the proportion above 4·02 in would be 0·1587 and the proportion below 3·98 in would be 0·0013. The total outside the tolerance limits would therefore be 16%.

C.8.   If demand is random, the number of boxes asked for per week will conform to the Poisson distribution with an average $(m) = 5$.

Using Table I:

(a) $P(5) = 0.1755$

(b) He will run out of stock whenever 9 or more boxes are demanded.

$$P(9 \text{ or more}) = P(9) + P(10) + \dots$$
$$= 0.0680$$

This corresponds to approximately $50 \times 0.0680 = 3.4$ times per year on average.

He will, however, only be unable to satisfy demand if 10 or more boxes are required which will occur approximately $50 \times 0.0317 = 1.6$ times per year on average.

C.9.   (a) P(both alive) = P(man alive) × P(wife alive)

$$= \frac{3}{5} \times \frac{2}{3} = \frac{2}{5}$$

(b) P(only man alive) = P(man alive) × P(wife dead)

$$= \frac{3}{5} \times \frac{1}{3} = \frac{1}{5}$$

(c) P(only wife alive) = P(man dead) × P(wife alive)

$$= \frac{2}{5} \times \frac{2}{3} = \frac{4}{15}$$

(d) There are three possibilities here; both alive, man only alive or wife only alive. These have been worked out separately above, therefore by the addition rule;

$$P(\text{at least one alive}) = \frac{2}{5} + \frac{1}{5} + \frac{4}{15} = \frac{13}{15}$$

Alternatively:

P(at least one alive) = 1 − P(both dead)

$$= 1 - \left(\frac{2}{5} \times \frac{1}{3}\right) = \frac{13}{15}$$

C.10. (a) The probabilities that the individual components will work efficiently for at least 1000 hours may be found from e^{-mt} with $t = 1000$ and m successively equal to $\dfrac{1}{1000}, \dfrac{1}{2000}, \dfrac{1}{3000}$ as follows:

Component number	Average life $(1/m)$	m	P(> 1000 hours) $= e^{-1000m}$
1	1000	$\dfrac{1}{1000}$	$e^{-1\cdot0} = 0\cdot3679$
2	2000	$\dfrac{1}{2000}$	$e^{-0\cdot5} = 0\cdot6065$
3	3000	$\dfrac{1}{3000}$	$e^{-0\cdot33} = 0\cdot7189$

In order for the whole sub-assembly to work, all three components must function efficiently. By the multiplication rule, the probability of this is $0\cdot3679 \times 0\cdot6065 \times 0\cdot7189 = 0\cdot16$.

(b) The calculations are identical to those above with $t = 2000$.

Component number	P(> 2000 h) $= e^{-2000m}$
1	$e^{-2\cdot0} = 0\cdot1353$
2	$e^{-1\cdot0} = 0\cdot3679$
3	$e^{-0\cdot67} = 0\cdot5117$

$0\cdot1353 \times 0\cdot3679 \times 0\cdot5117 = 0\cdot025$

(c)

Component number	P(> 3000 h) $= e^{-3000m}$
1	$e^{-3\cdot0} = 0\cdot0498$
2	$e^{-1\cdot5} = 0\cdot2231$
3	$e^{-1\cdot0} = 0\cdot3679$

$0\cdot0498 \times 0\cdot2231 \times 0\cdot3679 = 0\cdot004$

C.11. The number of sets requested each evening will follow the binomial distribution with $n = 10$ and $p = 0.5$.

(a) P(6 or more) = P(6) + P(7) + P(8) + P(9) + P(10)

$$P(6) = \frac{10!}{6!4!}(0.5)^6(0.5)^4 = 0.2051$$

$$P(7) = \frac{10!}{7!3!}(0.5)^{10} = 0.1172$$

$$P(8) = \frac{10!}{8!2!}(0.5)^{10} = 0.0440$$

$$P(9) = \frac{10!}{9!1!}(0.5)^{10} = 0.0097$$

$$P(10) = (0.5)^{10} = 0.0010$$

$\therefore$ P(6 or more) = 0.3770

(b) We need to find the average number of sets in use per day, from which the daily depreciation cost of the 5 sets purchased must be recovered.

The probability distribution of sets in use is:

P(0 sets in use) = 0.0010
P(1 set in use) = 0.0097
P(2 sets in use) = 0.0440
P(3 sets in use) = 0.1172
P(4 sets in use) = 0.2051
P(5 sets in use) = 0.6230

Notice that this follows the binomial distribution up to 4 sets in use, but as only 5 sets are available, the probability of 5 sets in use is the probability that 5 *or more* are requested.

The average number of sets in use per day may now be calculated as:

$$(0 \times 0.0010) + (1 \times 0.0097) + (2 \times 0.0440) + (3 \times 0.1172)$$
$$+ (4 \times 0.2051) + (5 \times 0.6230) = 4.38$$

Daily depreciation cost of 5 sets $= \dfrac{£50}{1000} \times 5 = £0.25$

$\therefore$ break-even rental per set $= \dfrac{£0.25}{4.38} = 5.7$p, say 6p.

C.12.   The distribution of clearance (cylinder – plunger) will have parameters:

$$\mu = \mu_1 - \mu_2 = 100 - 98\cdot4 = 1\cdot6$$
$$\sigma = \sqrt{\sigma_1{}^2 + \sigma_2{}^2} = \sqrt{0\cdot25 + 0\cdot09} = 0\cdot58$$

where μ_1, μ_2 and σ_1, σ_2 are the means and standard deviations of the cylinders and plungers respectively.

(a) The plunger will not fit the cylinder if the clearance is negative (plunger bigger than cylinder). The appropriate section of the clearance distribution is therefore that to the left of zero.

$$z = \frac{0 - 1\cdot6}{0\cdot58} = -2\cdot76$$

The proportion between 0 and 1·6 is therefore 0·4971 (from Table II), giving a proportion of $0\cdot5000 - 0\cdot4971 = 0\cdot0029$ with negative clearance.

(b) $z = \dfrac{1\cdot5 - 1\cdot6}{0\cdot58} = -0\cdot17$

$\therefore$ proportion above $1\cdot5 = 0\cdot0675 + 0\cdot5000 = 0\cdot5675$

C.13.   If accidents occur at random, the number per day will follow the Poisson distribution.

From the observed data, the average number per day (m)

$$= \frac{(21 \times 0) + (18 \times 1) + (7 \times 2) + (3 \times 3) + (1 \times 4)}{50} = 0\cdot9$$

Using Table I, with $m = 0\cdot9$ the following results may be obtained:

No. of accidents	Probability	Theoretical frequency	Observed frequency
0	0·4066	20·33	21
1	0·3659	18·29	18
2	0·1647	8·23	7
3	0·0494	2·47	3
4	0·0111	0·55	1
5	0·0020	0·10	0

C.14.   (a) $P(0 \text{ hits}) = \dfrac{3}{4} \times \dfrac{3}{4} \times \dfrac{2}{3} \times \dfrac{2}{3} = \dfrac{1}{4}$

$\therefore$ P(at least one hit) $= 1 - \dfrac{1}{4} = \dfrac{3}{4}$

(b) P(0 hits) must be not more than 0·1.
If A fires twice and B fires n times, then

$$P(0 \text{ hits}) = \left(\frac{3}{4}\right)^2 \left(\frac{2}{3}\right)^n$$

We require the smallest value of n which will make this not more than 0·1.
The required value is $n = 5$.

C.15.   The number of defectives per sample will follow the binomial distribution with $n = 400$ and $p = 0.10$. However, n is large enough to use the normal approximation with

$$\mu = np = 40$$
$$\sigma = \sqrt{np(1-p)} = 6$$

(a) $z = \dfrac{30 \cdot 5 - 40}{6} = -1 \cdot 58$

$\therefore$ P(30 or less) $= 0 \cdot 5000 - 0 \cdot 4429 = 0 \cdot 0571$

(b) $z_1 = \dfrac{29 \cdot 5 - 40}{6} = -1 \cdot 75$

$z_2 = \dfrac{40 \cdot 5 - 40}{6} = 0 \cdot 08$

$\therefore$ P(between 30 and 40) $= 0 \cdot 4599 + 0 \cdot 0319 = 0 \cdot 4918$

C.16.   The probability of getting a correct answer purely by chance is 0·5. The number of correct answers to 10 questions will therefore follow the binomial distribution with $n = 10$ and $p = 0.5$.

$$P(5 \text{ or more correct}) = P(5) + P(6) + \ldots P(10)$$

$$P(5) = 0 \cdot 2460$$
$$P(6) = 0 \cdot 2051$$
$$P(7) = 0 \cdot 1172$$
$$P(8) = 0 \cdot 0440$$
$$P(9) = 0 \cdot 0097$$
$$P(10) = 0 \cdot 0010$$

$$\therefore \text{ P(5 or more correct)} = 0.623$$

Anyone who is completely ignorant about the subject matter of the test has therefore a much better than even chance of getting at least 50%!

If there are four choices of answer, the probability of getting each answer correct falls to 0·25.

A similar calculation to the above shows that the probability of 5 or more correct has now fallen dramatically to only 0·0781.

C.17. The number of individuals who suffer a reaction in a sample of 2000 will conform to the binomial distribution with $n = 2000$ and $p = 0.001$.

It is, however, much easier to use the Poisson approximation with $m = np = 2.0$. This is valid, since n is large and p is small.

Using Table I:

(a) P(more than 2) = P(3) + P(4) + . . .   = 0·3232
(b) P(3 or less) = P(0) + P(1) + P(2) + P(3) = 0·8571
(c) P(at least 1) = 1 – P(0)   = 0·8647
(d) P(just 1)   = 0·2707

C.18. Assuming that widget length is distributed normally with $\mu = 6.00$ in and $\sigma = 0.30$ in,

(a) All widgets less than 5·60 in are too short.

$$z = \frac{5.60 - 6.00}{0.30} = -1.33$$

∴ proportion too short $= 0.5000 - 0.4082 = 0.0918$

(b) All above 6·50 in are too long.

$$z = \frac{6.50 - 6.00}{0.30} = 1.67$$

∴ proportion too long $= 0.5000 - 0.4525 = 0.0475$

(c) Proportion satisfactory $= 0.4082 + 0.4525 = 0.8607$

C.19. (a) The number of ways in which the 26 cards held by opponents can be arranged between the two hands is

$$\frac{26!}{13!13!} = n$$

Of these 26 cards, 4 are trumps and 22 are non-trumps. The number of hands containing 2 trumps and 11 non-trumps will therefore be $\dfrac{4!}{2!2!} \times \dfrac{22!}{11!11!} = m$

Required probability $= \dfrac{m}{n} = 0 \cdot 407$

(b) n is the same as above, but now we require 3 trumps and 10 non-trumps in one hand.

The number of ways in which this can happen is

$$\dfrac{4!}{3!1!} \times \dfrac{22!}{10!12!} \times 2 = m$$

The factor 2 is necessary because there are two distinct sets of hands; one set in which Opponent A holds 3 trumps and an equivalent set in which Opponent B holds 3 trumps.

Required probability $= \dfrac{m}{n} = 0 \cdot 497$

The 3–1 trump break is thus more likely than 2–2, as all bridge players know from experience!

C.20. (a) $P(0 \text{ boys}) = \left(\dfrac{1}{2}\right)^4 = \dfrac{1}{16}$

$\therefore$ P(at least 1 boy) $= 1 - P(0 \text{ boys}) = \dfrac{15}{16}$

(b) P(at least 1 boy and 1 girl) $= 1 - P(0 \text{ boys}) - P(0 \text{ girls})$

$$= 1 - \dfrac{1}{16} - \dfrac{1}{16} = \dfrac{14}{16} = \dfrac{7}{8}$$

C.21. $\mu = 0 \cdot 502$ in $\qquad \sigma = 0 \cdot 005$ in

$$z = \dfrac{0 \cdot 508 - 0 \cdot 502}{0 \cdot 005} = 1 \cdot 20$$

$\therefore$ proportion above $0 \cdot 508 = 0 \cdot 5000 - 0 \cdot 3849 = 0 \cdot 1151$

Similarly, the proportion below $0 \cdot 496$ is also $0 \cdot 1151$

The total proportion defective is therefore $0 \cdot 2302$, or $23 \cdot 02\%$.

C.22. The correct distribution of the number of customers buying additional items will be the binomial with $n = 20$ and $p = 0 \cdot 4$. The normal approximation to this distribution will have $\mu = np = 8$ and $\sigma = \sqrt{np(1-p)} = 2 \cdot 19$

$$z_1 = \frac{10 \cdot 5 - 8}{2 \cdot 19} = 1 \cdot 14$$

$$z_2 = \frac{9 \cdot 5 - 8}{2 \cdot 19} = 0 \cdot 68$$

$$\therefore \ P(10) = 0 \cdot 3729 - 0 \cdot 2517 = 0 \cdot 1212$$

This compares reasonably well with the much more tedious exact calculation:

$$P(10) = \frac{20!}{10!10!} \ (0 \cdot 4)^{10} \ (0 \cdot 6)^{10} = 0 \cdot 1172$$

C.23. 25 tins will cover an average of $25 \times 1000 = 25\,000$ sq. ft with a standard deviation of $\sqrt{25 \times 400} = 100$ sq. ft.

$$z = \frac{24{,}850 - 25{,}000}{100} = -1 \cdot 50$$

The probability of having enough paint to cover 24 850 sq. ft is therefore $0 \cdot 5000 + 0 \cdot 4332 = 0 \cdot 9332$.

C.24. The probability that any particular car does not have a faulty gearbox is $0 \cdot 99$. The probability of none in a sample of 50 will therefore be $(0 \cdot 99)^{50} = 0 \cdot 6050$.

C.25. $n = 2000 \quad \mu = 151$ lb $\quad \sigma = 15$ lb.

(a) $z_1 = \dfrac{120 - 151}{15} = -2 \cdot 07$

$$z_2 = \frac{150 - 151}{15} = -0 \cdot 07$$

$\therefore$ proportion between 120 lb and 150 lb $= 0 \cdot 4808 - 0 \cdot 0279$
$$= 0 \cdot 4529$$

$\therefore$ Expected number $= 2000 \times 0 \cdot 4529 = 905 \cdot 8$, say 906

(b) $z = \dfrac{185 - 151}{15} = 2 \cdot 27$

$\therefore$ proportion over 185 lb $= 0 \cdot 5000 - 0 \cdot 4884 = 0 \cdot 0116$

$\therefore$ Expected number $= 2000 \times 0 \cdot 0116 = 23 \cdot 2$, say 23

(c) $z = \dfrac{128 - 151}{15} = -1 \cdot 53$

$\therefore$ proportion less than 128 lb $= 0 \cdot 5000 - 0 \cdot 4370 = 0 \cdot 0630$

$\therefore$ Expected number $= 2000 \times 0 \cdot 0630 = 126$

Appendix D

D.1.   1. Null hypothesis: $\pi = 60\%$
        2. Alternative hypothesis: $\pi \neq 60\%$
        3. Significance level: 0·05
        4. Assuming the null hypothesis to be true, the appropriate sampling distribution will have a mean of 60 and a

standard error of $\sqrt{\dfrac{60 \times 40}{120}} = 4\cdot5$

The rejection area will be the extreme $2\frac{1}{2}\%$ in each tail of the distribution.

5. $z = \dfrac{P - \pi}{\text{S.E.}} = \dfrac{53\cdot3 - 60}{4.5} = -1\cdot49$

This does not reach the level required to reject the null hypothesis (1·96). The sample is therefore consistent with the manager's claim.

D.2.   (*a*) $n = 10$

$$\bar{x} = \frac{\sum x}{n} = \frac{£57\cdot5}{10} = £5\cdot75$$

$$s = \sqrt{\frac{\sum(x - \bar{x})^2}{n - 1}} = \sqrt{\frac{5\cdot4639}{9}} = £0\cdot78$$

For 95% confidence limits:

μ lies between $\bar{x} \pm t_{0\cdot025}\dfrac{s}{\sqrt{n}}$ ($t_{0\cdot025}$ with 9 d.f. = 2·262)

$$= 5\cdot75 \pm \frac{2\cdot262 \times 0\cdot78}{\sqrt{10}} = 5\cdot75 \pm 0\cdot56$$

or between £5.19 and £6.31.
For 99% confidence limits:

μ lies between $\bar{x} \pm t_{0\cdot005}\dfrac{s}{\sqrt{n}}$ ($t_{0\cdot005}$ with 9 d.f. = 3·250)

$$= 5\cdot75 \pm \frac{3\cdot250 \times 0\cdot78}{\sqrt{10}} = 5\cdot75 \pm 0\cdot80$$

or between £4.95 and £6.55.

(b) $n_1 = 7$ $n_2 = 10$

  $\bar{x}_1 = £4\cdot83$ $\bar{x}_2 = £5\cdot75$

  $s_1 = \sqrt{\dfrac{2\cdot342}{6}} = £0\cdot62$ $s_2 = £0\cdot78$

1. Null hypothesis: $\mu_1 = \mu_2$
2. Alternative hypothesis: $\mu_1 < \mu_2$
3. Significance level: 0·05
4. To calculate the appropriate standard error, we first must pool the sample variances. A prior F test is hardly necessary, as they are so similar:

$$s = \sqrt{\frac{(n_1 - 1)s_1^2 + (n_2 - 1)s_2^2}{n_1 + n_2 - 2}}$$

$$= \sqrt{\frac{(6 \times 0\cdot390) + (9 \times 0\cdot607)}{15}}$$

$$= 0\cdot72$$

$$\text{S.E.} = s\sqrt{\left(\frac{1}{n_1} + \frac{1}{n_2}\right)}$$

$$= 0\cdot72\sqrt{\left(\frac{1}{7} + \frac{1}{10}\right)}$$

$$= 0\cdot355$$

The alternative hypothesis indicates that a one-tail test is appropriate, therefore a t value in excess of $t_{0\cdot05}$ is required to enable the null hypothesis to be rejected. The value of $t_{0\cdot05}$ with 15 d.f. $= 1\cdot753$.

5. $t = \dfrac{\bar{x}_1 - \bar{x}_2}{\text{S.E.}} = \dfrac{4\cdot83 - 5\cdot75}{0\cdot355} = -2\cdot59$

This exceeds 1·753, thus we may reject the null hypothesis. We are justified in concluding, at the 5% significance level, that costs have risen.

D.3.

	Bankers	Industrialists	Farmers	Totals
Poor prospects	40 (36)	50 (60)	30 (24)	120
Average prospects	80 (78)	120 (130)	60 (52)	260
Good prospects	30 (36)	80 (60)	10 (24)	120
Totals	150	250	100	500

$$\chi^2 = \frac{4^2}{36} + \frac{10^2}{60} + \frac{6^2}{24} + \frac{2^2}{78} + \frac{10^2}{130} + \frac{8^2}{52} + \frac{6^2}{36} + \frac{20^2}{60} + \frac{14^2}{24}$$

$$= 21 \cdot 49$$

The $\chi^2_{0 \cdot 05}$ value, with $(3-1)(3-1) = 4$ d.f. is $9 \cdot 488$. These data therefore indicate that there are real differences of opinion about future prospects.

D.4. $n = 9$ $\bar{x} = 52$ $s = 2 \cdot 74$

   1. Null hypothesis: $\mu = 50$
   2. Alternative hypothesis: $\mu > 50$
   3. Significance level: $0 \cdot 05$

   4. S.E. $= \dfrac{s}{\sqrt{n}} = \dfrac{2 \cdot 74}{3} = 0 \cdot 91$

     $t_{0 \cdot 05}$ with 8 d.f. $= 1 \cdot 860$

   5. $t = \dfrac{\bar{x} - \mu}{\text{S.E.}} = \dfrac{52 - 50}{0 \cdot 91} = 2.20$

This is large enough to reject the null hypothesis. We may conclude that the new method has improved the production rate.

To calculate the sample size required to be 95% certain of an estimate which is not in error by more than 1 unit, we use the formula:

$$n = \left(\frac{t_{0 \cdot 025} s}{L} \right)^2$$

with
$$L = 1$$
$$s = 2.74$$
$$t_{0.025} \text{ with 8 d.f.} = 2.306$$
$$n = \left(\frac{2.306 \times 2.74}{1} \right)^2 = 40$$

A further 31 trials are therefore necessary.

D.5. 1. Null hypothesis: $\sigma_1{}^2 = \sigma_2{}^2$
where $\sigma_1{}^2$ = variance before modification
$\sigma_2{}^2$ = variance after modification
2. Alternative hypothesis: $\sigma_1{}^2 > \sigma_2{}^2$
3. Significance level: 0·05
4. The alternative hypothesis indicates that a one-tail test is appropriate. The critical value of F will therefore be $F_{0.05}$ with ∞ d.f. for the numerator and 19 d.f. for the denominator. This is 1·88.
5. $F = \dfrac{(2.8)^2}{(1.7)^2} = 2.71$

This exceeds 1·88, so we may conclude that the modification has successfully reduced variability.

D.6. $n = 9 \qquad \bar{x} = 510 \qquad s = 20.15$
1. Null hypothesis: $\mu = 500$
2. Alternative hypothesis: $\mu > 500$
3. Significance level: 0·05
4. The appropriate standard error $= \dfrac{20.15}{\sqrt{9}} = 6.72$

A one-tail test is required, therefore the critical value of t will be $t_{0.05}$ with 8 d.f. This is 1·860.
5. $t = \dfrac{\bar{x} - \mu}{\text{S.E.}} = \dfrac{510 - 500}{6.72} = 1.49$

We are therefore not able to claim at the 5% significance level that the allowance is inadequate.

D.7. $n = 600 \qquad P = 56.67\%$
1. Null hypothesis: $\pi = 50\%$
2. Alternative hypothesis: $\pi > 50\%$
3. Significance level: 0·05

4. S.E. $= \sqrt{\dfrac{\pi(100-\pi)}{n}} = \sqrt{\dfrac{50 \times 50}{600}} = 2 \cdot 04$

Critical value of z is $1 \cdot 64$.

5. $z = \dfrac{P - \pi}{\text{S.E.}} = \dfrac{6 \cdot 67}{2 \cdot 04} = 3 \cdot 27$

This is significant, therefore the data do indicate that a majority of shoppers are in favour of self-service.

D.8. $n_1 = 36$ $n_2 = 49$
$\bar{x}_1 = £1500$ $\bar{x}_2 = £1800$
$s_1 = £600$ $s_2 = £700$

1. Null hypothesis: $\mu_1 = \mu_2$
2. Alternative hypothesis: $\mu_1 \neq \mu_2$
3. Significance level: $0 \cdot 05$

4. S.E. $= \sqrt{\dfrac{s_1{}^2}{n_1} + \dfrac{s_2{}^2}{n_2}} = \sqrt{\dfrac{600^2}{36} + \dfrac{700^2}{49}} = 141 \cdot 4$

Critical value of $z = 1 \cdot 96$.

5. $z = \dfrac{\bar{x}_1 - \bar{x}_2}{\text{S.E.}} = \dfrac{300}{141 \cdot 4} = 2 \cdot 12$

There is a significant difference in average income between the two towns.

D.9.

	A	B	C	D	Totals
Good	65 (57)	112 (114)	85 (91)	80 (80)	342
Average	27 (33)	67 (66)	60 (53)	44 (46)	198
Poor	8 (10)	21 (20)	15 (16)	16 (14)	60
Totals	100	200	160	140	600

$$\chi^2 = \frac{8^2}{57} + \frac{2^2}{114} + \ldots + \frac{2^2}{14} = 4\cdot46$$

$\chi^2_{0\cdot05}$ with 6 d.f. $= 12\cdot592$

There are thus no significant differences in opinions between departments.

D.10. (a) $n = 400$ $P = 20\%$

$$\pi \text{ lies between } P \pm 2 \sqrt{\frac{P(100 - P)}{n}}$$

$$= 20 \pm 2 \sqrt{\frac{20 \times 80}{400}}$$

$$= 20\% \pm 4\%, \text{ or between } 16\% \text{ and } 24\%$$

(b) $n_1 = 400$ $n_2 = 500$
$P_1 = 20\%$ $P_2 = 14\%$

1. Null hypothesis: $\pi_1 = \pi_2 = \pi$
2. Alternative hypothesis: $\pi_1 \neq \pi_2$
3. Significance level: $0\cdot05$

4. The appropriate standard error

$$= \sqrt{\frac{\pi(100 - \pi)}{n_1} + \frac{\pi(100 - \pi)}{n_2}}$$

To obtain an estimate of the assumed common percentage π, we pool both samples, giving

$$\pi = \frac{80 + 70}{900} \times 100\% = 16\cdot67\%$$

$$\therefore \text{ S.E.} = \sqrt{\frac{16\cdot67 \times 83\cdot33}{400} + \frac{16\cdot67 \times 83\cdot33}{500}} = 2\cdot5$$

5. $z = \dfrac{P_1 - P_2}{\text{S.E.}} = \dfrac{6}{2\cdot5} = 2\cdot4$

This exceeds the critical value of $1\cdot96$, therefore we may conclude that there is a significant difference between the two suppliers.

The remaining solutions do not give the full logic of the significance tests in detail. When one becomes familiar with the reasoning, the test statistic may be evaluated immediately and interpreted for significance.

D.11.   We may first test the difference in variability of hardness for significance:

$$F = \frac{(15)^2}{(12)^2} = 1 \cdot 56$$

The $F_{0 \cdot 025}$ value with 29 d.f. for the numerator and 39 d.f. for the denominator is approximately $1 \cdot 94$. There is therefore no significant difference in the variability of hardness.

Testing the difference between the mean hardnesses for signficance:

$$\text{S.E.} = \sqrt{\frac{s_1^2}{n_1} + \frac{s_2^2}{n_2}} = \sqrt{\frac{(15)^2}{30} + \frac{(12)^2}{40}} = 3 \cdot 33$$

$$z = \frac{\bar{x}_1 - \bar{x}_2}{\text{S.E.}} = \frac{126 - 120}{3 \cdot 33} = 1 \cdot 80$$

This just fails to reach significance on a two-tail test at the $0 \cdot 05$ level.

D.12. $n = \dfrac{4P(100 - P)}{L^2}$ with $P = 15\%$
$\qquad\qquad\qquad\qquad\qquad\qquad\qquad L = \ 1\%$

$$n = \frac{4 \times 15 \times 85}{1} = 5100$$

D.13. $n_1 = 50 \qquad\qquad n_2 = 40$
$\qquad\ \ \bar{x}_1 = 24 \cdot 2 \qquad\ \ \bar{x}_2 = 22 \cdot 8$
$\qquad\ \ s_1 = 1 \cdot 5 \qquad\qquad s_2 = 2 \cdot 0$

$$\text{S.E.} = \sqrt{\frac{s_1^2}{n_1} + \frac{s_2^2}{n_2}} = \sqrt{\frac{(1 \cdot 5)^2}{50} + \frac{(2 \cdot 0)^2}{40}} = 0 \cdot 38$$

$$z = \frac{\bar{x}_1 - \bar{x}_2}{\text{S.E.}} = \frac{1 \cdot 4}{0 \cdot 38} = 3 \cdot 68$$

This is significant even at the $0 \cdot 01$ level.

D.14.

Score	Probability	Expected frequency (E)	Observed frequency (O)
2	$\frac{1}{36}$	10	8
3	$\frac{2}{36}$	20	18
4	$\frac{3}{36}$	30	28
5	$\frac{4}{36}$	40	41
6	$\frac{5}{36}$	50	50
7	$\frac{6}{36}$	60	68
8	$\frac{5}{36}$	50	54
9	$\frac{4}{36}$	40	39
10	$\frac{3}{36}$	30	28
11	$\frac{2}{36}$	20	19
12	$\frac{1}{36}$	10	7

$$\chi^2 = \frac{(8-10)^2}{10} + \frac{(18-20)^2}{20} + \ldots + \frac{(7-10)^2}{10} = 3\cdot24$$

$\chi^2_{0\cdot05}$ with 10 d.f. $= 18\cdot307$

The observed frequencies are thus consistent with the dice being unbiased.

D.15. $n_1 = 12$ $n_2 = 12$
$\bar{x}_1 = 152$ $\bar{x}_2 = 160$
$s_1 = 15$ $s_2 = 12$

$$F = \frac{(15)^2}{(12)^2} = 1\cdot56$$

This is not significant, so the two variances may be pooled:

$$s = \sqrt{\frac{(11 \times 225) + (11 \times 144)}{22}} = 13 \cdot 58$$

$$\text{Standard error} = s \sqrt{\frac{1}{n_1} + \frac{1}{n_2}} = 13 \cdot 58 \sqrt{\frac{1}{12} + \frac{1}{12}} = 5 \cdot 54$$

$$t = \frac{\bar{x}_1 - \bar{x}_2}{\text{S.E.}} = \frac{152 - 160}{5 \cdot 54} = -1 \cdot 44$$

The $t_{0 \cdot 025}$ value with 22 d.f. is $2 \cdot 074$, so there is no significant difference between the sales levels of the two bottles.

D.16.　$n = 500$
　　　　$P = 40\%$

$$\pi \text{ lies between } P \pm z \sqrt{\frac{P(100 - P)}{n}}$$

Using the approximate values of $z = 2$ and $z = 3$ for 95% and 99% confidence respectively:

$$95\% \text{ confidence limits are } 40\% \pm 2 \sqrt{\frac{40 \times 60}{500}}$$
$$= 40\% \pm 4 \cdot 38\%$$
$$99\% \text{ confidence limits are } 40\% \pm 6 \cdot 57\%$$

For the sample size necessary to get $\pm 2\%$ accuracy:

$$n = \frac{4P(100 - P)}{L^2} \text{ with } P = 40\% \text{ and } L = 2\%$$

$$n = \frac{4 \times 40 \times 60}{4} = 2400$$

An additional 1900 students would thus be required.

D.17.　$n = 30$
　　　　$\bar{x} = 19,000$
　　　　$s = 2,000$

To test the null hypothesis $\mu = 20\ 000$,

$$\text{S.E.} = \frac{s}{\sqrt{n}} = \frac{2000}{\sqrt{30}} = 365 \cdot 2$$

$$z = \frac{\bar{x} - \mu}{\text{S.E.}} = \frac{19\,000 - 20\,000}{365 \cdot 2} = -2 \cdot 74$$

On a one-tail test, this is significant at the 0·01 level. The manufacturer's claim is therefore unfounded, on the evidence of this sample.

D.18. $n_1 = 1000$ $n_2 = 800$
        $P_1 = 45\%$ $P_2 = 40\%$

$$\text{S.E.} = \sqrt{\frac{\pi(100 - \pi)}{n_1} + \frac{\pi(100 - \pi)}{n_2}}$$

where π is the assumed common percentage, under the null hypothesis of no difference in support.

The best available estimate of π is obtained by pooling the two samples:

$$\pi = \frac{450 + 320}{1800} \times 100\% = 42 \cdot 8\%$$

This gives S.E. $= \sqrt{\dfrac{42 \cdot 8 \times 57 \cdot 2}{1000} + \dfrac{42 \cdot 8 \times 57 \cdot 2}{800}} = 2 \cdot 35$

The hypothesis of no difference in support between the two constituencies may now be tested by:

$$z = \frac{P_1 - P_2}{\text{S.E.}} = \frac{5}{2 \cdot 35} = 2 \cdot 13$$

This is significant at the 0·05 level, indicating that there very probably is a difference in Conservative support.

D.19. $n_1 = 6$ $n_2 = 6$
        $\bar{x}_1 = 85 \cdot 3$ $\bar{x}_2 = 92 \cdot 7$
        $s_1 = 5 \cdot 8$ $s_2 = 6 \cdot 1$

The hypothesis of no difference in average yield may be tested by computing:

$$t = \frac{\bar{x}_1 - \bar{x}_2}{\text{S.E.}}$$

where the appropriate S.E. $= s \sqrt{\dfrac{1}{n_1} + \dfrac{1}{n_2}}$

s is the pooled standard deviation $= \sqrt{\dfrac{(5 \times 5\cdot8^2) + (5 \times 6\cdot1^2)}{10}} = 5\cdot95$

$$\text{S.E.} = 5.95\sqrt{\dfrac{1}{6} + \dfrac{1}{6}} = 3\cdot43$$

$$t = \dfrac{85\cdot3 - 92\cdot7}{3\cdot43} = -2\cdot16$$

The $t_{0\cdot025}$ value with 10 d.f. $= 2\cdot228$, so the result just fails to reach significance.

D.20. $n_1 = 1000$ $n_2 = 1000$
        $P_1 = 13\%$ $P_2 = 16\%$ estimate of common $\pi = 14\cdot5\%$

$$\text{S.E.} = \sqrt{\dfrac{14\cdot5 \times 85\cdot5 \times 2}{1000}} = 1\cdot57$$

$$z = \dfrac{P_1 - P_2}{\text{S.E.}} = \dfrac{-3}{1\cdot57} = -1\cdot91$$

On a one-tail test, this is significant at the 0·05 level. This supports the view that the second unit is inferior.

D.21

Number of Heads	Probability	Expected frequency	Observed frequency
0	$\dfrac{1}{8}$	30	22
1	$\dfrac{3}{8}$	90	105
2	$\dfrac{3}{8}$	90	92
3	$\dfrac{1}{8}$	30	21

$$\chi^2 = \dfrac{8^2}{30} + \dfrac{15^2}{90} + \dfrac{2^2}{90} + \dfrac{9^2}{30} = 7\cdot38$$

$$\chi^2_{0\cdot05} \text{ with 3 d.f.} = 7\cdot815$$

The hypothesis of no bias in the coins is therefore not rejected.

D.22. $n_1 = 6$ $n_2 = 5$
       $\bar{x}_1 = 4.73$ $\bar{x}_2 = 4 \cdot 94$
       $s_1 = 0 \cdot 163$ $s_2 = 0 \cdot 182$

$$F = \frac{(0 \cdot 182)^2}{(0 \cdot 163)^2} = 1 \cdot 25$$

which is not significant, so the sample variances may be pooled:

$$s = \sqrt{\frac{5(0 \cdot 163)^2 + 4(0 \cdot 182)^2}{9}} = 0 \cdot 172$$

$$\text{S.E.} = s \sqrt{\frac{1}{n_1} + \frac{1}{n_2}} = 0 \cdot 172 \sqrt{\frac{1}{6} + \frac{1}{5}}$$
$$= 0 \cdot 104$$

$$t = \frac{\bar{x}_1 - \bar{x}_2}{\text{S.E.}} = \frac{4 \cdot 73 - 4 \cdot 94}{0 \cdot 104} = -2 \cdot 02$$

$$t_{0 \cdot 05} \text{ with 9 d.f.} = 1 \cdot 833$$

There is thus a significant difference between the two samples and the second manufacturer's claim is upheld.

D.23. $n = 800$
       $P = 25\%$
       $\pi = 30\%$

$$\text{S.E.} = \sqrt{\frac{\pi(100 - \pi)}{n}} = \sqrt{\frac{30 \times 70}{800}} = 1 \cdot 62$$

$$z = \frac{P - \pi}{\text{S.E.}} = \frac{25 - 30}{1 \cdot 62} = -3 \cdot 09$$

This is significant, even at the 0·01 level, so the manufacturer's claim is almost certainly false.

D.24. $n_1 = 30$ $n_2 = 30$
       $\bar{x}_1 = £25$ $\bar{x}_2 = £30$
       $s_1 = £5$ $s_2 = £6$

$$\text{S.E.} = \sqrt{\frac{s_1^2}{n_1} + \frac{s_2^2}{n_2}} = \sqrt{\frac{25}{30} + \frac{36}{30}} = 1 \cdot 43$$

$$z = \frac{\bar{x}_1 - \bar{x}_2}{\text{S.E.}} = \frac{25 - 30}{1 \cdot 43} = -3 \cdot 5$$

This is highly significant. Assuming that other factors were constant over the two periods, therefore, the picture display does increase sales.

D.25.

	21–30	31–40	41–50	51–60	61–70	Totals
0	748 (770)	821 (818)	786 (773)	720 (721)	672 (665)	3747
1	74 (62)	60 (66)	51 (62)	66 (58)	50 (53)	301
2	31 (22)	25 (24)	22 (23)	16 (21)	15 (19)	109
>2	9 (8)	10 (8)	6 (7)	5 (7)	7 (7)	37
Totals	862	916	865	807	744	4194

$$\chi^2 = \frac{(22)^2}{770} + \frac{(3)^2}{818} + \ldots + \frac{(0)^2}{7} = 14 \cdot 16$$

$\chi^2_{0 \cdot 05}$ with $(4 - 1)(5 - 1) = 12$ d.f. is $21 \cdot 026$

There is thus no significant association between age and number of accidents.

STATISTICAL TABLES

					m					
x	0.1	0.2	0.3	0.4	0.5	0.6	0.7	0.8	0.9	1.0
0	.9048	.8187	.7408	.6703	.6065	.5488	.4966	.4493	.4066	.3679
1	.0905	.1637	.2222	.2681	.3033	.3293	.3476	.3595	.3659	.3679
2	.0045	.0164	.0333	.0536	.0758	.0988	.1217	.1438	.1647	.1839
3	.0002	.0011	.0033	.0072	.0126	.0198	.0284	.0383	.0494	.0613
4	.0000	.0001	.0002	.0007	.0016	.0030	.0050	.0077	.0111	.0153
5	.0000	.0000	.0000	.0001	.0002	.0004	.0007	.0012	.0020	.0031
6	.0000	.0000	.0000	.0000	.0000	.0000	.0001	.0002	.0003	.0005
7	.0000	.0000	.0000	.0000	.0000	.0000	.0000	.0000	.0000	.0001

					m					
x	1.1	1.2	1.3	1.4	1.5	1.6	1.7	1.8	1.9	2.0
0	.3329	.3012	.2725	.2466	.2231	.2019	.1827	.1653	.1496	.1353
1	.3662	.3614	.3543	.3452	.3347	.3230	.3106	.2975	.2842	.2707
2	.2014	.2169	.2303	.2417	.2510	.2584	.2640	.2678	.2700	.2707
3	.0738	.0867	.0998	.1128	.1255	.1378	.1496	.1607	.1710	.1804
4	.0203	.0260	.0324	.0395	.0471	.0551	.0636	.0723	.0812	.0902
5	.0045	.0062	.0084	.0111	.0141	.0176	.0216	.0260	.0309	.0361
6	.0008	.0012	.0018	.0026	.0035	.0047	.0061	.0078	.0098	.0120
7	.0001	.0002	.0003	.0005	.0008	.0011	.0015	.0020	.0027	.0034
8	.0000	.0000	.0001	.0001	.0001	.0002	.0003	.0005	.0006	.0009
9	.0000	.0000	.0000	.0000	.0000	.0000	.0001	.0001	.0001	.0002

					m					
x	2.1	2.2	2.3	2.4	2.5	2.6	2.7	2.8	2.9	3.0
0	.1225	.1108	.1003	.0907	.0821	.0743	.0672	.0608	.0550	.0498
1	.2572	.2438	.2306	.2177	.2052	.1931	.1815	.1703	.1596	.1494
2	.2700	.2681	.2652	.2613	.2565	.2510	.2450	.2384	.2314	.2240
3	.1890	.1966	.2033	.2090	.2138	.2176	.2205	.2225	.2237	.2240
4	.0992	.1082	.1169	.1254	.1336	.1414	.1488	.1557	.1622	.1680
5	.0417	.0476	.0538	.0602	.0668	.0735	.0804	.0872	.0940	.1008
6	.0146	.0174	.0206	.0241	.0278	.0319	.0362	.0407	.0455	.0504
7	.0044	.0055	.0068	.0083	.0099	.0118	.0139	.0163	.0188	.0216
8	.0011	.0015	.0019	.0025	.0031	.0038	.0047	.0057	.0068	.0081
9	.0003	.0004	.0005	.0007	.0009	.0011	.0014	.0018	.0022	.0027
10	.0001	.0001	.0001	.0002	.0002	.0003	.0004	.0005	.0006	.0008
11	.0000	.0000	.0000	.0000	.0000	.0001	.0001	.0001	.0002	.0002
12	.0000	.0000	.0000	.0000	.0000	.0000	.0000	.0000	.0000	.0001

					m					
x	3.1	3.2	3.3	3.4	3.5	3.6	3.7	3.8	3.9	4.0
0	.0450	.0408	.0369	.0334	.0302	.0273	.0247	.0224	.0202	.0183
1	.1397	.1304	.1217	.1135	.1057	.0984	.0915	.0850	.0789	.0733
2	.2165	.2087	.2008	.1929	.1850	.1771	.1692	.1615	.1539	.1465
3	.2237	.2226	.2209	.2186	.2158	.2125	.2087	.2046	.2001	.1954
4	.1734	.1781	.1823	.1858	.1888	.1912	.1931	.1944	.1951	.1954
5	.1075	.1140	.1203	.1264	.1322	.1377	.1429	.1477	.1522	.1563
6	.0555	.0608	.0662	.0716	.0771	.0826	.0881	.0936	.0989	.1042
7	.0246	.0278	.0312	.0348	.0385	.0425	.0466	.0508	.0551	.0595
8	.0095	.0111	.0129	.0148	.0169	.0191	.0215	.0241	.0269	.0298
9	.0033	.0040	.0047	.0056	.0066	.0076	.0089	.0102	.0116	.0132
10	.0010	.0013	.0016	.0019	.0023	.0028	.0033	.0039	.0045	.0053
11	.0003	.0004	.0005	.0006	.0007	.0009	.0011	.0013	.0016	.0019
12	.0001	.0001	.0001	.0002	.0002	.0003	.0003	.0004	.0005	.0006
13	.0000	.0000	.0000	.0000	.0001	.0001	.0001	.0001	.0002	.0002
14	.0000	.0000	.0000	.0000	.0000	.0000	.0000	.0000	.0000	.0001

Entries in the table give the probabilities that an event will occur x times when the average number of occurrences is m.

					m					
x	4.1	4.2	4.3	4.4	4.5	4.6	4.7	4.8	4.9	5.0
0	.0166	.0150	.0136	.0123	.0111	.0101	.0091	.0082	.0074	.0067
1	.0679	.0630	.0583	.0540	.0500	.0462	.0427	.0395	.0365	.0337
2	.1393	.1323	.1254	.1188	.1125	.1063	.1005	.0948	.0894	.0842
3	.1904	.1852	.1798	.1743	.1687	.1631	.1574	.1517	.1460	.1404
4	.1951	.1944	.1933	.1917	.1898	.1875	.1849	.1820	.1789	.1755
5	.1600	.1633	.1662	.1687	.1708	.1725	.1738	.1747	.1753	.1755
6	.1093	.1143	.1191	.1237	.1281	.1323	.1362	.1398	.1432	.1462
7	.0640	.0686	.0732	.0778	.0824	.0869	.0914	.0959	.1002	.1044
8	.0328	.0360	.0393	.0428	.0463	.0500	.0537	.0575	.0614	.0653
9	.0150	.0168	.0188	.0209	.0232	.0255	.0280	.0307	.0334	.0363
10	.0061	.0071	.0081	.0092	.0104	.0118	.0132	.0147	.0164	.0181
11	.0023	.0027	.0032	.0037	.0043	.0049	.0056	.0064	.0073	.0082
12	.0008	.0009	.0011	.0014	.0016	.0019	.0022	.0026	.0030	.0034
13	.0002	.0003	.0004	.0005	.0006	.0007	.0008	.0009	.0011	.0013
14	.0001	.0001	.0001	.0001	.0002	.0002	.0003	.0003	.0004	.0005
15	.0000	.0000	.0000	.0000	.0001	.0001	.0001	.0001	.0001	.0002

					m					
x	5.1	5.2	5.3	5.4	5.5	5.6	5.7	5.8	5.9	6.0
0	.0061	.0055	.0050	.0045	.0041	.0037	.0033	.0030	.0027	.0025
1	.0311	.0287	.0265	.0244	.0225	.0207	.0191	.0176	.0162	.0149
2	.0793	.0746	.0701	.0659	.0618	.0580	.0544	.0509	.0477	.0446
3	.1348	.1293	.1239	.1185	.1133	.1082	.1033	.0985	.0938	.0892
4	.1719	.1681	.1641	.1600	.1558	.1515	.1472	.1428	.1383	.1339
5	.1753	.1748	.1740	.1728	.1714	.1697	.1678	.1656	.1632	.1606
6	.1490	.1515	.1537	.1555	.1571	.1584	.1594	.1601	.1605	.1606
7	.1086	.1125	.1163	.1200	.1234	.1267	.1298	.1326	.1353	.1377
8	.0692	.0731	.0771	.0810	.0849	.0887	.0925	.0962	.0998	.1033
9	.0392	.0423	.0454	.0486	.0519	.0552	.0586	.0620	.0654	.0688
10	.0200	.0220	.0241	.0262	.0285	.0309	.0334	.0359	.0386	.0413
11	.0093	.0104	.0116	.0129	.0143	.0157	.0173	.0190	.0207	.0225
12	.0039	.0045	.0051	.0058	.0065	.0073	.0082	.0092	.0102	.0113
13	.0015	.0018	.0021	.0024	.0028	.0032	.0036	.0041	.0046	.0052
14	.0006	.0007	.0008	.0009	.0011	.0013	.0015	.0017	.0019	.0022
15	.0002	.0002	.0003	.0003	.0004	.0005	.0006	.0007	.0008	.0009
16	.0001	.0001	.0001	.0001	.0001	.0002	.0002	.0002	.0003	.0003
17	.0000	.0000	.0000	.0000	.0000	.0001	.0001	.0001	.0001	.0001

					m					
x	6.1	6.2	6.3	6.4	6.5	6.6	6.7	6 8	6.9	7.0
0	.0022	.0020	.0018	.0017	.0015	.0014	.0012	.0011	.0010	.0009
1	.0137	.0126	.0116	.0106	.0098	.0090	.0082	.0076	.0070	.0064
2	.0417	.0390	.0364	.0340	.0318	.0296	.0276	.0258	.0240	.0223
3	.0848	.0806	.0765	.0726	.0688	.0652	.0617	.0584	.0552	.0521
4	.1294	.1249	.1205	.1162	.1118	.1076	.1034	.0992	.0952	.0912
5	.1579	.1549	.1519	.1487	.1454	.1420	.1385	.1349	.1314	.1277
6	.1605	.1601	.1595	.1586	.1575	.1562	.1546	.1529	.1511	.1490
7	.1399	.1418	.1435	.1450	.1462	.1472	.1480	.1486	.1489	.1490
8	.1066	.1099	.1130	.1160	.1188	.1215	.1240	.1263	.1284	.1304
9	.0723	.0757	.0791	.0825	.0858	.0891	.0923	.0954	.0985	.1014
10	.0441	.0469	.0498	.0528	.0558	.0588	.0618	.0649	.0679	.0710
11	.0245	.0265	.0285	.0307	.0330	.0353	.0377	.0401	.0426	.0452
12	.0124	.0137	.0150	.0164	.0179	.0194	.0210	.0227	.0245	.0264
13	.0058	.0065	.0073	.0081	.0089	.0098	.0108	.0119	.0130	.0142
14	.0025	.0029	.0033	.0037	.0041	.0046	.0052	.0058	.0064	.0071
15	.0010	.0012	.0014	.0016	.0018	.0020	.0023	.0026	.0029	.0033
16	.0004	.0005	.0005	.0006	.0007	.0008	.0010	.0011	.0013	.0014
17	.0001	.0002	.0002	.0002	.0003	.0003	.0004	.0004	.0005	.0006
18	.0000	.0001	.0001	.0001	.0001	.0001	.0001	.0002	.0002	.0002
19	.0000	.0000	.0000	.0000	.0000	.0000	.0000	.0001	.0001	.0001

x	m 7.1	7.2	7.3	7.4	7.5	7.6	7.7	7.8	7.9	8.0
0	.0008	.0007	.0007	.0006	.0006	.0005	.0005	.0004	.0004	.0003
1	.0059	.0054	.0049	.0045	.0041	.0038	.0035	.0032	.0029	.0027
2	.0208	.0194	.0180	.0167	.0156	.0145	.0134	.0125	.0116	.0107
3	.0492	.0464	.0438	.0413	.0389	.0366	.0345	.0324	.0305	.0286
4	.0874	.0836	.0799	.0764	.0729	.0696	.0663	.0632	.0602	.0573
5	.1241	.1204	.1167	.1130	.1094	.1057	.1021	.0986	.0951	.0916
6	.1468	.1445	.1420	.1394	.1367	.1339	.1311	.1282	.1252	.1221
7	.1489	.1486	.1481	.1474	.1465	.1454	.1442	.1428	.1413	.1396
8	.1321	.1337	.1351	.1363	.1373	.1382	.1388	.1392	.1395	.1396
9	.1042	.1070	.1096	.1121	.1144	.1167	.1187	.1207	.1224	.1241
10	.0740	.0770	.0800	.0829	.0858	.0887	.0914	.0941	.0967	.0993
11	.0478	.0504	.0531	.0558	.0585	.0613	.0640	.0667	.0695	.0722
12	.0283	.0303	.0323	.0344	.0366	.0388	.0411	.0434	.0457	.0481
13	.0154	.0168	.0181	.0196	.0211	.0227	.0243	.0260	.0278	.0296
14	.0078	.0086	.0095	.0104	.0113	.0123	.0134	.0145	.0157	.0169
15	.0037	.0041	.0046	.0051	.0057	.0062	.0069	.0075	.0083	.0090
16	.0016	.0019	.0021	.0024	.0026	.0030	.0033	.0037	.0041	.0045
17	.0007	.0008	.0009	.0010	.0012	.0013	.0015	.0017	.0019	.0021
18	.0003	.0003	.0004	.0004	.0005	.0006	.0006	.0007	.0008	.0009
19	.0001	.0001	.0001	.0002	.0002	.0002	.0003	.0003	.0003	.0004
20	.0000	.0000	.0001	.0001	.0001	.0001	.0001	.0001	.0001	.0002
21	.0000	.0000	.0000	.0000	.0000	.0000	.0000	.0000	.0001	.0001

x	m 8.1	8.2	8.3	8.4	8.5	8.6	8.7	8.8	8.9	9.0
0	.0003	.0003	.0002	.0002	.0002	.0002	.0002	.0002	.0001	.0001
1	.0025	.0023	.0021	.0019	.0017	.0016	.0014	.0013	.0012	.0011
2	.0100	.0092	.0086	.0079	.0074	.0068	.0063	.0058	.0054	.0050
3	.0269	.0252	.0237	.0222	.0208	.0195	.0183	.0171	.0160	.0150
4	.0544	.0517	.0491	.0466	.0443	.0420	.0398	.0377	.0357	.0337
5	.0882	.0849	.0816	.0784	.0752	.0722	.0692	.0663	.0635	.0607
6	.1191	.1160	.1128	.1097	.1066	.1034	.1003	.0972	.0941	.0911
7	.1378	.1358	.1338	.1317	.1294	.1271	.1247	.1222	.1197	.1171
8	.1395	.1392	.1388	.1382	.1375	.1366	.1356	.1344	.1332	.1318
9	.1256	.1269	.1280	.1290	.1299	.1306	.1311	.1315	.1317	.1318
10	.1017	.1040	.1063	.1084	.1104	.1123	.1140	.1157	.1172	.1186
11	.0749	.0776	.0802	.0828	.0853	.0878	.0902	.0925	.0948	.0970
12	.0505	.0530	.0555	.0579	.0604	.0629	.0654	.0679	.0703	.0728
13	.0315	.0334	.0354	.0374	.0395	.0416	.0438	.0459	.0481	.0504
14	.0182	.0196	.0210	.0225	.0240	.0256	.0272	.0289	.0306	.0324
15	.0098	.0107	.0116	.0126	.0136	.0147	.0158	.0169	.0182	.0194
16	.0050	.0055	.0060	.0066	.0072	.0079	.0086	.0093	.0101	.0109
17	.0024	.0026	.0029	.0033	.0036	.0040	.0044	.0048	.0053	.0058
18	.0011	.0012	.0014	.0015	.0017	.0019	.0021	.0024	.0026	.0029
19	.0005	.0005	.0006	.0007	.0008	.0009	.0010	.0011	.0012	.0014
20	.0002	.0002	.0002	.0003	.0003	.0004	.0004	.0005	.0005	.0006
21	.0001	.0001	.0001	.0001	.0001	.0002	.0002	.0002	.0002	.0003
22	.0000	.0000	.0000	.0000	.0001	.0001	.0001	.0001	.0001	.0001

x	m 9.1	9.2	9.3	9.4	9.5	9.6	9.7	9.8	9.9	10
0	.0001	.0001	.0001	.0001	.0001	.0001	.0001	.0001	.0001	.0000
1	.0010	.0009	.0009	.0008	.0007	.0007	.0006	.0005	.0005	.0005
2	.0046	.0043	.0040	.0037	.0034	.0031	.0029	.0027	.0025	.0023
3	.0140	.0131	.0123	.0115	.0107	.0100	.0093	.0087	.0081	.0076
4	.0319	.0302	.0285	.0269	.0254	.0240	.0226	.0213	.0201	.0189
5	.0581	.0555	.0530	.0506	.0483	.0460	.0439	.0418	.0398	.0378
6	.0881	.0851	.0822	.0793	.0764	.0736	.0709	.0682	.0656	.0631
7	.1145	.1118	.1091	.1064	.1037	.1010	.0982	.0955	.0928	.0901
8	.1302	.1286	.1269	.1251	.1232	.1212	.1191	.1170	.1148	.1126
9	.1317	.1315	.1311	.1306	.1300	.1293	.1284	.1274	.1263	.1251

					m					
x	9.1	9.2	9.3	9.4	9.5	9.6	9.7	9.8	9.9	10
10	.1198	.1210	.1219	.1228	.1235	.1241	.1245	.1249	.1250	.1251
11	.0991	.1012	.1031	.1049	.1067	.1083	.1098	.1112	.1125	.1137
12	.0752	.0776	.0799	.0822	.0844	.0866	.0888	.0908	.0928	.0948
13	.0526	.0549	.0572	.0594	.0617	.0640	.0662	.0685	.0707	.0729
14	.0342	.0361	.0380	.0399	.0419	.0439	.0459	.0479	.0500	.0521
15	.0208	.0221	.0235	.0250	.0265	.0281	.0297	.0313	.0330	.0347
16	.0118	.0127	.0137	.0147	.0157	.0168	.0180	.0192	.0204	.0217
17	.0063	.0069	.0075	.0081	.0088	.0095	.0103	.0111	.0119	.0128
18	.0032	.0035	.0039	.0042	.0046	.0051	.0055	.0060	.0065	.0071
19	.0015	.0017	.0019	.0021	.0023	.0026	.0028	.0031	.0034	.0037
20	.0007	.0008	.0009	.0010	.0011	.0012	.0014	.0015	.0017	.0019
21	.0003	.0003	.0004	.0004	.0005	.0006	.0006	.0007	.0008	.0009
22	.0001	.0001	.0002	.0002	.0002	.0002	.0003	.0003	.0004	.0004
23	.0000	.0001	.0001	.0001	.0001	.0001	.0001	.0001	.0002	.0002
24	.0000	.0000	.0000	.0000	.0000	.0000	.0000	.0001	.0001	.0001

					m					
x	11	12	13	14	15	16	17	18	19	20
0	.0000	.0000	.0000	.0000	.0000	.0000	.0000	.0000	.0000	.0000
1	.0002	.0001	.0000	.0000	.0000	.0000	.0000	.0000	.0000	.0000
2	.0010	.0004	.0002	.0001	.0000	.0000	.0000	.0000	.0000	.0000
3	.0037	.0018	.0008	.0004	.0002	.0001	.0000	.0000	.0000	.0000
4	.0102	.0053	.0027	.0013	.0006	.0003	.0001	.0001	.0000	.0000
5	.0224	.0127	.0070	.0037	.0019	.0010	.0005	.0002	.0001	.0001
6	.0411	.0255	.0152	.0087	.0048	.0026	.0014	.0007	.0004	.0002
7	.0646	.0437	.0281	.0174	.0104	.0060	.0034	.0018	.0010	.0005
8	.0888	.0655	.0457	.0304	.0194	.0120	.0072	.0042	.0024	.0013
9	.1085	.0874	.0661	.0473	.0324	.0213	.0135	.0083	.0050	.0029
10	.1194	.1048	.0859	.0663	.0486	.0341	.0230	.0150	.0095	.0058
11	.1194	.1144	.1015	.0844	.0663	.0496	.0355	.0245	.0164	.0106
12	.1094	.1144	.1099	.0984	.0829	.0661	.0504	.0368	.0259	.0176
13	.0926	.1056	.1099	.1060	.0956	.0814	.0658	.0509	.0378	.0271
14	.0728	.0905	.1021	.1060	.1024	.0930	.0800	.0655	.0514	.0387
15	.0534	.0724	.0885	.0989	.1024	.0992	.0906	.0786	.0650	.0516
16	.0367	.0543	.0719	.0866	.0960	.0992	.0963	.0884	.0772	.0646
17	.0237	.0383	.0550	.0713	.0847	.0934	.0963	.0936	.0863	.0760
18	.0145	.0256	.0397	.0554	.0706	.0830	.0909	.0936	.0911	.0844
19	.0084	.0161	.0272	.0409	.0557	.0699	.0814	.0887	.0911	.0888
20	.0046	.0097	.0177	.0286	.0418	.0559	.0692	.0798	.0866	.0888
21	.0024	.0055	.0109	.0191	.0299	.0426	.0560	.0684	.0783	.0846
22	.0012	.0030	.0065	.0121	.0204	.0310	.0433	.0560	.0676	.0769
23	.0006	.0016	.0037	.0074	.0133	.0216	.0320	.0438	.0559	.0669
24	.0003	.0008	.0020	.0043	.0083	.0144	.0226	.0328	.0442	.0557
25	.0001	.0004	.0010	.0024	.0050	.0092	.0154	.0237	.0336	.0446
26	.0000	.0002	.0005	.0013	.0029	.0057	.0101	.0164	.0246	.0343
27	.0000	.0001	.0002	.0007	.0016	.0034	.0063	.0109	.0173	.0254
28	.0000	.0000	.0001	.0003	.0009	.0019	.0038	.0070	.0117	.0181
29	.0000	.0000	.0001	.0002	.0004	.0011	.0023	.0044	.0077	.0125
30	.0000	.0000	.0000	.0001	.0002	.0006	.0013	.0026	.0049	.0083
31	.0000	.0000	.0000	.0000	.0001	.0003	.0007	.0015	.0030	.0054
32	.0000	.0000	.0000	.0000	.0001	.0001	.0004	.0009	.0018	.0034
33	.0000	.0000	.0000	.0000	.0000	.0001	.0002	.0005	.0010	.0020
34	.0000	.0000	.0000	.0000	.0000	.0000	.0001	.0002	.0006	.0012
35	.0000	.0000	.0000	.0000	.0000	.0000	.0000	.0001	.0003	.0007
36	.0000	.0000	.0000	.0000	.0000	.0000	.0000	.0001	.0002	.0004
37	.0000	.0000	.0000	.0000	.0000	.0000	.0000	.0000	.0001	.0002
38	.0000	.0000	.0000	.0000	.0000	.0000	.0000	.0000	.0000	.0001
39	.0000	.0000	.0000	.0000	.0000	.0000	.0000	.0000	.0000	.0001

TABLE II NORMAL DISTRIBUTION

The table gives the area under the normal curve between the mean and a point z standard deviations above the mean.

z	.00	.01	.02	.03	.04	.05	.06	.07	.08	.09
0.0	.0000	.0040	.0080	.0120	.0160	.0199	.0239	.0279	.0319	.0359
0.1	.0398	.0438	.0478	.0517	.0557	.0596	.0636	.0675	.0714	.0753
0.2	.0793	.0832	.0871	.0910	.0948	.0987	.1026	.1064	.1103	.1141
0.3	.1179	.1217	.1255	.1293	.1331	.1368	.1406	.1443	.1480	.1517
0.4	.1554	.1591	.1628	.1664	.1700	.1736	.1772	.1808	.1844	.1879
0.5	.1915	.1950	.1985	.2019	.2054	.2088	.2123	.2157	.2190	.2224
0.6	.2257	.2291	.2324	.2357	.2389	.2422	.2454	.2486	.2517	.2549
0.7	.2580	.2611	.2642	.2673	.2704	.2734	.2764	.2794	.2823	.2852
0.8	.2881	.2910	.2939	.2967	.2995	.3023	.3051	.3078	.3106	.3133
0.9	.3159	.3186	.3212	.3238	.3264	.3289	.3315	.3340	.3365	.3389
1.0	.3413	.3438	.3461	.3485	.3508	.3531	.3554	.3577	.3599	.3621
1.1	.3643	.3665	.3686	.3708	.3729	.3749	.3770	.3790	.3810	.3830
1.2	.3849	.3869	.3888	.3907	.3925	.3944	.3962	.3980	.3997	.4015
1.3	.4032	.4049	.4066	.4082	.4099	.4115	.4131	.4147	.4162	.4177
1.4	.4192	.4207	.4222	.4236	.4251	.4265	.4279	.4292	.4306	.4319
1.5	.4332	.4345	.4357	.4370	.4382	.4394	.4406	.4418	.4429	.4441
1.6	.4452	.4463	.4474	.4484	.4495	.4505	.4515	.4525	.4535	.4545
1.7	.4554	.4564	.4573	.4582	.4591	.4599	.4608	.4616	.4625	.4633
1.8	.4641	.4649	.4656	.4664	.4671	.4678	.4686	.4693	.4699	.4706
1.9	.4713	.4719	.4726	.4732	.4738	.4744	.4750	.4756	.4761	.4767
2.0	.4772	.4778	.4783	.4788	.4793	.4798	.4803	.4808	.4812	.4817
2.1	.4821	.4826	.4830	.4834	.4838	.4842	.4846	.4850	.4854	.4857
2.2	.4861	.4864	.4868	.4871	.4875	.4878	.4881	.4884	.4887	.4890
2.3	.4893	.4896	.4898	.4901	.4904	.4906	.4909	.4911	.4913	.4916
2.4	.4918	.4920	.4922	.4925	.4927	.4929	.4931	.4932	.4934	.4936
2.5	.4938	.4940	.4941	.4943	.4945	.4946	.4948	.4949	.4951	.4952
2.6	.4953	.4955	.4956	.4957	.4959	.4960	.4961	.4962	.4963	.4964
2.7	.4965	.4966	.4967	.4968	.4969	.4970	.4971	.4972	.4973	.4974
2.8	.4974	.4975	.4976	.4977	.4977	.4978	.4979	.4979	.4980	.4981
2.9	.4981	.4982	.4982	.4983	.4984	.4984	.4985	.4985	.4986	.4986
3.0	.4987	.4987	.4987	.4988	.4988	.4989	.4989	.4989	.4990	.4990

Reproduced from *Modern Business Statistics* by J. E. Freund and F. J. Williams (Pitman). After a table in J. Neyman, *First Course in Probability and Statistics* (Holt, Rinehart).

TABLE III   STUDENT-t DISTRIBUTION   247

The value of t_α given in the table has a probability α of being exceeded.

d.f.	$t_{.100}$	$t_{.050}$	$t_{.025}$	$t_{.010}$	$t_{.005}$	d.f.
1	3.078	6.314	12.706	31.821	63.657	1
2	1.886	2.920	4.303	6.965	9.925	2
3	1.638	2.353	3.182	4.541	5.841	3
4	1.533	2.132	2.776	3.747	4.604	4
5	1.476	2.015	2.571	3.365	4.032	5
6	1.440	1.943	2.447	3.143	3.707	6
7	1.415	1.895	2.365	2.998	3.499	7
8	1.397	1.860	2.306	2.896	3.355	8
9	1.383	1.833	2.262	2.821	3.250	9
10	1.372	1.812	2.228	2.764	3.169	10
11	1.363	1.796	2.201	2.718	3.106	11
12	1.356	1.782	2.179	2.681	3.055	12
13	1.350	1.771	2.160	2.650	3.012	13
14	1.345	1.761	2.145	2.624	2.977	14
15	1.341	1.753	2.131	2.602	2.947	15
16	1.337	1.746	2.120	2.583	2.921	16
17	1.333	1.740	2.110	2.567	2.898	17
18	1.330	1.734	2.101	2.552	2.878	18
19	1.328	1.729	2.093	2.539	2.861	19
20	1.325	1.725	2.086	2.528	2.845	20
21	1.323	1.721	2.080	2.518	2.831	21
22	1.321	1.717	2.074	2.508	2.819	22
23	1.319	1.714	2.069	2.500	2.807	23
24	1.318	1.711	2.064	2.492	2.797	24
25	1.316	1.708	2.060	2.485	2.787	25
26	1.315	1.706	2.056	2.479	2.779	26
27	1.314	1.703	2.052	2.473	2.771	27
28	1.313	1.701	2.048	2.467	2.763	28
29	1.311	1.699	2.045	2.462	2.756	29
inf.	1.282	1.645	1.960	2.326	2.576	inf.

$$F._{05}$$

ν_2 \ ν_1	1	2	3	4	5	6	7	8	9	10
1	161·4	199·5	215·7	224·6	230·2	234·0	236·8	238·9	240·5	241·9
2	18·51	19·00	19·16	19·25	19·30	19·33	19·35	19·37	19·38	19·40
3	10·13	9·55	9·28	9·12	9·01	8·94	8·89	8·85	8·81	8·79
4	7·71	6·94	6·59	6·39	6·26	6·16	6·09	6·04	6·00	5·96
5	6·61	5·79	5·41	5·19	5·05	4·95	4·88	4·82	4·77	4·74
6	5·99	5·14	4·76	4·53	4·39	4·28	4·21	4·15	4·10	4·06
7	5·59	4·74	4·35	4·12	3·97	3·87	3·79	3·73	3·68	3·64
8	5·32	4·46	4·07	3·84	3·69	3·58	3·50	3·44	3·39	3·35
9	5·12	4·26	3·86	3·63	3·48	3·37	3·29	3·23	3·18	3·14
10	4·96	4·10	3·71	3·48	3·33	3·22	3·14	3·07	3·02	2·98
11	4·84	3·98	3·59	3·36	3·20	3·09	3·01	2·95	2·90	2·85
12	4·75	3·89	3·49	3·26	3·11	3·00	2·91	2·85	2·80	2·75
13	4·67	3·81	3·41	3·18	3·03	2·92	2·83	2·77	2·71	2·67
14	4·60	3·74	3·34	3·11	2·96	2·85	2·76	2·70	2·65	2·60
15	4·54	3·68	3·29	3·06	2·90	2·79	2·71	2·64	2·59	2·54
16	4·49	3·63	3·24	3·01	2·85	2·74	2·66	2·59	2·54	2·49
17	4·45	3·59	3·20	2·96	2·81	2·70	2·61	2·55	2·49	2·45
18	4·41	3·55	3·16	2·93	2·77	2·66	2·58	2·51	2·46	2·41
19	4·38	3·52	3·13	2·90	2·74	2·63	2·54	2·48	2·42	2·38
20	4·35	3·49	3·10	2·87	2·71	2·60	2·51	2·45	2·39	2·35
21	4·32	3·47	3·07	2·84	2·68	2·57	2·49	2·42	2·37	2·32
22	4·30	3·44	3·05	2·82	2·66	2·55	2·46	2·40	2·34	2·30
23	4·28	3·42	3·03	2·80	2·64	2·53	2·44	2·37	2·32	2·27
24	4·26	3·40	3·01	2·78	2·62	2·51	2·42	2·36	2·30	2·25
25	4·24	3·39	2·99	2·76	2·60	2·49	2·40	2·34	2·28	2·24
26	4·23	3·37	2·98	2·74	2·59	2·47	2·39	2·32	2·27	2·22
27	4·21	3·35	2·96	2·73	2·57	2·46	2·37	2·31	2·25	2·20
28	4·20	3·34	2·95	2·71	2·56	2·45	2·36	2·29	2·24	2·19
29	4·18	3·33	2·93	2·70	2·55	2·43	2·35	2·28	2·22	2·18
30	4·17	3·32	2·92	2·69	2·53	2·42	2·33	2·27	2·21	2·16
40	4·08	3·23	2·84	2·61	2·45	2·34	2·25	2·18	2·12	2·08
60	4·00	3·15	2·76	2·53	2·37	2·25	2·17	2·10	2·04	1·99
120	3·92	3·07	2·68	2·45	2·29	2·17	2·09	2·02	1·96	1·91
∞	3·84	3·00	2·60	2·37	2·21	2·10	2·01	1·94	1·88	1·83

Reproduced from *Biometrika Tables for Statisticians*, edited by E. S. Pearson and H. O. Hartley (Cambridge University Press).

The table for F_α gives the value of F which has a probability α of being exceeded. ν_1 gives the number of degrees of freedom for the numerator and ν_2 the number of degrees of freedom for the denominator.

10	12	15	20	24	30	40	60	120	∞
241·9	243·9	245·9	248·0	249·1	250·1	251·1	252·2	253·3	254·3
19·40	19·41	19·43	19·45	19·45	19·46	19·47	19·48	19·49	19·50
8·79	8·74	8·70	8·66	8·64	8·62	8·59	8·57	8·55	8·53
5·96	5·91	5·86	5·80	5·77	5·75	5·72	5·69	5·66	5·63
4·74	4·68	4·62	4·56	4·53	4·50	4·46	4·43	4·40	4·36
4·06	4·00	3·94	3·87	3·84	3·81	3·77	3·74	3·70	3·67
3·64	3·57	3·51	3·44	3·41	3·38	3·34	3·30	3·27	3·23
3·35	3·28	3·22	3·15	3·12	3·08	3·04	3·01	2·97	2·93
3·14	3·07	3·01	2·94	2·90	2·86	2·83	2·79	2·75	2·71
2·98	2·91	2·85	2·77	2·74	2·70	2·66	2·62	2·58	2·54
2·85	2·79	2·72	2·65	2·61	2·57	2·53	2·49	2·45	2·40
2·75	2·69	2·62	2·54	2·51	2·47	2·43	2·38	2·34	2·30
2·67	2·60	2·53	2·46	2·42	2·38	2·34	2·30	2·25	2·21
2·60	2·53	2·46	2·39	2·35	2·31	2·27	2·22	2·18	2·13
2·54	2·48	2·40	2·33	2·29	2·25	2·20	2·16	2·11	2·07
2·49	2·42	2·35	2·28	2·24	2·19	2·15	2·11	2·06	2·01
2·45	2·38	2·31	2·23	2·19	2·15	2·10	2·06	2·01	1·96
2·41	2·34	2·27	2·19	2·15	2·11	2·06	2·02	1·97	1·92
2·38	2·31	2·23	2·16	2·11	2·07	2·03	1·98	1·93	1·88
2·35	2·28	2·20	2·12	2·08	2·04	1·99	1·95	1·90	1·84
2·32	2·25	2·18	2·10	2·05	2·01	1·96	1·92	1·87	1·81
2·30	2·23	2·15	2·07	2·03	1·98	1·94	1·89	1·84	1·78
2·27	2·20	2·13	2·05	2·01	1·96	1·91	1·86	1·81	1·76
2·25	2·18	2·11	2·03	1·98	1·94	1·89	1·84	1·79	1·73
2·24	2·16	2·09	2·01	1·96	1·92	1·87	1·82	1·77	1·71
2·22	2·15	2·07	1·99	1·95	1·90	1·85	1·80	1·75	1·69
2·20	2·13	2·06	1·97	1·93	1·88	·1·84	1·79	1·73	1·67
2·19	2·12	2·04	1·96	1·91	1·87	1·82	1·77	1·71	1·65
2·18	2·10	2·03	1·94	1·90	1·85	1·81	1·75	1·70	1·64
2·16	2·09	2·01	1·93	1·89	1·84	1·79	1·74	1·68	1·62
2·08	2·00	1·92	1·84	1·79	1·74	1·69	1·64	1·58	1·51
1·99	1·92	1·84	1·75	1·70	1·65	1·59	1·53	1·47	1·39
1·91	1·83	1·75	1·66	1·61	1·55	1·50	1·43	1·35	1·25
1·83	1·75	1·67	1·57	1·52	1·46	1·39	1·32	1·22	1·00

$$F._{025}$$

ν_1 ν_2	1	2	3	4	5	6	7	8	9	10
1	647·8	799·5	864·2	899·6	921·8	937·1	948·2	956·7	963·3	968·6
2	38·51	39·00	39·17	39·25	39·30	39·33	39·36	39·37	39·39	39·40
3	17·44	16·04	15·44	15·10	14·88	14·73	14·62	14·54	14·47	14·42
4	12·22	10·65	9·98	9·60	9·36	9·20	9·07	8·98	8·90	8·84
5	10·01	8·43	7·76	7·39	7·15	6·98	6·85	6·76	6·68	6·62
6	8·81	7·26	6·60	6·23	5·99	5·82	5·70	5·60	5·52	5·46
7	8·07	6·54	5·89	5·52	5·29	5·12	4·99	4·90	4·82	4·76
8	7·57	6·06	5·42	5·05	4·82	4·65	4·53	4·43	4·36	4·30
9	7·21	5·71	5·08	4·72	4·48	4·32	4·20	4·10	4·03	3·96
10	6·94	5·46	4·83	4·47	4·24	4·07	3·95	3·85	3·78	3·72
11	6·72	5·26	4·63	4·28	4·04	3·88	3·76	3·66	3·59	3·53
12	6·55	5·10	4·47	4·12	3·89	3·73	3·61	3·51	3·44	3·37
13	6·41	4·97	4·35	4·00	3·77	3·60	3·48	3·39	3·31	3·25
14	6·30	4·86	4·24	3·89	3·66	3·50	3·38	3·29	3·21	3·15
15	6·20	4·77	4·15	3·80	3·58	3·41	3·29	3·20	3·12	3·06
16	6·12	4·69	4·08	3·73	3·50	3·34	3·22	3·12	3·05	2·99
17	6·04	4·62	4·01	3·66	3·44	3·28	3·16	3·06	2·98	2·92
18	5·98	4·56	3·95	3·61	3·38	3·22	3·10	3·01	2·93	2·87
19	5·92	4·51	3·90	3·56	3·33	3·17	3·05	2·96	2·88	2·82
20	5·87	4·46	3·86	3·51	3·29	3·13	3·01	2·91	2·84	2·77
21	5·83	4·42	3·82	3·48	3·25	3·09	2·97	2·87	2·80	2·73
22	5·79	4·38	3·78	3·44	3·22	3·05	2·93	2·84	2·76	2·70
23	5·75	4·35	3·75	3·41	3·18	3·02	2·90	2·81	2·73	2·67
24	5·72	4·32	3·72	3·38	3·15	2·99	2·87	2·78	2·70	2·64
25	5·69	4·29	3·69	3·35	3·13	2·97	2·85	2·75	2·68	2·61
26	5·66	4·27	3·67	3·33	3·10	2·94	2·82	2·73	2·65	2·59
27	5·63	4·24	3·65	3·31	3·08	2·92	2·80	2·71	2·63	2·57
28	5·61	4·22	3·63	3·29	3·06	.2·90	2·78	2·69	2·61	2·55
29	5·59	4·20	3·61	3·27	3·04	2·88	2·76	2·67	2·59	2·53
30	5·57	4·18	3·59	3·25	3·03	2·87	2·75	2·65	2·57	2·51
40	5·42	4·05	3·46	3·13	2·90	2·74	2·62	2·53	2·45	2·39
60	5·29	3·93	3·34	3·01	2·79	2·63	2·51	2·41	2·33	2·27
120	5·15	3·80	3·23	2·89	2·67	2·52	2·39	2·30	2·22	2·16
∞	5·02	3·69	3·12	2·79	2·57	2·41	2·29	2·19	2·11	2·05

10	12	15	20	24	30	40	60	120	∞
968·6	976·7	984·9	993·1	997·2	1001	1006	1010	1014	1018
39·40	39·41	39·43	39·45	39·46	39·46	39·47	39·48	39·49	39·50
14·42	14·34	14·25	14·17	14·12	14·08	14·04	13·99	13·95	13·90
8·84	8·75	8·66	8·56	8·51	8·46	8·41	8·36	8·31	8·26
6·62	6·52	6·43	6·33	6·28	6·23	6·18	6·12	6·07	6·02
5·46	5·37	5·27	5·17	5·12	5·07	5·01	4·96	4·90	4·85
4·76	4·67	4·57	4·47	4·42	4·36	4·31	4·25	4·20	4·14
4·30	4·20	4·10	4·00	3·95	3·89	3·84	3·78	3·73	3·67
3·96	3·87	3·77	3·67	3·61	3·56	3·51	3·45	3·39	3·33
3·72	3·62	3·52	3·42	3·37	3·31	3·26	3·20	3·14	3·08
3·53	3·43	3·33	3·23	3·17	3·12	3·06	3·00	2·94	2·88
3·37	3·28	3·18	3·07	3·02	2·96	2·91	2·85	2·79	2·72
3·25	3·15	3·05	2·95	2·89	2·84	2·78	2·72	2·66	2·60
3·15	3·05	2·95	2·84	2·79	2·73	2·67	2·61	2·55	2·49
3·06	2·96	2·86	2·76	2·70	2·64	2·59	2·52	2·46	2·40
2·99	2·89	2·79	2·68	2·63	2·57	2·51	2·45	2·38	2·32
2·92	2·82	2·72	2·62	2·56	2·50	2·44	2·38	2·32	2·25
2·87	2·77	2·67	2·56	2·50	2·44	2·38	2·32	2·26	2·19
2·82	2·72	2·62	2·51	2·45	2·39	2·33	2·27	2·20	2·13
2·77	2·68	2·57	2·46	2·41	2·35	2·29	2·22	2·16	2·09
2·73	2·64	2·53	2·42	2·37	2·31	2·25	2·18	2·11	2·04
2·70	2·60	2·50	2·39	2·33	2·27	2·21	2·14	2·08	2·00
2·67	2·57	2·47	2·36	2·30	2·24	2·18	2·11	2·04	1·97
2·64	2·54	2·44	2·33	2·27	2·21	2·15	2·08	2·01	1·94
2·61	2·51	2·41	2·30	2·24	2·18	2·12	2·05	1·98	1·91
2·59	2·49	2·39	2·28	2·22	2·16	2·09	2·03	1·95	1·88
2·57	2·47	2·36	2·25	2·19	2·13	2·07	2·00	1·93	1·85
2·55	2·45	2·34	2·23	2·17	2·11	2·05	1·98	1·91	1·83
2·53	2·43	2·32	2·21	2·15	2·09	2·03	1·96	1·89	1·81
2·51	2·41	2·31	2·20	2·14	2·07	2·01	1·94	1·87	1·79
2·39	2·29	2·18	2·07	2·01	1·94	1·88	1·80	1·72	1·64
2·27	2·17	2·06	1·94	1·88	1·82	1·74	1·67	1·58	1·48
2·16	2·05	1·94	1·82	1·76	1·69	1·61	1·53	1·43	1·31
2·05	1·94	1·83	1·71	1·64	1·57	1·48	1·39	1·27	1·00

$$F_{.01}$$

ν_1 / ν_2	1	2	3	4	5	6	7	8	9	10
1	4052	4999·5	5403	5625	5764	5859	5928	5982	6022	6056
2	98·50	99·00	99·17	99·25	99·30	99·33	99·36	99·37	99·39	99·4
3	34·12	30·82	29·46	28·71	28·24	27·91	27·67	27·49	27·35	27·2
4	21·20	18·00	16·69	15·98	15·52	15·21	14·98	14·80	14·66	14·5
5	16·26	13·27	12·06	11·39	10·97	10·67	10·46	10·29	10·16	10·0
6	13·75	10·92	9·78	9·15	8·75	8·47	8·26	8·10	7·98	7·8
7	12·25	9·55	8·45	7·85	7·46	7·19	6·99	6·84	6·72	6·6
8	11·26	8·65	7·59	7·01	6·63	6·37	6·18	6·03	5·91	5·8
9	10·56	8·02	6·99	6·42	6·06	5·80	5·61	5·47	5·35	5·2
10	10·04	7·56	6·55	5·99	5·64	5·39	5·20	5·06	4·94	4·8
11	9·65	7·21	6·22	5·67	5·32	5·07	4·89	4·74	4·63	4·5
12	9·33	6·93	5·95	5·41	5·06	4·82	4·64	4·50	4·39	4·3
13	9·07	6·70	5·74	5·21	4·86	4·62	4·44	4·30	4·19	4·1
14	8·86	6·51	5·56	5·04	4·69	4·46	4·28	4·14	4·03	3·9
15	8·68	6·36	5·42	4·89	4·56	4·32	4·14	4·00	3·89	3·8
16	8·53	6·23	5·29	4·77	4·44	4·20	4·03	3·89	3·78	3·6
17	8·40	6·11	5·18	4·67	4·34	4·10	3·93	3·79	3·68	3·5
18	8·29	6·01	5·09	4·58	4·25	4·01	3·84	3·71	3·60	3·5
19	8·18	5·93	5·01	4·50	4·17	3·94	3·77	3·63	3·52	3·4
20	8·10	5·85	4·94	4·43	4·10	3·87	3·70	3·56	3·46	3·3
21	8·02	5·78	4·87	4·37	4·04	3·81	3·64	3·51	3·40	3·3
22	7·95	5·72	4·82	4·31	3·99	3·76	3·59	3·45	3·35	3·2
23	7·88	5·66	4·76	4·26	3·94	3·71	3·54	3·41	3·30	3·2
24	7·82	5·61	4·72	4·22	3·90	3·67	3·50	3·36	3·26	3·1
25	7·77	5·57	4·68	4·18	3·85	3·63	3·46	3·32	3·22	3·1
26	7·72	5·53	4·64	4·14	3·82	3·59	3·42	3·29	3·18	3·0
27	7·68	5·49	4·60	4·11	3·78	3·56	3·39	3·26	3·15	3·0
28	7·64	5·45	4·57	4·07	3·75	3·53	3·36	3·23	3·12	3·0
29	7·60	5·42	4·54	4·04	3·73	3·50	3·33	3·20	3·09	3·0
30	7·56	5·39	4·51	4·02	3·70	3·47	3·30	3·17	3·07	2·9
40	7·31	5·18	4·31	3·83	3·51	3·29	3·12	2·99	2·89	2·8
60	7·08	4·98	4·13	3·65	3·34	3·12	2·95	2·82	2·72	2·6
120	6·85	4·79	3·95	3·48	3·17	2·96	2·79	2·66	2·56	2·4
∞	6·63	4·61	3·78	3·32	3·02	2·80	2·64	2·51	2·41	2·3

10	12	15	20	24	30	40	60	120	∞
6056	6106	6157	6209	6235	6261	6287	6313	6339	6366
99·40	99·42	99·43	99·45	99·46	99·47	99·47	99·48	99·49	99·50
27·23	27·05	26·87	26·69	26·60	26·50	26·41	26·32	26·22	26·13
14·55	14·37	14·20	14·02	13·93	13·84	13·75	13·65	13·56	13·46
10·05	9·89	9·72	9·55	9·47	9·38	9·29	9·20	9·11	9·02
7·87	7·72	7·56	7·40	7·31	7·23	7·14	7·06	6·97	6·88
6·62	6·47	6·31	6·16	6·07	5·99	5·91	5·82	5·74	5·65
5·81	5·67	5·52	5·36	5·28	5·20	5·12	5·03	4·95	4·86
5·26	5·11	4·96	4·81	4·73	4·65	4·57	4·48	4·40	4·31
4·85	4·71	4·56	4·41	4·33	4·25	4·17	4·08	4·00	3·91
4·54	4·40	4·25	4·10	4·02	3·94	3·86	3·78	3·69	3·60
4·30	4·16	4·01	3·86	3·78	3·70	3·62	3·54	3·45	3·36
4·10	3·96	3·82	3·66	3·59	3·51	3·43	3·34	3·25	3·17
3·94	3·80	3·66	3·51	3·43	3·35	3·27	3·18	3·09	3·00
3·80	3·67	3·52	3·37	3·29	3·21	3·13	3·05	2·96	2·87
3·69	3·55	3·41	3·26	3·18	3·10	3·02	2·93	2·84	2·75
3·59	3·46	3·31	3·16	3·08	3·00	2·92	2·83	2·75	2·65
3·51	3·37	3·23	3·08	3·00	2·92	2·84	2·75	2·66	2·57
3·43	3·30	3·15	3·00	2·92	2·84	2·76	2·67	2·58	2·49
3·37	3·23	3·09	2·94	2·86	2·78	2·69	2·61	2·52	2·42
3·31	3·17	3·03	2·88	2·80	2·72	2·64	2·55	2·46	2·36
3·26	3·12	2·98	2·83	2·75	2·67	2·58	2·50	2·40	2·31
3·21	3·07	2·93	2·78	2·70	2·62	2·54	2·45	2·35	2·26
3·17	3·03	2·89	2·74	2·66	2·58	2·49	2·40	2·31	2·21
3·13	2·99	2·85	2·70	2·62	2·54	2·45	2·36	2·27	2·17
3·09	2·96	2·81	2·66	2·58	2·50	2·42	2·33	2·23	2·13
3·06	2·93	2·78	2·63	2·55	2·47	2·38	2·29	2·20	2·10
3·03	2·90	2·75	2·60	2·52	2·44	2·35	2·26	2·17	2·06
3·00	2·87	2·73	2·57	2·49	2·41	2·33	2·23	2·14	2·03
2·98	2·84	2·70	2·55	2·47	2·39	2·30	2·21	2·11	2·01
2·80	2·66	2·52	2·37	2·29	2·20	2·11	2·02	1·92	1·80
2·63	2·50	2·35	2·20	2·12	2·03	1·94	1·84	1·73	1·60
2·47	2·34	2·19	2·03	1·95	1·86	1·76	1·66	1·53	1·38
2·32	2·18	2·04	1·88	1·79	1·70	1·59	1·47	1·32	1·00

$F_{.005}$

ν_2 \ ν_1	1	2	3	4	5	6	7	8	9	10
1	16211	20000	21615	22500	23056	23437	23715	23925	24091	24224
2	198·5	199·0	199·2	199·2	199·3	199·3	199·4	199·4	199·4	199·4
3	55·55	49·80	47·47	46·19	45·39	44·84	44·43	44·13	43·88	43·69
4	31·33	26·28	24·26	23·15	22·46	21·97	21·62	21·35	21·14	20·97
5	22·78	18·31	16·53	15·56	14·94	14·51	14·20	13·96	13·77	13·62
6	18·63	14·54	12·92	12·03	11·46	11·07	10·79	10·57	10·39	10·25
7	16·24	12·40	10·88	10·05	9·52	9·16	8·89	8·68	8·51	8·38
8	14·69	11·04	9·60	8·81	8·30	7·95	7·69	7·50	7·34	7·21
9	13·61	10·11	8·72	7·96	7·47	7·13	6·88	6·69	6·54	6·42
10	12·83	9·43	8·08	7·34	6·87	6·54	6·30	6·12	5·97	5·85
11	12·23	8·91	7·60	6·88	6·42	6·10	5·86	5·68	5·54	5·42
12	11·75	8·51	7·23	6·52	6·07	5·76	5·52	5·35	5·20	5·09
13	11·37	8·19	6·93	6·23	5·79	5·48	5·25	5·08	4·94	4·82
14	11·06	7·92	6·68	6·00	5·56	5·26	5·03	4·86	4·72	4·60
15	10·80	7·70	6·48	5·80	5·37	5·07	4·85	4·67	4·54	4·42
16	10·58	7·51	6·30	5·64	5·21	4·91	4·69	4·52	4·38	4·27
17	10·38	7·35	6·16	5·50	5·07	4·78	4·56	4·39	4·25	4·14
18	10·22	7·21	6·03	5·37	4·96	4·66	4·44	4·28	4·14	4·03
19	10·07	7·09	5·92	5·27	4·85	4·56	4·34	4·18	4·04	3·93
20	9·94	6·99	5·82	5·17	4·76	4·47	4·26	4·09	3·96	3·85
21	9·83	6·89	5·73	5·09	4·68	4·39	4·18	4·01	3·88	3·77
22	9·73	6·81	5·65	5·02	4·61	4·32	4·11	3·94	3·81	3·70
23	9·63	6·73	5·58	4·95	4·54	4·26	4·05	3·88	3·75	3·64
24	9·55	6·66	5·52	4·89	4·49	4·20	3·99	3·83	3·69	3·59
25	9·48	6·60	5·46	4·84	4·43	4·15	3·94	3·78	3·64	3·54
26	9·41	6·54	5·41	4·79	4·38	4·10	3·89	3·73	3·60	3·49
27	9·34	6·49	5·36	4·74	4·34	4·06	3·85	3·69	3·56	3·45
28	9·28	6·44	5·32	4·70	4·30	4·02	3·81	3·65	3·52	3·41
29	9·23	6·40	5·28	4·66	4·26	3·98	3·77	3·61	3·48	3·38
30	9·18	6·35	5·24	4·62	4·23	3·95	3·74	3·58	3·45	3·34
40	8·83	6·07	4·98	4·37	3·99	3·71	3·51	3·35	3·22	3·12
60	8·49	5·79	4·73	4·14	3·76	3·49	3·29	3·13	3·01	2·90
120	8·18	5·54	4·50	3·92	3·55	3·28	3·09	2·93	2·81	2·71
∞	7·88	5·30	4·28	3·72	3·35	3·09	2·90	2·74	2·62	2·52

10	12	15	20	24	30	40	60	120	∞
24224	24426	24630	24836	24940	25044	25148	25253	25359	25465
199·4	199·4	199·4	199·4	199·5	199·5	199·5	199·5	199·5	199·5
43·69	43·39	43·08	42·78	42·62	42·47	42·31	42·15	41·99	41·83
20·97	20·70	20·44	20·17	20·03	19·89	19·75	19·61	19·47	19·32
13·62	13·38	13·15	12·90	12·78	12·66	12·53	12·40	12·27	12·14
10·25	10·03	9·81	9·59	9·47	9·36	9·24	9·12	9·00	8·88
8·38	8·18	7·97	7·75	7·65	7·53	7·42	7·31	7·19	7·08
7·21	7·01	6·81	6·61	6·50	6·40	6·29	6·18	6·06	5·95
6·42	6·23	6·03	5·83	5·73	5·62	5·52	5·41	5·30	5·19
5·85	5·66	5·47	5·27	5·17	5·07	4·97	4·86	4·75	4·64
5·42	5·24	5·05	4·86	4·76	4·65	4·55	4·44	4·34	4·23
5·09	4·91	4·72	4·53	4·43	4·33	4·23	4·12	4·01	3·90
4·82	4·64	4·46	4·27	4·17	4·07	3·97	3·87	3·76	3·65
4·60	4·43	4·25	4·06	3·96	3·86	3·76	3·66	3·55	3·44
4·42	4·25	4·07	3·88	3·79	3·69	3·58	3·48	3·37	3·26
4·27	4·10	3·92	3·73	3·64	3·54	3·44	3·33	3·22	3·11
4·14	3·97	3·79	3·61	3·51	3·41	3·31	3·21	3·10	2·98
4·03	3·86	3·68	3·50	3·40	3·30	3·20	3·10	2·99	2·87
3·93	3·76	3·59	3·40	3·31	3·21	3·11	3·00	2·89	2·78
3·85	3·68	3·50	3·32	3·22	3·12	3·02	2·92	2·81	2·69
3·77	3·60	3·43	3·24	3·15	3·05	2·95	2·84	2·73	2·61
3·70	3·54	3·36	3·18	3·08	2·98	2·88	2·77	2·66	2·55
3·64	3·47	3·30	3·12	3·02	2·92	2·82	2·71	2·60	2·48
3·59	3·42	3·25	3·06	2·97	2·87	2·77	2·66	2·55	2·43
3·54	3·37	3·20	3·01	2·92	2·82	2·72	2·61	2·50	2·38
3·49	3·33	3·15	2·97	2·87	2·77	2·67	2·56	2·45	2·33
3·45	3·28	3·11	2·93	2·83	2·73	2·63	2·52	2·41	2·29
3·41	3·25	3·07	2·89	2·79	2·69	2·59	2·48	2·37	2·25
3·38	3·21	3·04	2·86	2·76	2·66	2·56	2·45	2·33	2·21
3·34	3·18	3·01	2·82	2·73	2·63	2·52	2·42	2·30	2·18
3·12	2·95	2·78	2·60	2·50	2·40	2·30	2·18	2·06	1·93
2·90	2·74	2·57	2·39	2·29	2·19	2·08	1·96	1·83	1·69
2·71	2·54	2·37	2·19	2·09	1·98	1·87	1·75	1·61	1·43
2·52	2·36	2·19	2·00	1·90	1·79	1·67	1·53	1·36	1·00

The value of χ_α^2 given in the table is the value of χ^2 which has a probability α of being exceeded.

d.f.	$\chi_{.05}^2$	$\chi_{.025}^2$	$\chi_{.01}^2$	$\chi_{.005}^2$	d.f.
1	3.841	5.024	6.635	7.879	1
2	5.991	7.378	9.210	10.597	2
3	7.815	9.348	11.345	12.838	3
4	9.488	11.143	13.277	14.860	4
5	11.070	12.832	15.086	16.750	5
6	12.592	14.449	16.812	18.548	6
7	14.067	16.013	18.475	20.278	7
8	15.507	17.535	20.090	21.955	8
9	16.919	19.023	21.666	23.589	9
10	18.307	20.483	23.209	25.188	10
11	19.675	21.920	24.725	26.757	11
12	21.026	23.337	26.217	28.300	12
13	22.362	24.736	27.688	29.819	13
14	23.685	26.119	29.141	31.319	14
15	24.996	27.488	30.578	32.801	15
16	26.296	28.845	32.000	34.267	16
17	27.587	30.191	33.409	35.718	17
18	28.869	31.526	34.805	37.156	18
19	30.144	32.852	36.191	38.582	19
20	31.410	34.170	37.566	39.997	20
21	32.671	35.479	38.932	41.401	21
22	33.924	36.781	40.289	42.796	22
23	35.172	38.076	41.638	44.181	23
24	36.415	39.364	42.980	45.558	24
25	37.652	40.646	44.314	46.928	25
26	38.885	41.923	45.642	48.290	26
27	40.113	43.194	46.963	49.645	27
28	41.337	44.461	48.278	50.993	28
29	42.557	45.722	49.588	52.336	29
30	43.773	46.979	50.892	53.672	30

Reproduced from *Modern Business Statistics* by J. E. Freund and F. J. Williams (Pitman). After a table in Sir R. A. Fisher, *Statistical Methods for Research Workers* (Oliver & Boyd).

TABLE VI SIGNIFICANT VALUE OF THE CORRELATION COEFFICIENT

If the calculated value of r exceeds the table value of r_α, a significant correlation has been established at the α significance level.

d.f.	$r_{.1}$	$r_{.05}$	$r_{.02}$	$r_{.01}$	$r_{.001}$
1	·98769	·99692	·999507	·999877	·9999988
2	·90000	·95000	·98000	·990000	·99900
3	·8054	·8783	·93433	·95873	·99116
4	·7293	·8114	·8822	·91720	·97406
5	·6694	·7545	·8329	·8745	·95074
6	·6215	·7067	·7887	·8343	·92493
7	·5822	·6664	·7498	·7977	·8982
8	·5494	·6319	·7155	·7646	·8721
9	·5214	·6021	·6851	·7348	·8471
10	·4973	·5760	·6581	·7079	·8233
11	·4762	·5529	·6339	·6835	·8010
12	·4575	·5324	·6120	·6614	·7800
13	·4409	·5139	·5923	·6411	·7603
14	·4259	·4973	·5742	·6226	·7420
15	·4124	·4821	·5577	·6055	·7246

d.f.	$r_{.1}$	$r_{.05}$	$r_{.02}$	$r_{.01}$	$r_{.001}$
16	·4000	·4683	·5425	·5897	·7084
17	·3887	·4555	·5285	·5751	·6932
18	·3783	·4438	·5155	·5614	·6787
19	·3687	·4329	·5034	·5487	·6652
20	·3598	·4227	·4921	·5368	·6524
25	·3233	·3809	·4451	·4869	·5974
30	·2960	·3494	·4093	·4487	·5541
35	·2746	·3246	·3810	·4182	·5189
40	·2573	·3044	·3578	·3932	·4896
45	·2428	·2875	·3384	·3721	·4648
50	·2306	·2732	·3218	·3541	·4433
60	·2108	·2500	·2948	·3248	·4078
70	·1954	·2319	·2737	·3017	·3799
80	·1829	·2172	·2565	·2830	·3568
90	·1726	·2050	·2422	·2673	·3375
100	·1638	·1946	·2301	·2540	·3211

The main part of the table is reproduced from Table VII of Sir R. A. Fisher and F. Yates, *Statistical Tables for Biological, Agricultural and Medical Research*, published by Oliver & Boyd Ltd, Edinburgh, by permission of the authors and publishers.

	0	1	2	3	4	5	6	7	8	9	Mean Differences 1 2 3	4 5 6	7 8 9
1·0	1·000	1·005	1·010	1·015	1·020	1·025	1·030	1·034	1·039	1·044	0 1 1	2 2 3	3 4 4
1·1	1·049	1·054	1·058	1·063	1·068	1·072	1·077	1·082	1·086	1·091	0 1 1	2 2 3	3 4 4
1·2	1·095	1·100	1·105	1·109	1·114	1·118	1·122	1·127	1·131	1·136	0 1 1	2 2 3	3 4 4
1·3	1·140	1·145	1·149	1·153	1·158	1·162	1·166	1·170	1·175	1·179	0 1 1	2 2 3	3 3 4
1·4	1·183	1·187	1·192	1·196	1·200	1·204	1·208	1·212	1·217	1·221	0 1 1	2 2 2	3 3 4
1·5	1·225	1·229	1·233	1·237	1·241	1·245	1·249	1·253	1·257	1·261	0 1 1	2 2 2	3 3 4
1·6	1·265	1·269	1·273	1·277	1·281	1·285	1·288	1·292	1·296	1·300	0 1 1	2 2 2	3 3 3
1·7	1·304	1·308	1·311	1·315	1·319	1·323	1·327	1·330	1·334	1·338	0 1 1	2 2 2	3 3 3
1·8	1·342	1·345	1·349	1·353	1·356	1·360	1·364	1·367	1·371	1·375	0 1 1	1 2 2	3 3 3
1·9	1·378	1·382	1·386	1·389	1·393	1·396	1·400	1·404	1·407	1·411	0 1 1	1 2 2	3 3 3
2·0	1·414	1·418	1·421	1·425	1·428	1·432	1·435	1·439	1·442	1·446	0 1 1	1 2 2	3 3 3
2·1	1·449	1·453	1·456	1·459	1·463	1·466	1·470	1·473	1·476	1·480	0 1 1	1 2 2	2 3 3
2·2	1·483	1·487	1·490	1·493	1·497	1·500	1·503	1·507	1·510	1·513	0 1 1	1 2 2	2 3 3
2·3	1·517	1·520	1·523	1·526	1·530	1·533	1·536	1·539	1·543	1·546	0 1 1	1 2 2	2 3 3
2·4	1·549	1·552	1·556	1·559	1·562	1·565	1·568	1·572	1·575	1·578	0 1 1	1 2 2	2 3 3
2·5	1·581	1·584	1·587	1·591	1·594	1·597	1·600	1·603	1·606	1·609	0 1 1	1 2 2	2 3 3
2·6	1·612	1·616	1·619	1·622	1·625	1·628	1·631	1·634	1·637	1·640	0 1 1	1 2 2	2 2 3
2·7	1·643	1·646	1·649	1·652	1·655	1·658	1·661	1·664	1·667	1·670	0 1 1	1 2 2	2 2 3
2·8	1·673	1·676	1·679	1·682	1·685	1·688	1·691	1·694	1·697	1·700	0 1 1	1 1 2	2 2 3
2·9	1·703	1·706	1·709	1·712	1·715	1·718	1·720	1·723	1·726	1·729	0 1 1	1 1 2	2 2 3
3·0	1·732	1·735	1·738	1·741	1·744	1·746	1·749	1·752	1·755	1·758	0 1 1	1 1 2	2 2 3
3·1	1·761	1·764	1·766	1·769	1·772	1·775	1·778	1·780	1·783	1·786	0 1 1	1 1 2	2 2 3
3·2	1·789	1·792	1·794	1·797	1·800	1·803	1·806	1·808	1·811	1·814	0 1 1	1 1 2	2 2 2
3·3	1·817	1·819	1·822	1·825	1·828	1·830	1·833	1·836	1·838	1·841	0 1 1	1 1 2	2 2 2
3·4	1·844	1·847	1·849	1·852	1·855	1·857	1·860	1·863	1·865	1·868	0 1 1	1 1 2	2 2 2
3·5	1·871	1·873	1·876	1·879	1·881	1·884	1·887	1·889	1·892	1·895	0 1 1	1 1 2	2 2 2
3·6	1·897	1·900	1·903	1·905	1·908	1·910	1·913	1·916	1·918	1·921	0 1 1	1 1 2	2 2 2
3·7	1·924	1·926	1·929	1·931	1·934	1·936	1·939	1·942	1·944	1·947	0 1 1	1 1 2	2 2 2
3·8	1·949	1·952	1·954	1·957	1·960	1·962	1·965	1·967	1·970	1·972	0 1 1	1 1 2	2 2 2
3·9	1·975	1·977	1·980	1·982	1·985	1·987	1·990	1·992	1·995	1·997	0 1 1	1 1 2	2 2 2
4·0	2·000	2·002	2·005	2·007	2·010	2·012	2·015	2·017	2·020	2·022	0 0 1	1 1 1	2 2 2
4·1	2·025	2·027	2·030	2·032	2·035	2·037	2·040	2·042	2·045	2·047	0 0 1	1 1 1	2 2 2
4·2	2·049	2·052	2·054	2·057	2·059	2·062	2·064	2·066	2·069	2·071	0 0 1	1 1 1	2 2 2
4·3	2·074	2·076	2·078	2·081	2·083	2·086	2·088	2·090	2·093	2·095	0 0 1	1 1 1	2 2 2
4·4	2·098	2·100	2·102	2·105	2·107	2·110	2·112	2·114	2·117	2·119	0 0 1	1 1 1	2 2 2
4·5	2·121	2·124	2·126	2·128	2·131	2·133	2·135	2·138	2·140	2·142	0 0 1	1 1 1	2 2 2
4·6	2·145	2·147	2·149	2·152	2·154	2·156	2·159	2·161	2·163	2·166	0 0 1	1 1 1	2 2 2
4·7	2·168	2·170	2·173	2·175	2·177	2·179	2·182	2·184	2·186	2·189	0 0 1	1 1 1	2 2 2
4·8	2·191	2·193	2·195	2·198	2·200	2·202	2·205	2·207	2·209	2·211	0 0 1	1 1 1	2 2 2
4·9	2·214	2·216	2·218	2·220	2·223	2·225	2·227	2·229	2·232	2·234	0 0 1	1 1 1	2 2 2
5·0	2·236	2·238	2·241	2·243	2·245	2·247	2·249	2·252	2·254	2·256	0 0 1	1 1 1	2 2 2
5·1	2·258	2·261	2·263	2·265	2·267	2·269	2·272	2·274	2·276	2·278	0 0 1	1 1 1	2 2 2
5·2	2·280	2·283	2·285	2·287	2·289	2·291	2·293	2·296	2·298	2·300	0 0 1	1 1 1	2 2 2
5·3	2·302	2·304	2·307	2·309	2·311	2·313	2·315	2·317	2·319	2·322	0 0 1	1 1 1	2 2 2
5·4	2·324	2·326	2·328	2·330	2·332	2·335	2·337	2·339	2·341	2·343	0 0 1	1 1 1	1 2 2

	0	1	2	3	4	5	6	7	8	9	Mean Differences.								
											1	2	3	4	5	6	7	8	9
5·5	2·345	2·347	2·349	2·352	2·354	2·356	2·358	2·360	2·362	2·364	0	0	1	1	1	1	1	2	2
5·6	2·366	2·369	2·371	2·373	2·375	2·377	2·379	2·381	2·383	2·385	0	0	1	1	1	1	1	2	2
5·7	2·387	2·390	2·392	2·394	2·396	2·398	2·400	2·402	2·404	2·406	0	0	1	1	1	1	1	2	2
5·8	2·408	2·410	2·412	2·415	2·417	2·419	2·421	2·423	2·425	2·427	0	0	1	1	1	1	1	2	2
5·9	2·429	2·431	2·433	2·435	2·437	2·439	2·441	2·443	2·445	2·447	0	0	1	1	1	1	1	2	2
6·0	2·449	2·452	2·454	2·456	2·458	2·460	2·462	2·464	2·466	2·468	0	0	1	1	1	1	1	2	2
6·1	2·470	2·472	2·474	2·476	2·478	2·480	2·482	2·484	2·486	2·488	0	0	1	1	1	1	1	2	2
6·2	2·490	2·492	2·494	2·496	2·498	2·500	2·502	2·504	2·506	2·508	0	0	1	1	1	1	1	2	2
6·3	2·510	2·512	2·514	2·516	2·518	2·520	2·522	2·524	2·526	2·528	0	0	1	1	1	1	1	2	2
6·4	2·530	2·532	2·534	2·536	2·538	2·540	2·542	2·544	2·546	2·548	0	0	1	1	1	1	1	2	2
6·5	2·550	2·551	2·553	2·555	2·557	2·559	2·561	2·563	2·565	2·567	0	0	1	1	1	1	1	2	2
6·6	2·569	2·571	2·573	2·575	2·577	2·579	2·581	2·583	2·585	2·587	0	0	1	1	1	1	1	2	2
6·7	2·588	2·590	2·592	2·594	2·596	2·598	2·600	2·602	2·604	2·606	0	0	1	1	1	1	1	2	2
6·8	2·608	2·610	2·612	2·613	2·615	2·617	2·619	2·621	2·623	2·625	0	0	1	1	1	1	1	2	2
6·9	2·627	2·629	2·631	2·632	2·634	2·636	2·638	2·640	2·642	2·644	0	0	1	1	1	1	1	2	2
7·0	2·646	2·648	2·650	2·651	2·653	2·655	2·657	2·659	2·661	2·663	0	0	1	1	1	1	1	2	2
7·1	2·665	2·666	2·668	2·670	2·672	2·674	2·676	2·678	2·680	2·681	0	0	1	1	1	1	1	1	2
7·2	2·683	2·685	2·687	2·689	2·691	2·693	2·694	2·696	2·698	2·700	0	0	1	1	1	1	1	1	2
7·3	2·702	2·704	2·706	2·707	2·709	2·711	2·713	2·715	2·717	2·718	0	0	1	1	1	1	1	1	2
7·4	2·720	2·722	2·724	2·726	2·728	2·729	2·731	2·733	2·735	2·737	0	0	1	1	1	1	1	1	2
7·5	2·739	2·740	2·742	2·744	2·746	2·748	2·750	2·751	2·753	2·755	0	0	1	1	1	1	1	1	2
7·6	2·757	2·759	2·760	2·762	2·764	2·766	2·768	2·769	2·771	2·773	0	0	1	1	1	1	1	1	2
7·7	2·775	2·777	2·778	2·780	2·782	2·784	2·786	2·787	2·789	2·791	0	0	1	1	1	1	1	1	2
7·8	2·793	2·795	2·796	2·798	2·800	2·802	2·804	2·805	2·807	2·809	0	0	1	1	1	1	1	1	2
7·9	2·811	2·812	2·814	2·816	2·818	2·820	2·821	2·823	2·825	2·827	0	0	1	1	1	1	1	1	2
8·0	2·828	2·830	2·832	2·834	2·835	2·837	2·839	2·841	2·843	2·844	0	0	1	1	1	1	1	1	2
8·1	2·846	2·848	2·850	2·851	2·853	2·855	2·857	2·858	2·860	2·862	0	0	1	1	1	1	1	1	2
8·2	2·864	2·865	2·867	2·869	2·871	2·872	2·874	2·876	2·877	2·879	0	0	1	1	1	1	1	1	2
8·3	2·881	2·883	2·884	2·886	2·888	2·890	2·891	2·893	2·895	2·897	0	0	1	1	1	1	1	1	2
8·4	2·898	2·900	2·902	2·903	2·905	2·907	2·909	2·910	2·912	2·914	0	0	1	1	1	1	1	1	2
8·5	2·915	2·917	2·919	2·921	2·922	2·924	2·926	2·927	2·929	2·931	0	0	1	1	1	1	1	1	2
8·6	2·933	2·934	2·936	2·938	2·939	2·941	2·943	2·944	2·946	2·948	0	0	1	1	1	1	1	1	2
8·7	2·950	2·951	2·953	2·955	2·956	2·958	2·960	2·961	2·963	2·965	0	0	1	1	1	1	1	1	2
8·8	2·966	2·968	2·970	2·972	2·973	2·975	2·977	2·978	2·980	2·982	0	0	1	1	1	1	1	1	2
8·9	2·983	2·985	2·987	2·988	2·990	2·992	2·993	2·995	2·997	2·998	0	0	1	1	1	1	1	1	2
9·0	3·000	3·002	3·003	3·005	3·007	3·008	3·010	3·012	3·013	3·015	0	0	0	1	1	1	1	1	1
9·1	3·017	3·018	3·020	3·022	3·023	3·025	3·027	3·028	3·030	3·032	0	0	0	1	1	1	1	1	1
9·2	3·033	3·035	3·036	3·038	3·040	3·041	3·043	3·045	3·046	3·048	0	0	0	1	1	1	1	1	1
9·3	3·050	3·051	3·053	3·055	3·056	3·058	3·059	3·061	3·063	3·064	0	0	0	1	1	1	1	1	1
9·4	3·066	3·068	3·069	3·071	3·072	3·074	3·076	3·077	3·079	3·081	0	0	0	1	1	1	1	1	1
9·5	3·082	3·084	3·085	3·087	3·089	3·090	3·092	3·094	3·095	3·097	0	0	0	1	1	1	1	1	1
9·6	3·098	3·100	3·102	3·103	3·105	3·106	3·108	3·110	3·111	3·113	0	0	0	1	1	1	1	1	1
9·7	3·114	3·116	3·118	3·119	3·121	3·122	3·124	3·126	3·127	3·129	0	0	0	1	1	1	1	1	1
9·8	3·130	3·132	3·134	3·135	3·137	3·138	3·140	3·142	3·143	3·145	0	0	0	1	1	1	1	1	1
9·9	3·146	3·148	3·150	3·151	3·153	3·154	3·156	3·158	3·159	3·161	0	0	0	1	1	1	1	1	1

	0	1	2	3	4	5	6	7	8	9	1 2 3	4 5 6	7 8 9
10	3·162	3·178	3·194	3·209	3·225	3·240	3·256	3·271	3·286	3·302	2 3 5	6 8 9	11 12 14
11	3·317	3·332	3·347	3·362	3·376	3·391	3·406	3·421	3·435	3·450	1 3 4	6 7 9	10 12 13
12	3·464	3·479	3·493	3·507	3·521	3·536	3·550	3·564	3·578	3·592	1 3 4	6 7 8	10 11 13
13	3·606	3·619	3·633	3·647	3·661	3·674	3·688	3·701	3·715	3·728	1 3 4	5 7 8	10 11 12
14	3·742	3·755	3·768	3·782	3·795	3·808	3·821	3·834	3·847	3·860	1 3 4	5 7 8	9 11 12
15	3·873	3·886	3·899	3·912	3·924	3·937	3·950	3·962	3·975	3·987	1 3 4	5 6 8	9 10 11
16	4·000	4·012	4·025	4·037	4·050	4·062	4·074	4·087	4·099	4·111	1 2 4	5 6 7	9 10 11
17	4·123	4·135	4·147	4·159	4·171	4·183	4·195	4·207	4·219	4·231	1 2 4	5 6 7	8 10 11
18	4·243	4·254	4·266	4·278	4·290	4·301	4·313	4·324	4·336	4·347	1 2 3	5 6 7	8 9 10
19	4·359	4·370	4·382	4·393	4·405	4·416	4·427	4·438	4·450	4·461	1 2 3	5 6 7	8 9 10
20	4·472	4·483	4·494	4·506	4·517	4·528	4·539	4·550	4·561	4·572	1 2 3	4 6 7	8 9 10
21	4·583	4·593	4·604	4·615	4·626	4·637	4·648	4·658	4·669	4·680	1 2 3	4 5 6	8 9 10
22	4·690	4·701	4·712	4·722	4·733	4·743	4·754	4·764	4·775	4·785	1 2 3	4 5 6	7 8 9
23	4·796	4·806	4·817	4·827	4·837	4·848	4·858	4·868	4·879	4·889	1 2 3	4 5 6	7 8 9
24	4·899	4·909	4·919	4·930	4·940	4·950	4·960	4·970	4·980	4·990	1 2 3	4 5 6	7 8 9
25	5·000	5·010	5·020	5·030	5·040	5·050	5·060	5·070	5·079	5·089	1 2 3	4 5 6	7 8 9
26	5·099	5·109	5·119	5·128	5·138	5·148	5·158	5·167	5·177	5·187	1 2 3	4 5 6	7 8 9
27	5·196	5·206	5·215	5·225	5·235	5·244	5·254	5·263	5·273	5·282	1 2 3	4 5 6	7 8 9
28	5·292	5·301	5·310	5·320	5·329	5·339	5·348	5·357	5·367	5·376	1 2 3	4 5 6	7 7 8
29	5·385	5·394	5·404	5·413	5·422	5·431	5·441	5·450	5·459	5·468	1 2 3	4 5 5	6 7 8
30	5·477	5·486	5·495	5·505	5·514	5·523	5·532	5·541	5·550	5·559	1 2 3	4 4 5	6 7 8
31	5·568	5·577	5·586	5·595	5·604	5·612	5·621	5·630	5·639	5·648	1 2 3	3 4 5	6 7 8
32	5·657	5·666	5·675	5·683	5·692	5·701	5·710	5·718	5·727	5·736	1 2 3	3 4 5	6 7 8
33	5·745	5·753	5·762	5·771	5·779	5·788	5·797	5·805	5·814	5·822	1 2 3	3 4 5	6 7 8
34	5·831	5·840	5·848	5·857	5·865	5·874	5·882	5·891	5·899	5·908	1 2 3	3 4 5	6 7 8
35	5·916	5·925	5·933	5·941	5·950	5·958	5·967	5·975	5·983	5·992	1 2 2	3 4 5	6 7 8
36	6·000	6·008	6·017	6·025	6·033	6·042	6·050	6·058	6·066	6·075	1 2 2	3 4 5	6 7 7
37	6·083	6·091	6·099	6·107	6·116	6·124	6·132	6·140	6·148	6·156	1 2 2	3 4 5	6 7 7
38	6·164	6·173	6·181	6·189	6·197	6·205	6·213	6·221	6·229	6·237	1 2 2	3 4 5	6 6 7
39	6·245	6·253	6·261	6·269	6·277	6·285	6·293	6·301	6·309	6·317	1 2 2	3 4 5	6 6 7
40	6·325	6·332	6·340	6·348	6·356	6·364	6·372	6·380	6·387	6·395	1 2 2	3 4 5	6 6 7
41	6·403	6·411	6·419	6·427	6·434	6·442	6·450	6·458	6·465	6·473	1 2 2	3 4 5	5 6 7
42	6·481	6·488	6·496	6·504	6·512	6·519	6·527	6·535	6·542	6·550	1 2 2	3 4 5	5 6 7
43	6·557	6·565	6·573	6·580	6·588	6·595	6·603	6·611	6·618	6·626	1 2 2	3 4 5	5 6 7
44	6·633	6·641	6·648	6·656	6·663	6·671	6·678	6·686	6·693	6·701	1 2 2	3 4 5	5 6 7
45	6·708	6·716	6·723	6·731	6·738	6·745	6·753	6·760	6·768	6·775	1 1 2	3 4 4	5 6 7
46	6·782	6·790	6·797	6·804	6·812	6·819	6·826	6·834	6·841	6·848	1 1 2	3 4 4	5 6 7
47	6·856	6·863	6·870	6·877	6·885	6·892	6·899	6·907	6·914	6·921	1 1 2	3 4 4	5 6 7
48	6·928	6·935	6·943	6·950	6·957	6·964	6·971	6·979	6·986	6·993	1 1 2	3 4 4	5 6 6
49	7·000	7·007	7·014	7·021	7·029	7·036	7·043	7·050	7·057	7·064	1 1 2	3 4 4	5 6 6
50	7·071	7·078	7·085	7·092	7·099	7·106	7·113	7·120	7·127	7·134	1 1 2	3 4 4	5 6 6
51	7·141	7·148	7·155	7·162	7·169	7·176	7·183	7·190	7·197	7·204	1 1 2	3 4 4	5 6 6
52	7·211	7·218	7·225	7·232	7·239	7·246	7·253	7·259	7·266	7·273	1 1 2	3 3 4	5 6 6
53	7·280	7·287	7·294	7·301	7·308	7·314	7·321	7·328	7·335	7·342	1 1 2	3 3 4	5 5 6
54	7·348	7·355	7·362	7·369	7·376	7·382	7·389	7·396	7·403	7·409	1 1 2	3 3 4	5 5 6

Mean Differences

	0	1	2	3	4	5	6	7	8	9	Mean Differences 1 2 3	4 5 6	7 8 9
55	7·416	7·423	7·430	7·436	7·443	7·450	7·457	7·463	7·470	7·477	1 1 2	3 3 4	5 5 6
56	7·483	7·490	7·497	7·503	7·510	7·517	7·523	7·530	7·537	7·543	1 1 2	3 3 4	5 5 6
57	7·550	7·556	7·563	7·570	7·576	7·583	7·589	7·596	7·603	7·609	1 1 2	3 3 4	5 5 6
58	7·616	7·622	7·629	7·635	7·642	7·649	7·655	7·662	7·668	7·675	1 1 2	3 3 4	5 5 6
59	7·681	7·688	7·694	7·701	7·707	7·714	7·720	7·727	7·733	7·740	1 1 2	3 3 4	4 5 6
60	7·746	7·752	7·759	7·765	7·772	7·778	7·785	7·791	7·797	7·804	1 1 2	3 3 4	4 5 6
61	7·810	7·817	7·823	7·829	7·836	7·842	7·849	7·855	7·861	7·868	1 1 2	3 3 4	4 5 6
62	7·874	7·880	7·887	7·893	7·899	7·906	7·912	7·918	7·925	7·931	1 1 2	3 3 4	4 5 6
63	7·937	7·944	7·950	7·956	7·962	7·969	7·975	7·981	7·987	7·994	1 1 2	3 3 4	4 5 6
64	8·000	8·006	8·012	8·019	8·025	8·031	8·037	8·044	8·050	8·056	1 1 2	2 3 4	4 5 6
65	8·062	8·068	8·075	8·081	8·087	8·093	8·099	8·106	8·112	8·118	1 1 2	2 3 4	4 5 6
66	8·124	8·130	8·136	8·142	8·149	8·155	8·161	8·167	8·173	8·179	1 1 2	2 3 4	4 5 5
67	8·185	8·191	8·198	8·204	8·210	8·216	8·222	8·228	8·234	8·240	1 1 2	2 3 4	4 5 5
68	8·246	8·252	8·258	8·264	8·270	8·276	8·283	8·289	8·295	8·301	1 1 2	2 3 4	4 5 5
69	8·307	8·313	8·319	8·325	8·331	8·337	8·343	8·349	8·355	8·361	1 1 2	2 3 4	4 5 5
70	8·367	8·373	8·379	8·385	8·390	8·396	8·402	8·408	8·414	8·420	1 1 2	2 3 4	4 5 5
71	8·426	8·432	8·438	8·444	8·450	8·456	8·462	8·468	8·473	8·479	1 1 2	2 3 4	4 5 5
72	8·485	8·491	8·497	8·503	8·509	8·515	8·521	8·526	8·532	8·538	1 1 2	2 3 3	4 5 5
73	8·544	8·550	8·556	8·562	8·567	8·573	8·579	8·585	8·591	8·597	1 1 2	2 3 3	4 5 5
74	8·602	8·608	8·614	8·620	8·626	8·631	8·637	8·643	8·649	8·654	1 1 2	2 3 3	4 5 5
75	8·660	8·666	8·672	8·678	8·683	8·689	8·695	8·701	8·706	8·712	1 1 2	2 3 3	4 5 5
76	8·718	8·724	8·729	8·735	8·741	8·746	8·752	8·758	8·764	8·769	1 1 2	2 3 3	4 5 5
77	8·775	8·781	8·786	8·792	8·798	8·803	8·809	8·815	8·820	8·826	1 1 2	2 3 3	4 4 5
78	8·832	8·837	8·843	8·849	8·854	8·860	8·866	8·871	8·877	8·883	1 1 2	2 3 3	4 4 5
79	8·888	8·894	8·899	8·905	8·911	8·916	8·922	8·927	8·933	8·939	1 1 2	2 3 3	4 4 5
80	8·944	8·950	8·955	8·961	8·967	8·972	8·978	8·983	8·989	8·994	1 1 2	2 3 3	4 4 5
81	9·000	9·006	9·011	9·017	9·022	9·028	9·033	9·039	9·044	9·050	1 1 2	2 3 3	4 4 5
82	9·055	9·061	9·066	9·072	9·077	9·083	9·088	9·094	9·099	9·105	1 1 2	2 3 3	4 4 5
83	9·110	9·116	9·121	9·127	9·132	9·138	9·143	9·149	9·154	9·160	1 1 2	2 3 3	4 4 5
84	9·165	9·171	9·176	9·182	9·187	9·192	9·198	9·203	9·209	9·214	1 1 2	2 3 3	4 4 5
85	9·220	9·225	9·230	9·236	9·241	9·247	9·252	9·257	9·263	9·268	1 1 2	2 3 3	4 4 5
86	9·274	9·279	9·284	9·290	9·295	9·301	9·306	9·311	9·317	9·322	1 1 2	2 3 3	4 4 5
87	9·327	9·333	9·338	9·343	9·349	9·354	9·359	9·365	9·370	9·375	1 1 2	2 3 3	4 4 5
88	9·381	9·386	9·391	9·397	9·402	9·407	9·413	9·418	9·423	9·429	1 1 2	2 3 3	4 4 5
89	9·434	9·439	9·445	9·450	9·455	9·460	9·466	9·471	9·476	9·482	1 1 2	2 3 3	4 4 5
90	9·487	9·492	9·497	9·503	9·508	9·513	9·518	9·524	9·529	9·534	1 1 2	2 3 3	4 4 5
91	9·539	9·545	9·550	9·555	9·560	9·566	9·571	9·576	9·581	9·586	1 1 2	2 3 3	4 4 5
92	9·592	9·597	9·602	9·607	9·612	9·618	9·623	9·628	9·633	9·638	1 1 2	2 3 3	4 4 5
93	9·644	9·649	9·654	9·659	9·664	9·670	9·675	9·680	9·685	9·690	1 1 2	2 3 3	4 4 5
94	9·695	9·701	9·706	9·711	9·716	9·721	9·726	9·731	9·737	9·742	1 1 2	2 3 3	4 4 5
95	9·747	9·752	9·757	9·762	9·767	9·772	9·778	9·783	9·788	9·793	1 1 2	2 3 3	4 4 5
96	9·798	9·803	9·808	9·813	9·818	9·823	9·829	9·834	9·839	9·844	1 1 2	2 3 3	4 4 5
97	9·849	9·854	9·859	9·864	9·869	9·874	9·879	9·884	9·889	9·894	1 1 1	2 3 3	4 4 5
98	9·899	9·905	9·910	9·915	9·920	9·925	9·930	9·935	9·940	9·945	0 1 1	2 2 3	3 4 4
99	9·950	9·955	9·960	9·965	9·970	9·975	9·980	9·985	9·990	9·995	0 1 1	2 2 3	3 4 4

	·00	·01	·02	·03	·04	·05	·06	·07	·08	·09	·001	·002	·003	·004	·005	·006	·007	·008	·009
1·0	·0000	·0043	·0086	·0128	·0170						5	9	13	17	21	26	30	34	38
						·0212	·0253	·0294	·0334	·0374	4	8	12	16	20	24	28	32	36
1·1	·0414	·0453	·0492	·0531	·0569						4	8	12	16	20	23	27	31	35
						·0607	·0645	·0682	·0719	·0755	4	7	11	15	18	22	26	29	33
1·2	·0792	·0828	·0864	·0899	·0934						3	7	11	14	18	21	25	28	32
						·0969	·1004	·1038	·1072	·1106	3	7	10	14	17	20	24	27	31
1·3	·1139	·1173	·1206	·1239	·1271		·				3	6	10	13	16	19	23	26	29
						·1303	·1335	·1367	·1399	·1430	3	7	10	13	16	19	22	25	29
1·4	·1461	·1492	·1523	·1553	·1584						3	6	9	12	15	19	22	25	28
						·1614	·1644	·1673	·1703	·1732	3	6	9	12	14	17	20	23	26
1·5	·1761	·1790	·1818	·1847	·1875						3	6	9	11	14	17	20	23	26
						·1903	·1931	·1959	·1987	·2014	3	6	8	11	14	17	19	22	25
1·6	·2041	·2068	·2095	·2122	·2148						3	6	8	11	14	16	19	22	24
						·2175	·2201	·2227	·2253	·2279	3	5	8	10	13	16	18	21	23
1·7	·2304	·2330	·2355	·2380	·2405						3	5	8	10	13	15	18	20	23
						·2430	·2455	·2480	·2504	·2529	3	5	8	10	12	15	17	20	22
1·8	·2553	·2577	·2601	·2625	·2648						2	5	7	9	12	14	17	19	21
						·2672	·2695	·2718	·2742	·2765	2	4	7	9	11	14	16	18	21
1·9	·2788	·2810	·2833	·2856	·2878						2	4	7	9	11	13	16	18	20
						·2900	·2923	·2945	·2967	·2989	2	4	6	8	11	13	15	17	19
2·0	·3010	·3032	·3054	·3075	·3096	·3118	·3139	·3160	·3181	·3201	2	4	6	8	11	13	15	17	19
2·1	·3222	·3243	·3263	·3284	·3304	·3324	·3345	·3365	·3385	·3404	2	4	6	8	10	12	14	16	18
2·2	·3424	·3444	·3464	·3483	·3502	·3522	·3541	·3560	·3579	·3598	2	4	6	8	10	12	14	15	17
2·3	·3617	·3636	·3655	·3674	·3692	·3711	·3729	·3747	·3766	·3784	2	4	6	7	9	11	13	15	17
2·4	·3802	·3820	·3838	·3856	·3874	·3892	·3909	·3927	·3945	·3962	2	4	5	7	9	11	12	14	16
2·5	·3979	·3997	·4014	·4031	·4048	·4065	·4082	·4099	·4116	·4133	2	3	5	7	9	10	12	14	15
2·6	·4150	·4166	·4183	·4200	·4216	·4232	·4249	·4265	·4281	·4298	2	3	5	7	8	10	11	13	15
2·7	·4314	·4330	·4346	·4362	·4378	·4393	·4409	·4425	·4440	·4456	2	3	5	6	8	9	11	13	14
2·8	·4472	·4487	·4502	·4518	·4533	·4548	·4564	·4579	·4594	·4609	2	3	5	6	8	9	11	12	14
2·9	·4624	·4639	·4654	·4669	·4683	·4698	·4713	·4728	·4742	·4757	1	3	4	6	7	9	10	12	13
3·0	·4771	·4786	·4800	·4814	·4829	·4843	·4857	·4871	·4886	·4900	1	3	4	6	7	9	10	11	13
3·1	·4914	·4928	·4942	·4955	·4969	·4983	·4997	·5011	·5024	·5038	1	3	4	6	7	8	10	11	12
3·2	·5051	·5065	·5079	·5092	·5105	·5119	·5132	·5145	·5159	·5172	1	3	4	5	7	8	9	11	12
3·3	·5185	·5198	·5211	·5224	·5237	·5250	·5263	·5276	·5289	·5302	1	3	4	5	6	8	9	10	12
3·4	·5315	·5328	·5340	·5353	·5366	·5378	·5391	·5403	·5416	·5428	1	3	4	5	6	8	9	10	11
3·5	·5441	·5453	·5465	·5478	·5490	·5502	·5514	·5527	·5539	·5551	1	2	4	5	6	7	9	10	11
3·6	·5563	·5575	·5587	·5599	·5611	·5623	·5635	·5647	·5658	·5670	1	2	4	5	6	7	8	10	11
3·7	·5682	·5694	·5705	·5717	·5729	·5740	·5752	·5763	·5775	·5786	1	2	3	5	6	7	8	9	10
3·8	·5798	·5809	·5821	·5832	·5843	·5855	·5866	·5877	·5888	·5899	1	2	3	5	6	7	8	9	10
3·9	·5911	·5922	·5933	·5944	·5955	·5966	·5977	·5988	·5999	·6010	1	2	3	4	5	7	8	9	10
4·0	·6021	·6031	·6042	·6053	·6064	·6075	·6085	·6096	·6107	·6117	1	2	3	4	5	6	8	9	10
4·1	·6128	·6138	·6149	·6160	·6170	·6180	·6191	·6201	·6212	·6222	1	2	3	4	5	6	7	8	9
4·2	·6232	·6243	·6253	·6263	·6274	·6284	·6294	·6304	·6314	·6325	1	2	3	4	5	6	7	8	9
4·3	·6335	·6345	·6355	·6365	·6375	·6385	·6395	·6405	·6415	·6425	1	2	3	4	5	6	7	8	9
4·4	·6435	·6444	·6454	·6464	·6474	·6484	·6493	·6503	·6513	·6522	1	2	3	4	5	6	7	8	9
4·5	·6532	·6542	·6551	·6561	·6571	·6580	·6590	·6599	·6609	·6618	1	2	3	4	5	6	7	8	9
4·6	·6628	·6637	·6646	·6656	·6665	·6675	·6684	·6693	·6702	·6712	1	2	3	4	5	6	7	7	8
4·7	·6721	·6730	·6739	·6749	·6758	·6767	·6776	·6785	·6794	·6803	1	2	3	4	5	5	6	7	8
4·8	·6812	·6821	·6830	·6839	·6848	·6857	·6866	·6875	·6884	·6893	1	2	3	4	4	5	6	7	8
4·9	·6902	·6911	·6920	·6928	·6937	·6946	·6955	·6964	·6972	·6981	1	2	3	4	4	5	6	7	8

10,000ths

	0·0	·01	·02	·03	·04	·05	·06	·07	·08	·09	·001	·002	·003	·004	·005	·006	·007	·008	·009
5·0	·6990	·6998	·7007	·7016	·7024	·7033	·7042	·7050	·7059	·7067	1	2	3	3	4	5	6	7	8
5·1	·7076	·7084	·7093	·7101	·7110	·7118	·7126	·7135	·7143	·7152	1	2	3	3	4	5	6	7	8
5·2	·7160	·7168	·7177	·7185	·7193	·7202	·7210	·7218	·7226	·7235	1	2	2	3	4	5	6	7	7
5·3	·7243	·7251	·7259	·7267	·7275	·7284	·7292	·7300	·7308	·7316	1	2	2	3	4	5	6	6	7
5·4	·7324	·7332	·7340	·7348	·7356	·7364	·7372	·7380	·7388	·7396	1	2	2	3	4	5	6	6	7
5·5	·7404	·7412	·7419	·7427	·7435	·7443	·7451	·7459	·7466	·7474	1	2	2	3	4	5	5	6	7
5·6	·7482	·7490	·7497	·7505	·7513	·7520	·7528	·7536	·7543	·7551	1	2	2	3	4	5	5	6	7
5·7	·7559	·7566	·7574	·7582	·7589	·7597	·7604	·7612	·7619	·7627	1	2	2	3	4	5	5	6	7
5·8	·7634	·7642	·7649	·7657	·7664	·7672	·7679	·7686	·7694	·7701	1	1	2	3	4	4	5	6	7
5·9	·7709	·7716	·7723	·7731	·7738	·7745	·7752	·7760	·7767	·7774	1	1	2	3	4	4	5	6	7
6·0	·7782	·7789	·7796	·7803	·7810	·7818	·7825	·7832	·7839	·7846	1	1	2	3	4	4	5	6	6
6·1	·7853	·7860	·7868	·7875	·7882	·7889	·7896	·7903	·7910	·7917	1	1	2	3	4	4	5	6	6
6·2	·7924	·7931	·7938	·7945	·7952	·7959	·7966	·7973	·7980	·7987	1	1	2	3	3	4	5	6	6
6·3	·7993	·8000	·8007	·8014	·8021	·8028	·8035	·8041	·8048	·8055	1	1	2	3	3	4	5	5	6
6·4	·8062	·8069	·8075	·8082	·8089	·8096	·8102	·8109	·8116	·8122	1	1	2	3	3	4	5	5	6
6·5	·8129	·8136	·8142	·8149	·8156	·8162	·8169	·8176	·8182	·8189	1	1	2	3	3	4	5	5	6
6·6	·8195	·8202	·8209	·8215	·8222	·8228	·8235	·8241	·8248	·8254	1	1	2	3	3	4	5	5	6
6·7	·8261	·8267	·8274	·8280	·8287	·8293	·8299	·8306	·8312	·8319	1	1	2	3	3	4	5	5	6
6·8	·8325	·8331	·8338	·8344	·8351	·8357	·8363	·8370	·8376	·8382	1	1	2	3	3	4	4	5	6
6·9	·8388	·8395	·8401	·8407	·8414	·8420	·8426	·8432	·8439	·8445	1	1	2	2	3	4	4	5	6
7·0	·8451	·8457	·8463	·8470	·8476	·8482	·8488	·8494	·8500	·8506	1	1	2	2	3	4	4	5	6
7·1	·8513	·8519	·8525	·8531	·8537	·8543	·8549	·8555	·8561	·8567	1	1	2	2	3	4	4	5	5
7·2	·8573	·8579	·8585	·8591	·8597	·8603	·8609	·8615	·8621	·8627	1	1	2	2	3	4	4	5	5
7·3	·8633	·8639	·8645	·8651	·8657	·8663	·8669	·8675	·8681	·8686	1	1	2	2	3	4	4	5	5
7·4	·8692	·8698	·8704	·8710	·8716	·8722	·8727	·8733	·8739	·8745	1	1	2	2	3	4	4	5	5
7·5	·8751	·8756	·8762	·8768	·8774	·8779	·8785	·8791	·8797	·8802	1	1	2	2	3	3	4	5	5
7·6	·8808	·8814	·8820	·8825	·8831	·8837	·8842	·8848	·8854	·8859	1	1	2	2	3	3	4	5	5
7·7	·8865	·8871	·8876	·8882	·8887	·8893	·8899	·8904	·8910	·8915	1	1	2	2	3	3	4	4	5
7·8	·8921	·8927	·8932	·8938	·8943	·8949	·8954	·8960	·8965	·8971	1	1	2	2	3	3	4	4	5
7·9	·8976	·8982	·8987	·8993	·8998	·9004	·9009	·9015	·9020	·9025	1	1	2	2	3	3	4	4	5
8·0	·9031	·9036	·9042	·9047	·9053	·9058	·9063	·9069	·9074	·9079	1	1	2	2	3	3	4	4	5
8·1	·9085	·9090	·9096	·9101	·9106	·9112	·9117	·9122	·9128	·9133	1	1	2	2	3	3	4	4	5
8·2	·9138	·9143	·9149	·9154	·9159	·9165	·9170	·9175	·9180	·9186	1	1	2	2	3	3	4	4	5
8·3	·9191	·9196	·9201	·9206	·9212	·9217	·9222	·9227	·9232	·9238	1	1	2	2	3	3	4	4	5
8·4	·9243	·9248	·9253	·9258	·9263	·9269	·9274	·9279	·9284	·9289	1	1	2	2	3	3	4	4	5
8·5	·9294	·9299	·9304	·9309	·9315	·9320	·9325	·9330	·9335	·9340	1	1	2	2	3	3	4	4	5
8·6	·9345	·9350	·9355	·9360	·9365	·9370	·9375	·9380	·9385	·9390	1	1	2	2	3	3	4	4	5
8·7	·9395	·9400	·9405	·9410	·9415	·9420	·9425	·9430	·9435	·9440	0	1	1	2	2	3	3	4	4
8·8	·9445	·9450	·9455	·9460	·9465	·9469	·9474	·9479	·9484	·9489	0	1	1	2	2	3	3	4	4
8·9	·9494	·9499	·9504	·9509	·9513	·9518	·9523	·9528	·9533	·9538	0	1	1	2	2	3	3	4	4
9·0	·9542	·9547	·9552	·9557	·9562	·9566	·9571	·9576	·9581	·9586	0	1	1	2	2	3	3	4	4
9·1	·9590	·9595	·9600	·9605	·9609	·9614	·9619	·9624	·9628	·9633	0	1	1	2	2	3	3	4	4
9·2	·9638	·9643	·9647	·9652	·9657	·9661	·9666	·9671	·9675	·9680	0	1	1	2	2	3	3	4	4
9·3	·9685	·9689	·9694	·9699	·9703	·9708	·9713	·9717	·9722	·9727	0	1	1	2	2	3	3	4	4
9·4	·9731	·9736	·9741	·9745	·9750	·9754	·9759	·9763	·9768	·9773	0	1	1	2	2	3	3	4	4
9·5	·9777	·9782	·9786	·9791	·9795	·9800	·9805	·9809	·9814	·9818	0	1	1	2	2	3	3	4	4
9·6	·9823	·9827	·9832	·9836	·9841	·9845	·9850	·9854	·9859	·9863	0	1	1	2	2	3	3	4	4
9·7	·9868	·9872	·9877	·9881	·9886	·9890	·9894	·9899	·9903	·9908	0	1	1	2	2	3	3	4	4
9·8	·9912	·9917	·9921	·9926	·9930	·9934	·9939	·9943	·9948	·9952	0	1	1	2	2	3	3	4	4
9·9	·9956	·9961	·9965	·9969	·9974	·9978	·9983	·9987	·9991	·9996	0	1	1	2	2	3	3	3	4

10,000ths

	0	1	2	3	4	5	6	7	8	9	1 2 3 4	5	6 7 8 9
·00	1000	1002	1005	1007	1009	1012	1014	1016	1019	1021	0 0 1 1	1	1 2 2 2
·01	1023	1026	1028	1030	1033	1035	1038	1040	1042	1045	0 0 1 1	1	1 2 2 2
·02	1047	1050	1052	1054	1057	1059	1062	1064	1067	1069	0 0 1 1	1	1 2 2 2
·03	1072	1074	1076	1079	1081	1084	1086	1089	1091	1094	0 0 1 1	1	1 2 2 2
·04	1096	1099	1102	1104	1107	1109	1112	1114	1117	1119	0 1 1 1	1	2 2 2 2
·05	1122	1125	1127	1130	1132	1135	1138	1140	1143	1146	0 1 1 1	1	2 2 2 2
·06	1148	1151	1153	1156	1159	1161	1164	1167	1169	1172	0 1 1 1	1	2 2 2 2
·07	1175	1178	1180	1183	1186	1189	1191	1194	1197	1199	0 1 1 1	1	2 2 2 2
·08	1202	1205	1208	1211	1213	1216	1219	1222	1225	1227	0 1 1 1	1	2 2 2 3
·09	1230	1233	1236	1239	1242	1245	1247	1250	1253	1256	0 1 1 1	1	2 2 2 3
·10	1259	1262	1265	1268	1271	1274	1276	1279	1282	1285	0 1 1 1	1	2 2 2 3
·11	1288	1291	1294	1297	1300	1303	1306	1309	1312	1315	0 1 1 1	2	2 2 2 3
·12	1318	1321	1324	1327	1330	1334	1337	1340	1343	1346	0 1 1 1	2	2 2 2 3
·13	1349	1352	1355	1358	1361	1365	1368	1371	1374	1377	0 1 1 1	2	2 2 3 3
·14	1380	1384	1387	1390	1393	1396	1400	1403	1406	1409	0 1 1 1	2	2 2 3 3
·15	1413	1416	1419	1422	1426	1429	1432	1435	1439	1442	0 1 1 1	2	2 2 3 3
·16	1445	1449	1452	1455	1459	1462	1466	1469	1472	1476	0 1 1 1	2	2 2 3 3
·17	1479	1483	1486	1489	1493	1496	1500	1503	1507	1510	0 1 1 1	2	2 2 3 3
·18	1514	1517	1521	1524	1528	1531	1535	1538	1542	1545	0 1 1 1	2	2 2 3 3
·19	1549	1552	1556	1560	1563	1567	1570	1574	1578	1581	0 1 1 1	2	2 3 3 3
·20	1585	1589	1592	1596	1600	1603	1607	1611	1614	1618	0 1 1 1	2	2 3 3 3
·21	1622	1626	1629	1633	1637	1641	1644	1648	1652	1656	0 1 1 2	2	2 3 3 3
·22	1660	1663	1667	1671	1675	1679	1683	1687	1690	1694	0 1 1 2	2	2 3 3 3
·23	1698	1702	1706	1710	1714	1718	1722	1726	1730	1734	0 1 1 2	2	2 3 3 4
·24	1738	1742	1746	1750	1754	1758	1762	1766	1770	1774	0 1 1 2	2	2 3 3 4
·25	1778	1782	1786	1791	1795	1799	1803	1807	1811	1816	0 1 1 2	2	2 3 3 4
·26	1820	1824	1828	1832	1837	1841	1845	1849	1854	1858	0 1 1 2	2	3 3 3 4
·27	1862	1866	1871	1875	1879	1884	1888	1892	1897	1901	0 1 1 2	2	3 3 3 4
·28	1905	1910	1914	1919	1923	1928	1932	1936	1941	1945	0 1 1 2	2	3 3 4 4
·29	1950	1954	1959	1963	1968	1972	1977	1982	1986	1991	0 1 1 2	2	3 3 4 4
·30	1995	2000	2004	2009	2014	2018	2023	2028	2032	2037	0 1 1 2	2	3 3 4 4
·31	2042	2046	2051	2056	2061	2065	2070	2075	2080	2084	0 1 1 2	2	3 3 4 4
·32	2089	2094	2099	2104	2109	2113	2118	2123	2128	2133	0 1 1 2	2	3 3 4 4
·33	2138	2143	2148	2153	2158	2163	2168	2173	2178	2183	0 1 1 2	2	3 3 4 4
·34	2188	2193	2198	2203	2208	2213	2218	2223	2228	2234	1 1 2 2	3	3 4 4 5
·35	2239	2244	2249	2254	2259	2265	2270	2275	2280	2286	1 1 2 2	3	3 4 4 5
·36	2291	2296	2301	2307	2312	2317	2323	2328	2333	2339	1 1 2 2	3	3 4 4 5
·37	2344	2350	2355	2360	2366	2371	2377	2382	2388	2393	1 1 2 2	3	3 4 4 5
·38	2399	2404	2410	2415	2421	2427	2432	2438	2443	2449	1 1 2 2	3	3 4 4 5
·39	2455	2460	2466	2472	2477	2483	2489	2495	2500	2506	1 1 2 2	3	3 4 5 5
·40	2512	2518	2523	2529	2535	2541	2547	2553	2559	2564	1 1 2 2	3	4 4 5 5
·41	2570	2576	2582	2588	2594	2600	2606	2612	2618	2624	1 1 2 2	3	4 4 5 5
·42	2630	2636	2642	2649	2655	2661	2667	2673	2679	2685	1 1 2 2	3	4 4 5 6
·43	2692	2698	2704	2710	2716	2723	2729	2735	2742	2748	1 1 2 3	3	4 4 5 6
·44	2754	2761	2767	2773	2780	2786	2793	2799	2805	2812	1 1 2 3	3	4 4 5 6
·45	2818	2825	2831	2838	2844	2851	2858	2864	2871	2877	1 1 2 3	3	4 5 5 6
·46	2884	2891	2897	2904	2911	2917	2924	2931	2938	2944	1 1 2 3	3	4 5 5 6
·47	2951	2958	2965	2972	2979	2985	2992	2999	3006	3013	1 1 2 3	3	4 5 5 6
·48	3020	3027	3034	3041	3048	3055	3062	3069	3076	3083	1 1 2 3	4	4 5 6 6
·49	3090	3097	3105	3112	3119	3126	3133	3141	3148	3155	1 1 2 3	4	4 5 6 6

	0	1	2	3	4	5	6	7	8	9	1 2 3 4	5	6 7 8 9
·50	3162	3170	3177	3184	3192	3199	3206	3214	3221	3228	1 1 2 3	4	4 5 6 7
·51	3236	3243	3251	3258	3266	3273	3281	3289	3296	3304	1 2 2 3	4	5 5 6 7
·52	3311	3319	3327	3334	3342	3350	3357	3365	3373	3381	1 2 2 3	4	5 5 6 7
·53	3388	3396	3404	3412	3420	3428	3436	3443	3451	3459	1 2 2 3	4	5 6 6 7
·54	3467	3475	3483	3491	3499	3508	3516	3524	3532	3540	1 2 2 3	4	5 6 6 7
·55	3548	3556	3565	3573	3581	3589	3597	3606	3614	3622	1 2 2 3	4	5 6 7 7
·56	3631	3639	3648	3656	3664	3673	3681	3690	3698	3707	1 2 3 3	4	5 6 7 8
·57	3715	3724	3733	3741	3750	3758	3767	3776	3784	3793	1 2 3 3	4	5 6 7 8
·58	3802	3811	3819	3828	3837	3846	3855	3864	3873	3882	1 2 3 4	4	5 6 7 8
·59	3890	3899	3908	3917	3926	3936	3945	3954	3963	3972	1 2 3 4	5	5 6 7 8
·60	3981	3990	3999	4009	4018	4027	4036	4046	4055	4064	1 2 3 4	5	6 6 7 8
·61	4074	4083	4093	4102	4111	4121	4130	4140	4150	4159	1 2 3 4	5	6 7 8 9
·62	4169	4178	4188	4198	4207	4217	4227	4236	4246	4256	1 2 3 4	5	6 7 8 9
·63	4266	4276	4285	4295	4305	4315	4325	4335	4345	4355	1 2 3 4	5	6 7 8 9
·64	4365	4375	4385	4395	4406	4416	4426	4436	4446	4457	1 2 3 4	5	6 7 8 9
·65	4467	4477	4487	4498	4508	4519	4529	4539	4550	4560	1 2 3 4	5	6 7 8 9
·66	4571	4581	4592	4603	4613	4624	4634	4645	4656	4667	1 2 3 4	5	6 7 9 10
·67	4677	4688	4699	4710	4721	4732	4742	4753	4764	4775	1 2 3 4	5	7 8 9 10
·68	4786	4797	4808	4819	4831	4842	4853	4864	4875	4887	1 2 3 4	6	7 8 9 10
·69	4898	4909	4920	4932	4943	4955	4966	4977	4989	5000	1 2 3 5	6	7 8 9 10
·70	5012	5023	5035	5047	5058	5070	5082	5093	5105	5117	1 2 4 5	6	7 8 9 10
·71	5129	5140	5152	5164	5176	5188	5200	5212	5224	5236	1 2 4 5	6	7 8 10 11
·72	5248	5260	5272	5284	5297	5309	5321	5333	5346	5358	1 2 4 5	6	7 9 10 11
·73	5370	5383	5395	5408	5420	5433	5445	5458	5470	5483	1 3 4 5	6	8 9 10 11
·74	5495	5508	5521	5534	5546	5559	5572	5585	5598	5610	1 3 4 5	6	8 9 10 12
·75	5623	5636	5649	5662	5675	5689	5702	5715	5728	5741	1 3 4 5	7	8 9 10 12
·76	5754	5768	5781	5794	5808	5821	5834	5848	5861	5875	1 3 4 5	7	8 9 11 12
·77	5888	5902	5916	5929	5943	5957	5970	5984	5998	6012	1 3 4 5	7	8 10 11 12
·78	6026	6039	6053	6067	6081	6095	6109	6124	6138	6152	1 3 4 6	7	8 10 11 13
·79	6166	6180	6194	6209	6223	6237	6252	6266	6281	6295	1 3 4 6	7	9 10 11 13
·80	6310	6324	6339	6353	6368	6383	6397	6412	6427	6442	1 3 4 6	7	9 10 12 13
·81	6457	6471	6486	6501	6516	6531	6546	6561	6577	6592	2 3 5 6	8	9 11 12 14
·82	6607	6622	6637	6653	6668	6683	6699	6714	6730	6745	2 3 5 6	8	9 11 12 14
·83	6761	6776	6792	6808	6823	6839	6855	6871	6887	6902	2 3 5 6	8	9 11 13 14
·84	6918	6934	6950	6966	6982	6998	7015	7033	7047	7063	2 3 5 6	8	10 11 13 15
·85	7079	7096	7112	7129	7145	7161	7178	7194	7211	7228	2 3 5 7	8	10 12 13 15
·86	7244	7261	7278	7295	7311	7328	7345	7362	7379	7396	2 3 5 7	8	10 12 13 15
·87	7413	7430	7447	7464	7482	7499	7516	7534	7551	7568	2 3 5 7	9	10 12 14 16
·88	7586	7603	7621	7638	7656	7674	7691	7709	7727	7745	2 4 5 7	9	11 12 14 16
·89	7762	7780	7798	7816	7834	7852	7870	7889	7907	7925	2 4 5 7	9	11 13 14 16
·90	7943	7962	7980	7998	8017	8035	8054	8072	8091	8110	2 4 6 7	9	11 13 15 17
·91	8128	8147	8166	8185	8204	8222	8241	8260	8279	8299	2 4 6 8	9	11 13 15 17
·92	8318	8337	8356	8375	8395	8414	8433	8453	8472	8492	2 4 6 8	10	12 14 15 17
·93	8511	8531	8551	8570	8590	8610	8630	8650	8670	8690	2 4 6 8	10	12 14 16 18
·94	8710	8730	8750	8770	8790	8810	8831	8851	8872	8892	2 4 6 8	10	12 14 16 18
·95	8913	8933	8954	8974	8995	9016	9036	9057	9078	9099	2 4 6 8	10	12 15 17 19
·96	9120	9141	9162	9183	9204	9226	9247	9268	9290	9311	2 4 6 8	11	13 15 17 19
·97	9333	9354	9376	9397	9419	9441	9462	9484	9506	9528	2 4 7 9	11	13 15 17 20
·98	9550	9572	9594	9616	9638	9661	9683	9705	9727	9750	2 4 7 9	11	13 16 18 20
·99	9772	9795	9817	9840	9863	9886	9908	9931	9954	9977	2 5 7 9	11	14 16 18 20

TABLE IX e^{-x}: NAPERIAN LOGARITHMS FROM 0.1 TO 1

x	e^{-x}	x	e^{-x}	x	e^{-x}	x	e^{-x}
0.00	1.00000	0.50	.60653	1.00	.36788	1.50	.22313
0.01	0.99005	0.51	.60050	1.01	.36422	1.51	.22091
0.02	.98020	0.52	.59452	1.02	.36059	1.52	.21871
0.03	.97045	0.53	.58860	1.03	.35701	1.53	.21654
0.04	.96079	0.54	.58275	1.04	.35345	1.54	.21438
0.05	.95123	0.55	.57695	1.05	.34994	1.55	.21225
0.06	.94176	0.56	.57121	1.06	.34646	1.56	.21014
0.07	.93239	0.57	.56553	1.07	.34301	1.57	.20805
0.08	.92312	0.58	.55990	1.08	.33960	1.58	.20598
0.09	.91393	0.59	.55433	1.09	.33622	1.59	.20393
0.10	.90484	0.60	.54881	1.10	.33287	1.60	.20190
0.11	.89583	0.61	.54335	1.11	.32956	1.61	.19989
0.12	.88692	0.62	.53794	1.12	.32628	1.62	.19790
0.13	.87810	0.63	.53259	1.13	.32303	1.63	.19593
0.14	.86936	0.64	.52729	1.14	.31982	1.64	.19398
0.15	.86071	0.65	.52205	1.15	.31664	1.65	.19205
0.16	.85214	0.66	.51685	1.16	.31349	1.66	.19014
0.17	.84366	0.67	.51171	1.17	.31037	1.67	.18825
0.18	.83527	0.68	.50662	1.18	.30728	1.68	.18637
0.19	.82696	0.69	.50158	1.19	.30422	1.69	.18452
0.20	.81873	0.70	.49659	1.20	.30119	1.70	.18268
0.21	.81058	0.71	.49164	1.21	.29820	1.71	.18087
0.22	.80252	0.72	.48675	1.22	.29523	1.72	.17907
0.23	.79453	0.73	.48191	1.23	.29229	1.73	.17728
0.24	.78663	0.74	.47711	1.24	.28938	1.74	.17552
0.25	.77880	0.75	.47237	1.25	.28650	1.75	.17377
0.26	.77105	0.76	.46767	1.26	.28365	1.76	.17204
0.27	.76338	0.77	.46301	1.27	.28083	1.77	.17033
0.28	.75578	0.78	.45841	1.28	.27804	1.78	.16864
0.29	.74826	0.79	.45384	1.29	.27527	1.79	.16696
0.30	.74082	0.80	.44933	1.30	.27253	1.80	.16530
0.31	.73345	0.81	.44486	1.31	.26982	1.81	.16365
0.32	.72615	0.82	.44043	1.32	.26714	1.82	.16203
0.33	.71892	0.83	.43605	1.33	.26448	1.83	.16041
0.34	.71177	0.84	.43171	1.34	.26185	1.84	.15882
0.35	.70469	0.85	.42741	1.35	.25924	1.85	.15724
0.36	.69768	0.86	.42316	1.36	.25666	1.86	.15567
0.37	.69073	0.87	.41895	1.37	.25411	1.87	.15412
0.38	.68386	0.88	.41478	1.38	.25158	1.88	.15259
0.39	.67706	0.89	.41066	1.39	.24908	1.89	.15107
0.40	.67032	0.90	.40657	1.40	.24660	1.90	.14957
0.41	.66365	0.91	.40252	1.41	.24414	1.91	.14808
0.42	.65705	0.92	.39852	1.42	.24171	1.92	.14661
0.43	.65051	0.93	.39455	1.43	.23931	1.93	.14515
0.44	.64404	0.94	.39063	1.44	.23693	1.94	.14370
0.45	.63763	0.95	.38674	1.45	.23457	1.95	.14227
0.46	.63128	0.96	.38289	1.46	.23224	1.96	.14086
0.47	.62500	0.97	.37908	1.47	.22993	1.97	.13946
0.48	.61878	0.98	.37531	1.48	.22764	1.98	.13807
0.49	.61263	0.99	.37158	1.49	.22537	1.99	.13670

x	e^{-x}	x	e^{-x}	x	e^{-x}	x	e^{-x}
2.00	.13534	2.40	.09072	2.80	.06081	4.00	.01832
2.01	.13399	2.41	.08982	2.81	.06020	4.10	.01657
2.02	.13266	2.42	.08892	2.82	.05961	4.20	.01500
2.03	.13134	2.43	.08804	2.83	.05901	4.30	.01357
2.04	.13003	2.44	.08716	2.84	.05843	4.40	.01228
2.05	.12873	2.45	.08629	2.85	.05784	4.50	.01111
2.06	.12745	2.46	.08544	2.86	.05727	4.60	.01005
2.07	.12619	2.47	.08458	2.87	.05670	4.70	.00910
2.08	.12493	2.48	.08374	2.88	.05613	4.80	.00823
2.09	.12369	2.49	.08291	2.89	.05558	4.90	.00745
2.10	.12246	2.50	.08208	2.90	.05502	5.00	.00674
2.11	.12124	2.51	.08127	2.91	.05448	5.10	.00610
2.12	.12003	2.52	.08046	2.92	.05393	5.20	.00552
2.13	.11884	2.53	.07966	2.93	.05340	5.30	.00499
2.14	.11765	2.54	.07887	2.94	.05287	5.40	.00452
2.15	.11648	2.55	.07808	2.95	.05234	5.50	.00409
2.16	.11533	2.56	.07730	2.96	.05182	5.60	.00370
2.17	.11418	2.57	.07654	2.97	.05130	5.70	.00335
2.18	.11304	2.58	.07577	2.98	.05079	5.80	.00303
2.19	.11192	2.59	.07502	2.99	.05029	5.90	.00274
2.20	.11080	2.60	.07427	3.00	.04979	6.00	.00248
2.21	.10970	2.61	.07353	3.05	.04736	6.25	.00193
2.22	.10861	2.62	.07280	3.10	.04505	6.50	.00150
2.23	.10753	2.63	.07208	3.15	.04285	6.75	.00117
2.24	.10646	2.64	.07136	3.20	.04076	7.00	.00091
2.25	.10540	2.65	.07065	3.25	.03877	7.50	.00055
2.26	.10435	2.66	.06995	3.30	.03688	8.00	.00034
2.27	.10331	2.67	.06925	3.35	.03508	8.50	.00020
2.28	.10228	2.68	.06856	3.40	.03337	9.00	.00012
2.29	.10127	2.69	.06788	3.45	.03175	9.50	.00007
2.30	.10026	2.70	.06721	3.50	.03020	10.00	.00005
2.31	.09926	2.71	.06654	3.55	.02872		
2.32	.09827	2.72	.06587	3.60	.02732		
2.33	.09730	2.73	.06522	3.65	.02599		
2.34	.09633	2.74	.06457	3.70	.02472		
2.35	.09537	2.75	.06393	3.75	.02352		
2.36	.09442	2.76	.06329	3.80	.02237		
2.37	.09348	2.77	.06266	3.85	.02128		
2.38	.09255	2.78	.06204	3.90	.02024		
2.39	.09163	2.79	.06142	3.95	.01925		

INDEX

269